W9-BRT-968

NASHVILLE

MARGARET LITTMAN

Contents

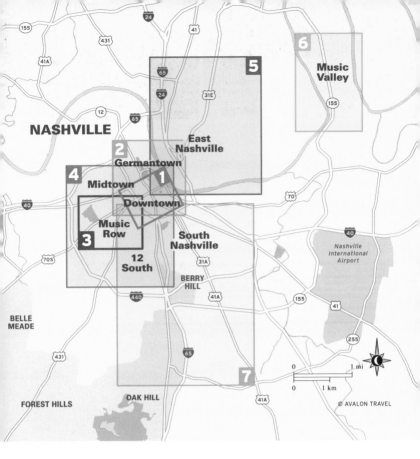

Maps

SIGHTS

9	The Arcade	51	Tennessee Sports Hall of Fame
24	Civil Rights Room at the Nashville Public Library	67	George Jones Museum
28	Downtown Presbyterian Church	70	The Johnny Cash Museum
43	Frist Center for the Visual Arts	71	Patsy Cline Museum
46	Hume-Fogg	76	John Seigenthaler Pedestrian Bridge
47	Customs House	78	Country Music Hall of Fame and Museum
48	Ryman Auditorium		

HOTELS

1	Sheraton Nashville Downtown	42	Holiday Inn Express Nashville-Downtown
4	Hermitage Hotel	62	Hilton Nashville Downtown
14	Noelle	84	Omni Nashville Hotel
16	Hotel Indigo Downtown	88	404 Hotel
22	21c Museum Hotel Nashville	92	Thompson
27	Courtyard by Marriott	94	Westin Nashville
27	Renaissance Hotel	101	SoBro Guest House
40	Union Station		

RESTAURANTS

2	Capitol Grille	56	Jack's Bar-B-Que
8	Puckett's Grocery & Restaurant	65	Merchants
12	Manny's House of Pizza	69	Sun Diner
13	The Greek Touch	72	Goo Goo Cluster Store
20	Gray & Dudley	74	The Southern Steak and Oyster
23	The Standard	82	The Diner
26	Provence	85	Fin & Pearl
33	Chauhan Ale & Masala House	90	Watermark
35	The Mockingbird	93	Biscuit Love
36	Tansuo	97	Arnold's Country Kitchen
37	Adele's	99	Party Fowl
38	Whiskey Kitchen	102	Pinewood
44	Frist Center Café	108	Husk Nashville

NIGHTLIFE

3	Oak Bar	64	Nudie's Honky Tonk
15	Skull's Rainbow Room	68	Wildhorse Saloon
17	Bourbon Street Blues and Boogie Bar	75	Acme Feed & Seed
18	Lonnie's Western Room	79	Country Music Hall of Fame and Museum
32	B. B. King's Blues Club	83	Ascend Amphitheater
39	Whiskey Kitchen	87	The Station Inn
41	Flying Saucer	95	Cannery Ballroom
49	Ryman Auditorium	96	Yazoo Tap Room
53	Legends Corner	98	Jackalope Brewing Company
54	Tootsie's Orchid Lounge	105	City Winery
55	Layla's	106	Tennessee Brew Works
57	Robert's Western World	107	The Listening Room Café
58	The Stage on Broadway	111	3rd and Lindsley
59	AJ's Good Time Bar		
63	Paradise Park Trailer Resort		

ARTS AND CULTURE

5	Tinney Contemporary	50	Bluegrass Nights at the Ryman
6	The Rymer Gallery	73	Nashville Symphony Orchestra
7	The Arts Company	80	Haley Gallery
10	The Arcade	100	Music City Roots
19	Herb Williams Studio	109	Nashville Children's Theatre
21	21c Museum Hotel Nashville		
25	Wishing Chair Productions		

SPORTS AND ACTIVITIES

31	iRide Nashville	77	Pontoon Saloon
34	Off the Wagon Tours	103	Sprocket Rocket
52	Nashville Predators	110	Explore Crawls
61	Experience Nashville		

SHOPS

11	Peanut Shop	66	Boot Country
30	Fire Finch Boutique	81	Hatch Show Print
45	Manuel Exclusive Clothier	86	Two Old Hippies
60	Ernest Tubb Record Shop	89	Lucchese Boot Co.
		91	The Frye Co.
		104	Third Man Records

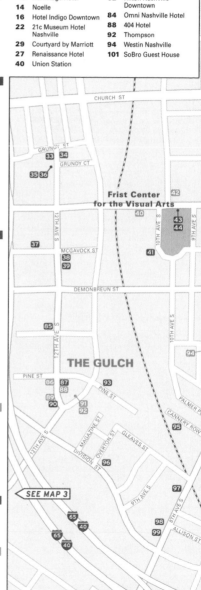

CHURCH ST

Frist Center for the Visual Arts

THE GULCH

SEE MAP 3

MAIN ST

CAPITOL HILL

SEE MAP 2

CHARLOTTE AVE

DEADERICK ST

Public Square Park

SEE MAP 5

WOODLAND ST

Legislative Plaza

UNION ST

The Arcade

9 10

RUSSELL ST

Cumberland River

1

2 3 4

THE ARCADE

14

16

17

20 21 22

5

6

7

8

11 12 13

15

BANK ALLEY

19

THE DISTRICT

18

CHURCH ST

24 25

26

28

Downtown Presbyterian Church

29

PRINTERS ALLEY

30

Civil Rights Room at the Nashville Public Library

4TH AVE N

3RD AVE N

2ND AVE N

1ST AVE N

23

COMMERCE ST

31

32

Fort Nashborough Interpretive Center

VICTORY AVE

Hume-Fogg

27

Ryman Auditorium

48 49 50

George Jones Museum

67

68

45

46

54 55 57 56 58

53

66

Cumberland Park

Customs House

47

BROADWAY

59

Tennessee Sports Hall of Fame

51

52

60 63 64

61

62

69

70 71 72

The Johnny Cash and Patsy Cline Museums

75

77

76

John Seigenthaler Pedestrian Bridge

SYMPHONY PL

Music City Walk of Fame Park

73

74

DEMONBREUN ST

82

Country Music Hall of Fame and Museum

78 79

MOLLOY ST

80 81

83

DOWNTOWN

84

KOREAN VETERAN'S BLVD

KOREAN VETERAN'S BLVD

8TH AVE S

LEA AVE

100

5TH AVE S

4TH AVE S

101

PEABODY ST

102

LAFAYETTE ST

103

HERMITAGE AVE

7TH AVE S

LEA AVE

LEA AVE

RUTLEDGE ST

104

6TH AVE S

108

70

MIDDLETON ST

105

107

3RD AVE S

MIDDLETON ST

109

ELM ST

FOGG ST

106

0   250 yds

0   250 m

110

111

SEE MAP 7

LINDSLEY AVE

DISTANCE ACROSS MAP
Approximate: 3 mi or 4.8 km

© AVALON TRAVEL

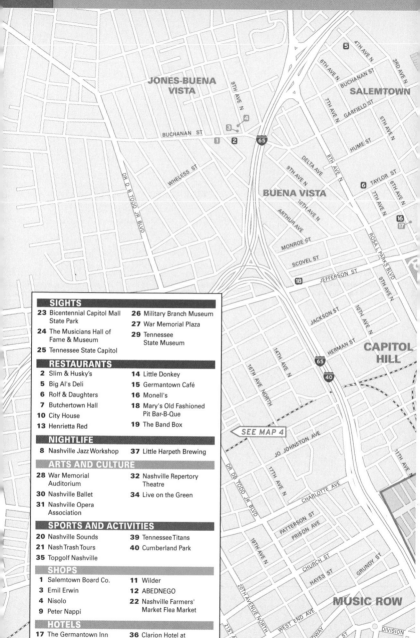

SIGHTS

23	Bicentennial Capitol Mall State Park	26	Military Branch Museum
24	The Musicians Hall of Fame & Museum	27	War Memorial Plaza
25	Tennessee State Capitol	29	Tennessee State Museum

RESTAURANTS

2	Slim & Husky's	14	Little Donkey
5	Big Al's Deli	15	Germantown Café
6	Rolf & Daughters	16	Monell's
7	Butchertown Hall	18	Mary's Old Fashioned Pit Bar-B-Que
10	City House	19	The Band Box
13	Henrietta Red		

NIGHTLIFE

| 8 | Nashville Jazz Workshop | 37 | Little Harpeth Brewing |

ARTS AND CULTURE

28	War Memorial Auditorium	32	Nashville Repertory Theatre
30	Nashville Ballet	34	Live on the Green
31	Nashville Opera Association		

SPORTS AND ACTIVITIES

20	Nashville Sounds	39	Tennessee Titans
21	Nash Trash Tours	40	Cumberland Park
35	Topgolf Nashville		

SHOPS

1	Salemtown Board Co.	11	Wilder
3	Emil Erwin	12	ABEDNEGO
4	Nisolo	22	Nashville Farmers' Market Flea Market
9	Peter Nappi		

HOTELS

| 17 | The Germantown Inn | 36 | Clarion Hotel at the Stadium |
| 33 | Doubletree Hotel Nashville | 38 | Quality Inn Nashville |

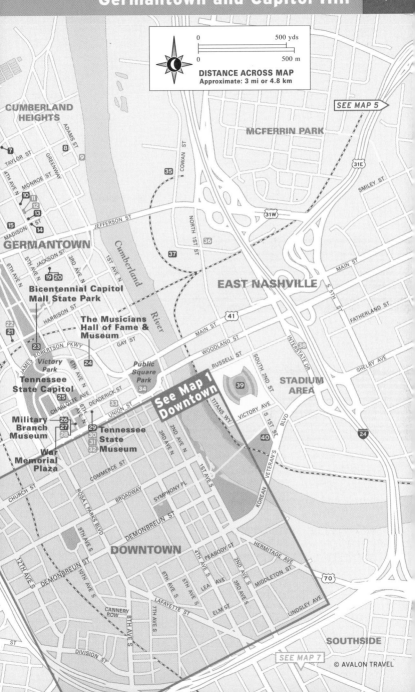

0 500 yds
0 500 m

DISTANCE ACROSS MAP
Approximate: 3 mi or 4.8 km

SEE MAP 5

CUMBERLAND
HEIGHTS

MCFERRIN PARK

31E

7
TAYLOR ST
8
ADAMS ST
9
4TH AVE N
MONROE ST
GREENWAY
SMILEY ST

COWAN ST
35
31W

10
11
12
13
JEFFERSON ST
NORTH 1ST ST
36

15
MADISON
14
37

GERMANTOWN

Cumberland River

EAST NASHVILLE

MAIN ST

S. 5TH ST

FATHERLAND ST

8TH AVE N
7TH AVE N
JACKSON ST
3RD AVE N
19 20
1ST AVE N

**Bicentennial Capitol
Mall State Park**
HARRISON ST

**The Musicians
Hall of Fame &
Museum**
GAY ST

MAIN ST
41

WOODLAND ST

INTERSTATE DR
38

22
21
JAMES ROBERTSON PKWY
23
*Victory
Park*
24
8TH AVE N

*Public
Square
Park*
34

RUSSELL ST

SOUTH 2ND ST
STADIUM
AREA

SHELBY AVE

**Tennessee
State Capitol**
25
CHARLOTTE AVE
DEADERICK ST
33
UNION ST

See Map 1
Downtown

TITANS WY

VICTORY AVE

1ST AVE S

39

S 1ST ST
BLVD

40

24

**Military
Branch
Museum**
26
27
28
6TH AVE N
29
**Tennessee
State
Museum**
30
31
32

3RD AVE N
2ND AVE N

KOREAN VETERANS

**War
Memorial
Plaza**
CHURCH ST

COMMERCE ST

ROSA PARKS BLVD
9TH AVE S
BROADWAY
SYMPHONY PL

1ST AVE S

DEMONBREUN ST

DOWNTOWN

4TH AVE S
2ND AVE S
3RD AVE S
HERMITAGE AVE

MIDDLETON ST
70

12TH AVE S
DEMONBREUN ST
10TH AVE S
8TH AVE S
PEABODY ST
5TH AVE S
LEA AVE
LAFAYETTE ST
ELM ST
LINDSLEY AVE

CANNERY
ROW
7TH AVE S

DIVISION ST

SOUTHSIDE

SEE MAP 7

© AVALON TRAVEL

SIGHTS

18 RCA Studio B
21 Parthenon
26 Vanderbilt University
30 The Upper Room

RESTAURANTS

4 Suzy Wong's House of Yum
9 Elliston Place Soda Shop
13 Hattie B's Hot Chicken
14 Americano
16 The Catbird Seat
24 Jake's Bakes
25 Rotier's
27 Caviar & Bananas
28 Henley
31 San Antonio Taco Co.
35 Hog Heaven
47 Tin Angel
54 Pancake Pantry
56 Fido

NIGHTLIFE

2 Play
3 Tribe
5 Café Coco
6 Exit/In
7 The End
8 The Gold Rush
17 Patterson House
32 Old Glory
36 Springwater
37 The Country Nashville
42 Commodore Grille
55 Cabana

ARTS AND CULTURE

22 Musicians Corner
45 Sarratt Gallery
46 Vanderbilt University Fine Arts Gallery
48 Blair School of Music
52 Belcourt Theatre

SPORTS AND ACTIVITIES

19 Nashville Pedal Tavern
23 Centennial Park
40 Cumberland Transit

SHOPS

33 Castilleja
34 Edgehill Village
38 UAL
39 Boutique Bella
41 Scarlett Begonia
49 Hillsboro Village
50 Hey Rooster General Store
51 Davis Cookware
53 Pangaea
57 Native + Nomad

Parthenon

Centennial Park

Vanderbilt University

VANDERBILT UNIVERSITY

HILLSBORO VILLAGE

PATTERSON ST
21ST AVE N
22ND AVE N
LOUISE AVE
ELLISTON PL
23RD AVE N
25TH AVE N
WEST END AVE
24TH AVE S
PARTHENON AVE
28TH AVE N
POSTON AVE
30TH AVE N
31ST AVE S
WEST END AVE
VANDERBILT PL
NATCHEZ TRCE
26TH AVE S
25TH AVE S
28TH AVE
BLAKEMORE AVE
BELCOURT AVE
ACKLEN AVE

SEE MAP 4

PATTERSON ST

20TH AVE N

CHURCH ST

19TH AVE N

18TH AVE N

HAYES ST

17TH AVE N

WEST END AVE

16TH AVE N

MUSIC ROW

DEMONBREUN ST

DIVISION ST

SEE MAP 1

BROADWAY

DIVISION ST

ROY ACUFF PL

RCA
Studio B

HAWKINS ST

ADELICIA ST

The Upper
Room

SOUTH ST

GRAND AVE

SCARRITT PL

21ST AVE S

19TH AVE S

18TH AVE S

MUSIC SQUARE W

MUSIC SQUARE E

17TH AVE S

TREMONT ST

EDGEHILL AVE

VILLA PLACE

14TH AVE S

HORTON AVE

17TH AVE S

21ST AVE

BELCOURT AVE

SEE MAP 4

MAGNOLIA BLVD

WEDGEWOOD AVE

BELMONT
UNIVERSITY

© AVALON TRAVEL

DISTANCE ACROSS MAP
Approximate: 4.9 mi or 7.9 km

0   500 yds
0   500 m

HOTELS

1 Music City Hostel

10 Loews Vanderbilt Hotel

11 Hampton Inn Vanderbilt

12 Hutton Hotel

15 Aloft West End

20 Best Western Plus
   Music Row

29 Kimpton Aertson Hotel

43 Holiday Inn Nashville-
   Vanderbilt

44 Nashville Marriott at
   Vanderbilt University

0 500 yds
0 500 m

DISTANCE ACROSS MAP
Approximate: 4.9 mi or 7.9 km

HADLEY PARK

40TH AVE N

CLIFTON AVE

40

CLIFTON AVE

11

MCKISSACK PARK

See Map 3 Music Row

CHARLOTTE AVE

PARK PLAZA

25TH AVE N

SYLVAN HEIGHTS

Centennial Park

Centennial Dog Park

40

PARTHENON AVE

CHEROKEE PARK

WEST END AVE

VANDERBILT PL

31ST AVE S

CENTENNIAL

440

NATCHEZ TRCE

SIGHTS

1 Meharry Medical College
2 Fisk University
10 Marathon Village
18 Belmont Mansion
19 Belmont University

RESTAURANTS

11 Swett's
20 Bongo Java
21 International Market and Restaurant
22 PM
29 Mafiaoza's Pizzeria and Neighborhood Pub
34 Las Paletas
35 Sloco
39 Athens Family

NIGHTLIFE

5 Marathon Music Works
6 Third Coast Comedy Club
9 Corsair Artisan Distillery
14 The Basement
24 Zanies
25 Douglas Corner Café
28 12 South Taproom and Grill
40 The Sutler Saloon

ARTS AND CULTURE

3 Aaron Douglas Gallery
4 Carl Van Vechten Gallery

SHOPS

7 Antique Archaeology
8 Bang Candy Company
12 Hatwrks
13 Flip
15 Grimey's New and Preloved Music
16 Howlin' Books
23 Eighth Avenue Antiques Mall
26 Gruhn Guitars
30 MODA
31 Imogene + Willie
32 Draper James
33 Halcyon Bike Shop
36 Ceri Hoover
37 White's Mercantile

HOTELS

17 Daisy Hill B&B
27 Linden Manor Bed and Breakfast
38 12 South Inn

BOWLING AVE

17

BLAIR BLVD

SUNSET PL

W LINDEN AVE

WOODLAWN DR

© AVALON TRAVEL

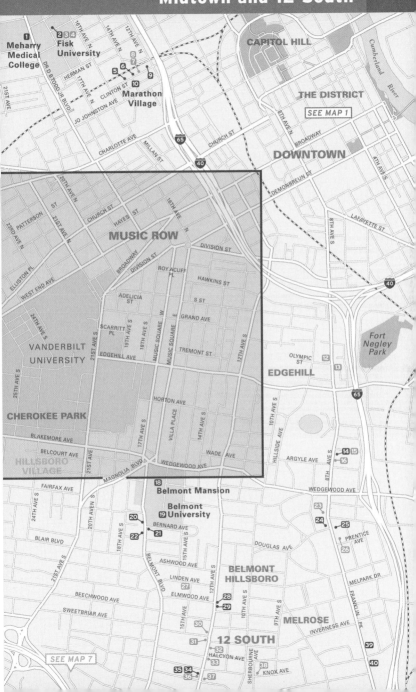

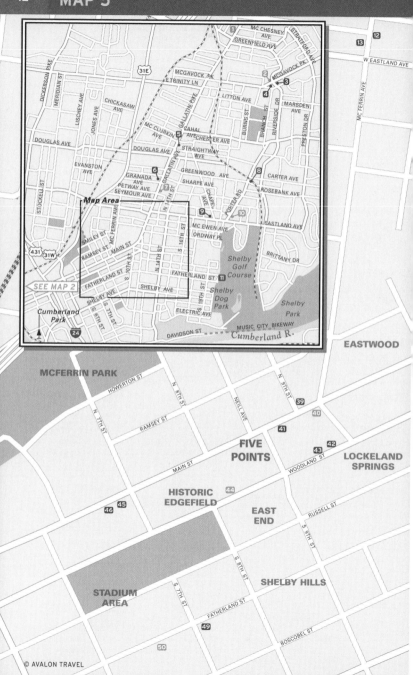

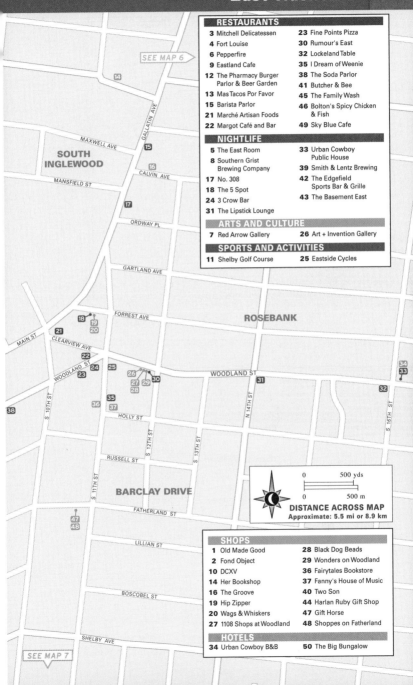

SEE MAP 6

SOUTH INGLEWOOD

MAXWELL AVE

GALLATIN AVE

MANSFIELD ST

CALVIN AVE

ORDWAY PL

GARTLAND AVE

FORREST AVE

ROSEBANK

MAIN ST

CLEARVIEW AVE

WOODLAND ST

WOODLAND ST

HOLLY ST

S 10TH ST

S 12TH ST

S 13TH ST

N 14TH ST

S 16TH ST

RUSSELL ST

S 11TH ST

BARCLAY DRIVE

FATHERLAND ST

LILLIAN ST

BOSCOBEL ST

SHELBY AVE

SEE MAP 7

RESTAURANTS

- 3 Mitchell Delicatessen
- 4 Fort Louise
- 6 Pepperfire
- 9 Eastland Cafe
- 12 The Pharmacy Burger Parlor & Beer Garden
- 13 Mas Tacos Por Favor
- 15 Barista Parlor
- 21 Marché Artisan Foods
- 22 Margot Café and Bar
- 23 Fine Points Pizza
- 30 Rumour's East
- 32 Lockeland Table
- 35 I Dream of Weenie
- 38 The Soda Parlor
- 41 Butcher & Bee
- 45 The Family Wash
- 46 Bolton's Spicy Chicken & Fish
- 49 Sky Blue Cafe

NIGHTLIFE

- 5 The East Room
- 8 Southern Grist Brewing Company
- 17 No. 308
- 18 The 5 Spot
- 24 3 Crow Bar
- 31 The Lipstick Lounge
- 33 Urban Cowboy Public House
- 39 Smith & Lentz Brewing
- 42 The Edgefield Sports Bar & Grille
- 43 The Basement East

ARTS AND CULTURE

- 7 Red Arrow Gallery
- 26 Art + Invention Gallery

SPORTS AND ACTIVITIES

- 11 Shelby Golf Course
- 25 Eastside Cycles

SHOPS

- 1 Old Made Good
- 2 Fond Object
- 10 DCXV
- 14 Her Bookshop
- 16 The Groove
- 19 Hip Zipper
- 20 Wags & Whiskers
- 27 1108 Shops at Woodland
- 28 Black Dog Beads
- 29 Wonders on Woodland
- 36 Fairytales Bookstore
- 37 Fanny's House of Music
- 40 Two Son
- 44 Harlan Ruby Gift Shop
- 47 Gift Horse
- 48 Shoppes on Fatherland

HOTELS

- 34 Urban Cowboy B&B
- 50 The Big Bungalow

0   500 yds
0   500 m

DISTANCE ACROSS MAP
Approximate: 5.5 mi or 8.9 km

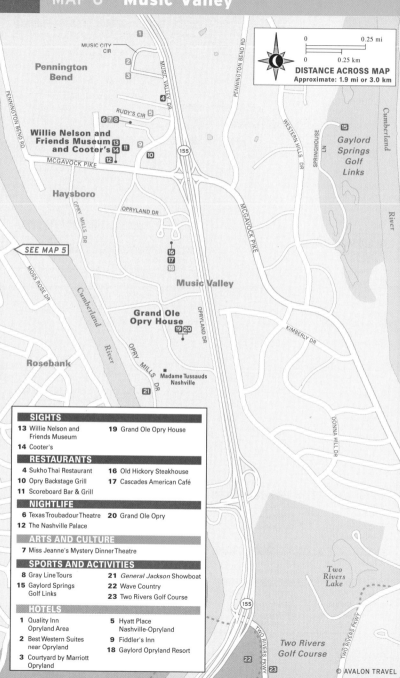

MUSIC CITY CIR

Pennington Bend

MUSIC VALLEY DR

PENNINGTON BEND RD

RUDY'S CIR

Willie Nelson and Friends Museum and Cooter's

MCGAVOCK PIKE

Haysboro

OPRY MILLS DR

OPRYLAND DR

SEE MAP 5

MOSS ROSE DR

Cumberland River

Music Valley

WESTERN HILLS DR

SPRINGHOUSE LN

MCGAVOCK PIKE

Cumberland River

Gaylord Springs Golf Links

0   0.25 mi
0   0.25 km

DISTANCE ACROSS MAP
Approximate: 1.9 mi or 3.0 km

Grand Ole Opry House

KIMBERLY DR

Rosebank

OPRY MILLS DR

Madame Tussauds Nashville

DONNA HILL DR

Two Rivers Lake

Two Rivers Golf Course

TWO RIVERS PKWY

© AVALON TRAVEL

SIGHTS

13 Willie Nelson and Friends Museum
14 Cooter's
19 Grand Ole Opry House

RESTAURANTS

4 Sukho Thai Restaurant
10 Opry Backstage Grill
11 Scoreboard Bar & Grill
16 Old Hickory Steakhouse
17 Cascades American Café

NIGHTLIFE

6 Texas Troubadour Theatre
12 The Nashville Palace
20 Grand Ole Opry

ARTS AND CULTURE

7 Miss Jeanne's Mystery Dinner Theatre

SPORTS AND ACTIVITIES

8 Gray Line Tours
15 Gaylord Springs Golf Links
21 *General Jackson* Showboat
22 Wave Country
23 Two Rivers Golf Course

HOTELS

1 Quality Inn Opryland Area
2 Best Western Suites near Opryland
3 Courtyard by Marriott Opryland
5 Hyatt Place Nashville-Opryland
9 Fiddler's Inn
18 Gaylord Opryland Resort

SIGHTS

1 Tennessee Central Railway Museum
3 City Cemetery
4 Adventure Science Center
5 Fort Negley Park
12 Lane Motor Museum
28 Nashville Zoo at Grassmere
30 Tennessee Agricultural Museum
31 Travellers Rest Plantation and Museum

RESTAURANTS

8 Gabby's Burgers & Fries
11 Bastion
17 The Pfunky Griddle
20 The Yellow Porch
21 Dunya Kabob
27 Plaza Mariachi
29 Back to Cuba Café

NIGHTLIFE

13 Trax
26 The Black Abbey Brewing Company

ARTS AND CULTURE

6 David Lusk Gallery Nashville
7 Zeitgeist Arts
9 Gallery Luperca
10 Track One
14 Nashville Shakespeare
15 Fort Houston

SPORTS AND ACTIVITIES

2 Tennessee Central Railway
24 Coleman Park Community Center

SHOPS

16 Nashville Flea Market
18 Gilchrist Gilchrist
19 Cat Shoppe/Dog Store
22 Phonoluxe Records
23 Hester & Cook
25 Gaslamp Antique and Decorating Mall

DISTANCE ACROSS MAP
Approximate: 4 mi or 6.4 km

0   0.5 mi
0   0.5 km

© AVALON TRAVEL

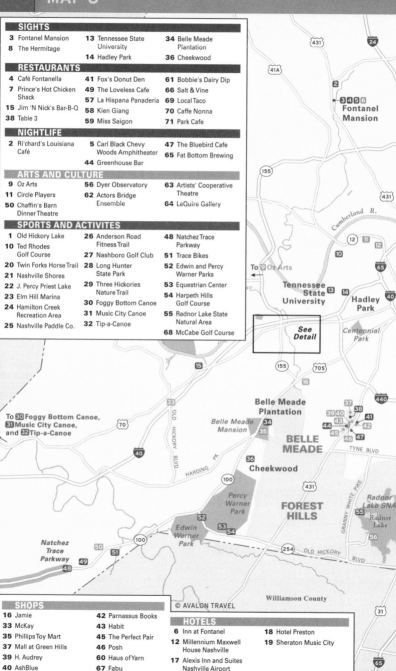

SIGHTS
- **3** Fontanel Mansion
- **8** The Hermitage
- **13** Tennessee State University
- **14** Hadley Park
- **34** Belle Meade Plantation
- **36** Cheekwood

RESTAURANTS
- **4** Café Fontanella
- **7** Prince's Hot Chicken Shack
- **15** Jim 'N Nick's Bar-B-Q
- **38** Table 3
- **41** Fox's Donut Den
- **49** The Loveless Cafe
- **57** La Hispana Panaderia
- **58** Kien Giang
- **59** Miss Saigon
- **61** Bobbie's Dairy Dip
- **66** Salt & Vine
- **69** Local Taco
- **70** Caffe Nonna
- **71** Park Cafe

NIGHTLIFE
- **2** Ri'chard's Louisiana Café
- **5** Carl Black Chevy Woods Amphitheater
- **44** Greenhouse Bar
- **47** The Bluebird Cafe
- **65** Fat Bottom Brewing

ARTS AND CULTURE
- **9** Oz Arts
- **11** Circle Players
- **50** Chaffin's Barn Dinner Theatre
- **56** Dyer Observatory
- **62** Actors Bridge Ensemble
- **63** Artists' Cooperative Theatre
- **64** LeQuire Gallery

SPORTS AND ACTIVITES
- **1** Old Hickory Lake
- **10** Ted Rhodes Golf Course
- **20** Twin Forks Horse Trail
- **21** Nashville Shores
- **22** J. Percy Priest Lake
- **23** Elm Hill Marina
- **24** Hamilton Creek Recreation Area
- **25** Nashville Paddle Co.
- **26** Anderson Road Fitness Trail
- **27** Nashboro Golf Club
- **28** Long Hunter State Park
- **29** Three Hickories Nature Trail
- **30** Foggy Bottom Canoe
- **31** Music City Canoe
- **32** Tip-a-Canoe
- **48** Natchez Trace Parkway
- **51** Trace Bikes
- **52** Edwin and Percy Warner Parks
- **53** Equestrian Center
- **54** Harpeth Hills Golf Course
- **55** Radnor Lake State Natural Area
- **68** McCabe Golf Course

SHOPS
- **16** Jamie
- **33** McKay
- **35** Phillips Toy Mart
- **37** Mall at Green Hills
- **39** H. Audrey
- **40** AshBlue
- **42** Parnassus Books
- **43** Habit
- **45** The Perfect Pair
- **46** Posh
- **60** Haus of Yarn
- **67** Fabu

HOTELS
- **6** Inn at Fontanel
- **12** Millennium Maxwell House Nashville
- **17** Alexis Inn and Suites Nashville Airport
- **18** Hotel Preston
- **19** Sheraton Music City

© AVALON TRAVEL

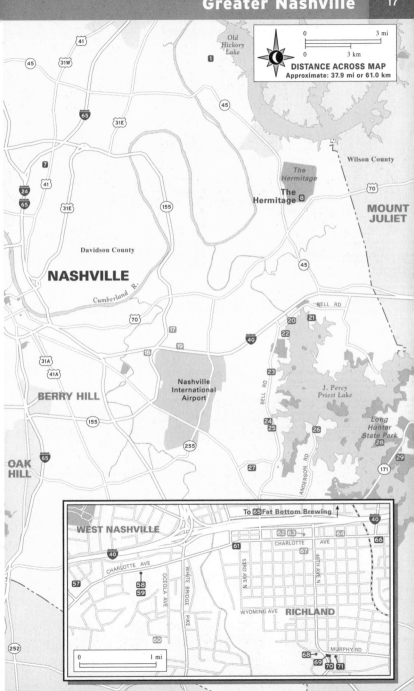

Old Hickory Lake

Wilson County

The Hermitage

The Hermitage 8

MOUNT JULIET

Davidson County

NASHVILLE

Cumberland R.

BELL RD

20 21

22

23

J. Percy Priest Lake

Long Hunter State Park

28

29

Nashville International Airport

24 25

26

27

ANDERSON RD

BELL RD

171

BERRY HILL

OAK HILL

DISTANCE ACROSS MAP
Approximate: 37.9 mi or 61.0 km

0 — 3 mi
0 — 3 km

To 65 Fat Bottom Brewing

40

WEST NASHVILLE

40

CHARLOTTE AVE

57

58 59

61

62 63

CHARLOTTE AVE

64

66

67

53RD AVE N

46TH AVE N

60

WYOMING AVE

RICHLAND

68

69

70 71

MURPHY RD

OCEOLA AVE

WHITE BRIDGE PIKE

252

0 — 1 mi

DISCOVER
Nashville

When it comes to creative energy, nowhere compares to Music City. People come here with big dreams, big talent, and big ideas. Even before Johnny Cash picked up a guitar or Elvis first entered RCA Studio B, this was a city that attracted mavericks and iconoclasts. And whether you have a banjo in the overhead bin or you can't tell a harmony from a melody, it doesn't matter. Because Nashville isn't just about the music. People here are willing to try new things and do things differently. You'll get to experience it even on a short visit.

Creativity of all kinds flows in the veins of folks who call this place home. Nashville is filled with hyphenates like chef-singer-songwriter and artist-poet-hula-hoop-maker. It fosters an entrepreneurial energy that results in funky music clubs for dancing, quirky boutiques for shopping, and one-of-a-kind roadside eateries for … well, eating.

And the "anything can happen" attitude isn't limited just to residents. You don't have to be here more than a day or two to encounter truly talented musicians singing on the curb on Lower Broadway or taste the creative genius emerging from the kitchens of the city's restaurants—both upscale and down home. Whether you're in town for the weekend or for good, take advantage of that optimism, offered with a dash of Southern hospitality. Move to the quirky, and always interesting, Nashville beat.

Clockwise from top left: Patsy Cline Museum; one of several *I Believe in Nashville* murals by T-shirt shop DCXV; the Nashville skyline at night; the Grand Ole Opry.

Planning Your Trip

Where to Go

Downtown

Downtown is Nashville's economic and tourism hub, not to mention the geographic center of the city. This is the heart of Music City's beat. **Lower Broad** is lined with **honky-tonks** with Western swing music playing almost any hour of the day. In addition to some of the city's biggest attractions, downtown is home to hotels, restaurants, and a great view of the **Cumberland River**. Nearby, **The Gulch** is populated by high-rises filled with **restaurants, bars,** and **shops.**

Germantown and Capitol Hill

Historic Germantown is chock-full of **boutiques, chef-driven restaurants,** and bars locals love to frequent. The adjacent **Buchanan Street** is in a burgeoning district of restaurants, **artists' studios, galleries,** and shops. North of downtown, Capitol Hill is home to the **Tennessee State Capitol.**

Music Row, Midtown, and 12 South

Midtown is where the work gets done: It's home to **Vanderbilt University** and Music Row, where record deals are signed. The 12 South neighborhood is abuzz with activity: It boasts well-curated **boutique shopping,** compelling restaurants, and an **active nightlife,** from **live music venues** to **comedy clubs.** The area lends itself to leisurely strolls down neighborhood streets. The **Belmont University** campus brings **youthful energy** to the area.

The Grand Ole Opry is synonymous with Nashville.

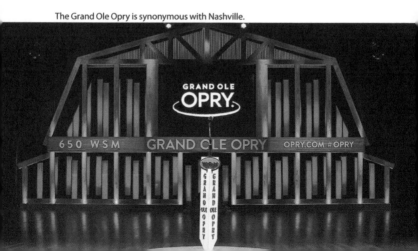

The Tennessee Titans play at Nissan Stadium.

East Nashville

East Nashville has a love-hate relationship with the "hip" moniker it has earned over the years. This gentrifying neighborhood just east of downtown is home to stylish **vintage boutiques** and purveyors of handcrafted goods, not to mention many of the city's **tastiest restaurants** and **best watering holes.** Leafy neighboring **Inglewood** is not as dense, but it also welcomes an **offbeat** collection of eateries and vintage shops.

Music Valley

Close to the airport and the home of the **Grand Ole Opry** and **Opry Mills,** Music Valley is designed for tourists. Here you'll find **affordable hotels** and motels, kitschy attractions, **family-friendly restaurants,** and a few attractions that even locals secretly love to frequent.

South Nashville

South Nashville isn't the cohesive neighborhood that other parts of the city do. As a result, it can be hard to define where one section of South Nashville ends and another neighborhood begins. What the area may lack in clear borders, however, it makes up for in worthy destinations: the **Nashville Zoo at Grassmere,** several **art galleries,** and the best **international cuisine** in Nashville.

Greater Nashville

Nashville's outlying areas and suburbs offer compelling reasons to jump in the car and explore. Out the window you'll see Middle Tennessee's **rolling hills** and the beauty of some of the area's best attractions, including **Cheekwood, Belle Meade Plantation,** Andrew Jackson's home, **The Hermitage,** and the mammoth log cabin **Fontanel Mansion,** once Barbara Mandrell's home.

When to Go

There's no wrong time to head to Music City; it just depends on your personal preference. **Spring** and **fall** are generally mild, filled with pleasant days and crisp nights. Wildflowers bloom in the Greenways, and streets are lined with flowering dogwoods and cherry trees. Weekends are filled with fun events. Nashville has become one of the country's biggest **bachelorette party** destinations; the windup to June and October wedding seasons are particularly popular.

Summer is **high tourist season.** Free and paid concerts alike are booked on indoor and outdoor stages most weekends, and Lower Broadway is filled with folks enjoying the honky-tonks, long summer days, and high-energy atmosphere. The downside of summer is that it will be **hot and humid**—even at night. If you are a high-energy, festival-going kind of traveler, come in the summer and pack accordingly. Remember to bring a sweater for overly air-conditioned hotels and restaurants.

Winter in Nashville is mild compared to cities farther north where snow and slush clog the streets. While Music City will get a light dusting of snow, generally winter means grabbing a coat and hat, not a shovel and gloves. Winter days may seem especially short due to Nashville's proximity to the eastern edge of the time zone. **Christmastime** at **Gaylord Opryland Resort** is magical for travelers with families, featuring thousands of lights, holiday displays, and annual stage performances.

The Two-Day Best of Nashville

Nashville has a 24/7 city-that-never-sleeps vibe, though there are still pockets that are traditionally Southern, with some businesses closed on Sunday and relatively early on weekday nights. The following itinerary assumes a Saturday-Sunday stay in Music City, but it can be adjusted for different days of the week (and seasons of the year).

Day 1

▶ Arrive in Nashville. Check in early to a swanky hotel, such as the historic **Hermitage** or the modern **21c Museum Hotel Nashville.** Store your bags early on so you can make the most of the day unencumbered.

▶ Set out on foot to the **Civil Rights Room at the Nashville Public Library,** where you'll learn about the city's role in the national movement.

▶ From there take in the **Tennessee State Capitol** and then head down the hill for lunch at one of the many tasty choices in **Germantown.**

▶ Next, take a walk through **Bicentennial Capitol Mall State Park,** which is between Germantown and downtown. After hearing the carillon bells play "The Tennessee Waltz," check out First Tennessee Park, home of baseball's **Nashville Sounds,** and head back downtown.

▶ Spend the afternoon at the **Country Music Hall of Fame and Museum** and **RCA Studio B.** Grab a Goo Goo Cluster from their flagship store as you head back to the hotel to clean up for the evening.

Nashville War Memorial Auditorium

Ryman Auditorium

Fisk University

▶ Start the night off with drinks and dinner at **Pinewood.** Walk down the hill to spend the evening strolling, dancing, and drinking at Lower Broadway's **honky-tonks.** Or check out the show playing at the **Ryman Auditorium** or the outdoor riverside **Ascend Amphitheater.** If you're in town between Thanksgiving and New Year's Eve, you'll be able to see the **Grand Ole Opry** at the Ryman.

Day 2

▶ Grab the car and drive through the historic **Fisk University** campus. Stop at both the **Carl Van Vechten Gallery** and the **Aaron Douglas Gallery** on campus.

▶ Make your way to **Arnold's Country Kitchen** for a late breakfast. Standing in line with a cross section of locals and tourists will whet your appetite.

▶ Sated with biscuits, head to bucolic **Centennial Park** and the majestic **Parthenon.** The replica is striking from the outside, but take the time to go inside and see the museum and the shining gold *Athena* sculpture. Grab a snack from one of the many food trucks that gather in Centennial Park.

▶ Drive through Midtown, looking at the **Vanderbilt University** campus and **Music Row,** where you might see celebs on their way to meetings with their record label executives.

▶ Shoppers will enjoy the boutiques in **Hillsboro Village.**

▶ Grab an afternoon pick-me-up from **Fido** or **Biscuit Love.**

Top: the Nashville sound was made in RCA Studio B. **Bottom:** Country Music Hall of Fame and Museum.

Music City on a Budget

It's Saturday night. You want to go out and hear some of the sound that makes Music City groove, but your wallet is empty. You forgot to get tickets. Not a problem! They call it Music City, USA. There's always somewhere to tap your toes without tapping yourself out.

- All the downtown honky-tonks (more than one dozen), including **Tootsie's Orchid Lounge** and **Robert's Western World** are cover-charge free, though you are expected to put money in the (actual) hat when the band passes it.

- **Midnite Jamboree** is an hour-long, always-free radio show starting at 10pm on Saturday nights. The show doesn't charge for admission or parking, and the caliber of talent that plays is always rich.

The Bluebird Cafe is one of Nashville's iconic music venues.

- Catch a songwriters' night, an evening where you can hear the people who literally write the music test out their new material and share old favorites. The ones at **The Bluebird Cafe** are the most famous, but **Puckett's Grocery & Restaurant** and **Douglas Corner Café** have good options, too. Several hotels, including the **Hotel Indigo Downtown** and the **Aloft West End** have listening rooms perfect for singer-songwriter nights.

- Record stores in Nashville are more than places to buy a CD (or vinyl). You can do that, but also hear live music played to enthusiastic fans. **Grimey's New and Preloved Music** and Jack White's **Third Man Records** are sure bets.

- If making your own music is more your groove, you'll need the right instrument. **Gruhn Guitars** is considered by some the best vintage guitar shop in the world. You'll likely walk into a jam session when you go to East Nashville's **Fanny's House of Music.** Like to sing-along karaoke-style? Head to **Lonnie's Western Room.**

▶ If the sun is shining, spend the afternoon checking out the museum and gardens at **Cheekwood.** If not, take shelter in a big pink bus and enjoy the rollicking humor of a **Nash Trash Tour.**

▶ Cross the bridge into East Nashville for your evening out. Choose to dine early at **Butcher & Bee,** where you can have both drinks and dinner in an open, high-energy environment.

▶ Then head across the river to Music Valley, to catch the **Grand Ole Opry** in all its grand ole glory.

▶ If you were lucky enough to catch the Opry downtown the night before, then you get a more leisurely night of enjoying East Nashville's cocktails and culinary delights. Spread the love around **No. 308, The 5 Spot,** and **Urban Cowboy Public House.**

Foodie Weekend

The city's kitchens are making one "best of" list after another. To that end, the following itinerary is a foodie's fantasy weekend.

Saturday

BREAKFAST

▶ Start with a well-edited and well-presented continental breakfast at **Barista Parlor.** The coffee is a work of art, but you'll also want a light meal considering the eating you've got planned for the rest of the day.

LUNCH

▶ Feast on smartly designed cocktails and plates of oysters at **The Southern Steak and Oyster,** which is conveniently located for a rest after touring the **Country Music Hall of Fame and Museum.**

▶ A midafternoon snack should involve some of Nashville's signature hot chicken, served on white bread, either from **Bolton's Spicy Chicken & Fish** or **Prince's Hot Chicken Shack.**

DINNER

▶ Do whatever it takes (which means making a reservation online 30 days in advance) to nab one of the coveted 32 seats at acclaimed **The Catbird Seat.** Your three-hour meal is a culinary performance as much as dinner. The evening includes drink pairings and dessert. Enjoy the experience.

Clockwise from top left: hot chicken, a signature Nashville dish; warm cookies from Jake's Bakes; the bowling lanes at Pinewood.

Sunday

BREAKFAST

▸ East Nashville's **Sky Blue Cafe** is known and beloved for its brisket bowl, a breakfast treat said to calm even the worst hangover.

LUNCH

▸ The city's movers and shakers dine at **Swett's,** an old-school cafeteria with tasty soul food. The gossip dished up here is as good as the food on the plate. Stop to fuel up after visiting the nearby **Parthenon** in Centennial Park.

▸ Afterward, grab a palate-cleansing frozen treat at **Las Paletas,** where you can stroll the boutiques (and people-watch) in the vibrant 12 South neighborhood before moving on to the next meal of the day.

DINNER

▸ Southern ingredients served in decidedly un-Southern ways are on the menu at **Husk Nashville.** Afterward, walk down from the leafy street to catch live music at nearby **3rd and Lindsley.**

▸ Didn't save room for dessert? No worries. Call **Jake's Bakes** and have some warm cookies delivered to your hotel room later.

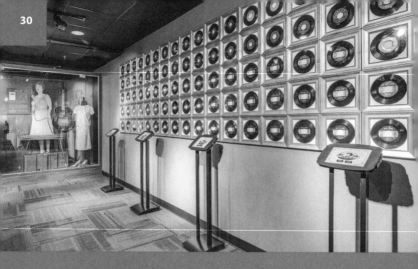

Sights

Nashville's location, within a day's drive for much of the U.S. population, and its recent popularity thanks to TV shows like *Nashville,* means it has become the "it" city for weekend getaways.

In just two days you can see many of the city's best attractions and catch a show at the Grand Ole Opry. But musical pilgrims, Civil War buffs, shoppers, and outdoorspeople should plan to spend more time in Music City. Even the most disciplined explorers will find themselves happily occupied if they choose to stay a full week—or more.

For a city of its size, Nashville takes up a lot of physical space. In fact, Nashville has the second-largest footprint of any major American city. But don't picture a concrete scene: Nashville is a leafy, green city. Outside downtown is a patchwork of traffic lights, strip malls, and tree-lined residential neighborhoods, several of which are incorporated towns with their own elected officials, city halls, and police.

Nashville's attractions are spread out among the city's various neighborhoods and exploring them is part of experiencing Music City's charms. A car is essential to reach some of the best attractions away from downtown. Prepare for traffic during rush hour. All that sprawl means watching the taillights in front of you from time to time. Look to your right or left. That person singing to the radio while in traffic? Next year, that voice might be *on* the radio.

Look for ★ to find
recommended sights.

Highlights

★ **Most Inspiring Place:** In the **Civil Rights Room at the Nashville Public Library,** you can see how a few people changed the world with peaceful contributions to U.S. desegregation efforts (page 33).

★ **First Stop for Getting Up to Speed on the Nashville Sound:** Head directly to the **Country Music Hall of Fame and Museum** to learn about the genre's complex roots and then be ready to explore the city's live music bounty (page 34).

★ **Most Iconic Music Venue:** The restored **Ryman Auditorium** is revered by performers and audiences alike (page 38).

★ **Where to Hear the Bells Ring:** Every hour on the hour you can hear "Rocky Top," "The Tennessee Waltz," and other songs played from 95 carillon bells on the north end of **Bicentennial Capitol Mall State Park** (page 40).

★ **Best Way to Experience Ancient Greece:** A life-size replica of the Greek wonder, the **Parthenon** is a gathering place, a museum, and one of the reasons Nashville is called "The Athens of the South" (page 44).

★ **Place of the Radio Show that Started It All:** Two hours at the **Grand Ole Opry House** introduces you to the depth and breadth of country music (page 49).

★ **Best Celebrity Mansion Tour:** Forget Hollywood: Head to **Fontanel Mansion** and get a glimpse of the lifestyle of legend Barbara Mandrell (page 57).

★ **Most Presidential Home:** The tours of **The Hermitage** home and plantation don't sugarcoat the complicated legacy of the seventh U.S. president, Andrew Jackson (page 58).

Sightseeing on a Budget

Nashville's popularity has caused some prices to skyrocket. But one of Nashville's continued strengths is that there are many free and low-budget options to explore. Check out these sights:

The **Civil Rights Room at the Nashville Public Library** showcases the city's essential role in the civil rights movement with the 1960s Nashville sit-ins.

Want to experience Nashville's amazing downtown? Parking is often free in Nissan Stadium's Lot R, which is close to **Cumberland Park,** a great place to play and learn about the river's role in the city. Then you can walk across the **John Seigenthaler Pedestrian Bridge** and explore downtown on foot. When there are big events downtown, there may be a fee to park in Lot R, but it will still be significantly cheaper than a downtown lot.

Many of the city's major attractions, including the **Frist Center for the Visual Arts** and **Cheekwood,** offer free days throughout the year. The city is also home to free events like the **East Nashville Tomato Art Festival** and **Independence Day** and **New Year's Eve** celebrations.

Downtown
Map 1

THE ARCADE

One of Nashville's distinctive downtown structures is the covered arcade that runs between 4th and 5th Avenues and parallel to Union Street. The two-story arcade with a gabled glass roof was built in 1903 by developer Daniel Buntin, who was inspired by similar arcades he saw in Europe. It has identical Palladian facades at both entrances, on both 4th and 5th Avenues. From the moment it opened, the Arcade was a bustling center for commerce. Famous for its **Peanut Shop** (19 Arcade, 615/256-3394, www.nashvillenut.com), the Arcade has also been the location of photo studios, jewelers, and a post office for many years. Today, restaurants—including **Manny's House of Pizza** (15 Arcade, 615/242-7144, www.mannyshouseofpizza.com)—crowd the lower level, while art galleries, artists' studios, and professional offices line the 2nd floor. Don't miss the bustling activities here during the **First Saturday Art Crawl** (www.nashvilledowntown.com), held on the first Saturday of the month.

MAP 1: 244 5th Ave. N.; http://thenashvillearcade.com; hours vary by merchant; free

★ CIVIL RIGHTS ROOM AT THE NASHVILLE PUBLIC LIBRARY

The 2nd floor of the main Nashville Public Library houses a powerful freestanding exhibit on the movement for civil rights that took place in Nashville in the 1950s and 1960s. Nashville was the first Southern city to desegregate public services, and it did so relatively peacefully, setting an example for activists throughout the South. This history is an important part of Nashville's legacy. The library is a fitting location for the exhibit, which includes photographs, videos, and displays, because the block below on Church Street was the epicenter of the Nashville sit-ins during the 1960s.

Inside the room, large-format photographs show school desegregation, sit-ins, and a silent march to the courthouse. A circular table at the center of the room is symbolic of the lunch counters where young students from Fisk, Meharry, American Baptist, and Tennessee A&I sat silently and peacefully at sit-ins. The table is engraved with the 10 rules of conduct set out for sit-in participants, including to be polite and courteous at all times, regardless of how you are treated. A timeline of the national and Nashville civil rights movements is presented above the table. Inside a glass-enclosed viewing room you can choose from six different documentary videos, including an hour-long 1960 NBC news documentary about the Nashville sit-ins. Many of the videos are 30 minutes or longer, so plan on spending several hours here if you are interested in exploring the topics in depth.

The centerpiece of the Civil Rights Room is a glass inscription by Martin Luther King Jr., who visited the city in 1960 and said, during a speech at Fisk University: "I came to Nashville not to bring inspiration, but to gain inspiration from the great movement that has taken place in this community." **MAP 1:** 615 Church St., 615/862-5782, http://library.nashville.org; 9am-8pm Mon.-Thurs., 9am-6pm Fri., 9am-5pm Sat., 2pm-5pm Sun.; free

★ COUNTRY MUSIC HALL OF FAME AND MUSEUM

The distinctive design of the Country Music Hall of Fame and Museum is the first thing you will notice about this monument to country music. Vertical windows at the front and back of the building resemble piano keys; the sweeping arch on the right side of the building portrays a 1950s Cadillac fin; and from above, the building resembles a bass clef. The hall of fame was first established in 1967, and its first inductees were Jimmie Rodgers, Hank Williams, and Fred Rose. The original hall was located on Music Row, but in 2002 it moved to this signature building two blocks off Broadway. Country music fans are drawn by the carload to the hall of fame, where they can pay homage to country's greatest stars, as well as the lesser-known men and women who influenced the music. Those who aren't fans when they walk in generally leave with an appreciation of the genre's varied roots. The hall's slogan is "Honor Thy Music."

The museum is arranged chronologically, beginning with country's roots and ending with displays on some of the genre's hottest stars of today. In between, exhibits detail themes including the rise of bluegrass, honky-tonk, and the world-famous Nashville Sound, which introduced country music to the world. There are half a dozen private listening booths where you can hear studio-quality recordings of seminal performances, as well as a special display of a few of the genre's most famous instruments. Here you can see Bill Monroe's mandolin, Maybelle Carter's Gibson, and Johnny Cash's Martin D-355. The hall of fame itself is set in a rotunda in the museum. Brass plaques honor the inductees, and around the room are the words Will the Circle Be Unbroken, from the hymn made famous by the Carter family.

The only way to visit Music Row's famous **RCA Studio B** (1611 Roy Acuff Pl., http://studiob.org), where Elvis once recorded, is to buy your ticket at the museum box office and hop on the hall of fame's guided tour bus. The tour takes about an hour, including the 10-minute drive to Music Row and back. The Studio B tour is an additional fee to your admission, but comes as part of a package ($40 adults, $30 children) with admission to the Country Music Hall of Fame.

The Taylor Swift Education Center is an interactive space upstairs where kids and parents can think creatively about songwriting and music making and, during scheduled programs, learn to play instruments (check schedules for dates and times for this programming). The museum has several gift shops, one of which is full of much of the music you hear in the museum. Also in the complex are the iconic **Hatch Show Print** poster designers and the **Haley Gallery.** For an additional fee, you can learn about letterpress printing and even bring home your own printed creation during the Hatch Experience ($40 adults, $30 children).

MAP 1: 222 5th Ave. S., 615/416-2001, http://countrymusichalloffame.com; 9am-5pm daily; regular admission $25 adults, $22.50 seniors, $15 children; with Bill Cody audio tour $27 adults, $18 children

CUSTOMS HOUSE

Located at 701 Broadway, the old Nashville Customs House is a historical landmark and architectural beauty. Construction on the Customs House began in 1875, and President Rutherford B. Hayes visited Nashville to lay the cornerstone in 1877. The building is an impressive example of the Victorian Gothic style. Designed by Treasury architect William Appleton Potter, it was completed in 1916. Although it is called a customs house, in truth the building served as the center of federal government operations in the city with government offices, courts, and treasury offices. The building still houses government offices, so it is open to the public during business hours. But only those who really love the details of ironwork and woodwork will want to peruse the interior. Otherwise this landmark's ornate design, including its lovely clock tower and Victorian windows, are easily admired from the outside.

MAP 1: 701 Broadway; 9am-5pm Mon.-Fri.; free

DOWNTOWN PRESBYTERIAN CHURCH

William Strickland, the architect for the Tennessee State Capitol, also designed the Downtown Presbyterian Church, now both a place of worship and the holder of a coveted spot on the National Register of Historic Places. Built in 1848 to replace an earlier church destroyed by fire, the church is in the Egyptian revival style that was popular at the time. It is one of only three surviving churches in the country built in this style. Downtown Presbyterian was used as a Union hospital during the Civil War, and it is where James K. Polk was inaugurated as Tennessee governor in 1839. Visitors are welcome to come for a **self-guided tour** (9am-3pm Mon.-Fri.); groups of five or more should call in advance for a guided tour. The church's **Waffle Shop** brunch, held in early December, is a popular local holiday tradition.

MAP 1: 154 5th Ave. N., 615/254-7584, http://dpchurch.com; services 11am Sun.; free

FRIST CENTER FOR THE VISUAL ARTS

Nashville's foremost visual art space is the Frist Center for the Visual Arts. The Frist is located in a stately building that once housed the 1930s downtown post office (and there's still a working post office in the basement). High ceilings, art deco finishes, and unique hardwood tiles distinguish the museum. Look carefully in the hallways and you can see the indentations in the walls from folks who leaned here waiting for their turn in line at the post office. The Frist has no permanent collection of its own (which is why it is called a visual arts center rather than a museum). The Frist puts on about 12 different major visiting exhibitions annually, many of which have garnered national attention. At any given time, you can see 3-4 different exhibits, many being regional or national premieres. There are typically plenty of ongoing educational activities paired with the exhibitions. The Martin ArtQuest Gallery, a permanent part of the Frist, is an excellent hands-on arts activity room for children and their parents. The **Frist Center Café** serves better-than-expected salads and sandwiches and has a nice outdoor patio for alfresco dining. There are many free-admission days throughout the year.

MAP 1: 919 Broadway, 615/244-3340, http://fristcenter.org; 10am-5:30pm Mon.-Wed. and Sat., 10am-9pm Thurs.-Fri., 1pm-5:30pm Sun.; $12 adults, $9 seniors and students, free for ages 18 and younger; audio tour $3

GEORGE JONES MUSEUM

Known as "the Possum," George Jones was a country music great who passed away in 2013 at the age of 81. He struggled with alcohol abuse: He famously once drove a John Deere tractor to the liquor store because his brother-in-law hid his car keys and was known for being a "No Show" for performances. His wife devoted her time to helping him get better when he was alive. Now she's devoted her time to preserving his musical legacy. The museum is filled with artifacts from his life and career, from stage costumes to awards to, yes, a replica of that John Deere tractor. Some exhibits include a hologram of Jones, to give the experience of seeing the legend. A **rooftop bar** (11am-10pm Sun.-Wed., 11am-1am Thurs.-Sat.) has one of the city's best views of the Cumberland River.

MAP 1: 128 2nd Ave. N., 615/818-0128, http://georgejonesmuseum.com; 10am-8pm daily; $17 adults, $10 seniors and military, $7 youth

Top: Country Music Hall of Fame and Museum. Bottom: The Johnny Cash Museum.

Located across Broadway from the Customs House is Hume-Fogg Magnet School. It sits on land formerly occupied by Hume School, which was Nashville's first public school. The four-story, stone-clad 1912 building was designed by William Ittner of St. Louis in the Norman Gothic style with Tudor Gothic details. Today, it is a public magnet school with a reputation for high academic standards. Hume-Fogg is not open to the public and can only be viewed from the outside.

MAP 1: 700 Broadway, 615/291-6300, http://schools.mnps.org

THE JOHNNY CASH MUSEUM

Opened in April 2013, this museum looks like a small storefront with a tiny gift shop. But back behind the cash register is a wealth of information on all things Johnny Cash. The collection was amassed by one fan-turned-collector and features interactive listening booths, the jumpsuit the Man in Black wore when he flipped the bird in public, and other memorabilia from a varied and lauded career. Locals are crazy for the rebuilt stone wall that was taken from Cash's fire-destroyed suburban home. In just a few years this has become one of the city's most visited attractions.

MAP 1: 119 3rd Ave. S., 615/256-1777, www.johnnycashmuseum.com; 9am-7pm daily; $19 adults, $18 seniors and military, $15 youth

PATSY CLINE MUSEUM

Housed above The Johnny Cash Museum, this small museum chronicling the life of legendary country artist Patsy Cline might seem like an afterthought from the outside. But once you get inside, you'll see it is anything but. Visitors can view Cline's personal belongings and relevant artifacts, many of which were donated by her family, who are delighted to have so many people learn about the vocalist's short but important life. Exhibits include a replica of the soda shop where she worked, her home, and videos about her career. Admission is separate from The Johnny Cash Museum.

MAP 1: 119 3rd Ave. S., 2nd floor, 615/454-4722, www.patsyclinemuseum.com; 9am-7pm daily; $19 adults, $15 children 6-15, children 5 and under free

★ RYMAN AUDITORIUM

The legendary Ryman Auditorium remains one of the best places in the United States to hear live music. Built in 1892 by Capt. Thomas Ryman, the Union Gospel Tabernacle (as the Ryman was then called) was designed as a venue for the charismatic preaching of Rev. Samuel P. Jones. During the first half of the 20th century, the Ryman began to showcase music and performances. In 1943, the Ryman began hosting a popular barn dance called the Grand Ole Opry. The legacy of this partnership gave the Ryman its place in history as the Mother Church of Country Music. After the Opry left in 1974, the Ryman fell into disrepair and was virtually condemned until Gaylord Entertainment, the same company that owns the Opry, decided to invest in the grand old tabernacle. Today it is a popular concert venue, booking rock, country, and classical

The Battle of Nashville

During most of the Civil War, Nashville was occupied by Federal forces. After Fort Donelson, 90 miles northeast of Nashville, fell in mid-February 1862, Nashville was in Union hands. Nashville became an important goods depot for the Northern cause, and the Federalists set strict rules for city residents during the occupation.

As the war drew to a close in late 1864, Nashville was the site of what war historians now say was the last major battle of the Western Theater.

The Battle of Nashville came after a string of defeats for the Confederate army of Tennessee, commanded by John Bell Hood. After his bloody and humiliating losses at Spring Hill and Franklin a few miles south, Hood moved north and set up headquarters at Travellers Rest, the home of John Overton. His plan was to set up his troops in an arc around the southern side of the city. Union Maj. Gen. George H. Thomas did not plan to wait for Hood's attack, however. He devised a plan to attack first and drive the Confederates away from Nashville.

A winter storm and frigid temperatures delayed the battle. For two weeks, from December 2 to 14, 1864, the two armies peered at one another across the no-man's-land between the two lines. Then at dawn on December 15, 1864, the Union attack began. Union troops on foot and horse, including at least four U.S. Colored Infantry brigades, attacked various Confederate posts around the city. By the close of the first day of fighting, Hood had withdrawn his troops two miles farther south from the city.

The dawn of the second day of battle augured more losses for the Confederates. Unable to hold their line against the Union assault, they fell back again. As darkness fell, Gen. Thomas wired Washington to announce his victory. Pursued by a Union cavalry commanded by Maj. Gen. James Wilson, what remained of the Confederate army of Tennessee marched south and, on the day after Christmas, crossed the Tennessee River into Alabama. Four months later, the war was over.

The **Battle of Nashville Preservation Society, Inc.** (http://bonps.org) offers tours of area battlefield sites.

---

acts, plus comedy and more. Performers like to show the building's acoustics off, playing a number or two without a mic. The Opry returns here during the Christmas season, and in the summer there's a weekly bluegrass series.

Seeing a show at the Ryman is by far the best way to experience this venue, but if you can't do that, pay the admission fee to see a short video and explore the auditorium, including museum-style exhibits about the musicians who have performed here through the ages. You can sit for a few minutes on the old wooden pews and even climb on stage to be photographed in front of the classic Opry backdrop. A backstage **guided tour** ($30 adults, $25 children) is available, and isn't just for die-hard fans. It gives lots of insight into how stars behaved when they were behind these famous walls. Plus, you get to walk on the storied stage yourself.

If you need a snack, visit the on-site **Cafe Lula** (www.cafelula.net). **MAP 1:** 116 5th Ave. N., 615/889-3060, http://ryman.com; 9am-4pm daily; $20 adults, $15 children

Built in 1909, what was once called the Sparkman Street Bridge (and still sometimes called the Shelby Street Bridge) was slated for demolition in 1998 after inspectors called its condition "poor." But citing the success of the Walnut Street Bridge in revitalizing downtown Chattanooga, advocates succeeded in saving the bridge. The Shelby Street Bridge reopened in 2003 as a pedestrian and bike bridge.

Today, the John Seigenthaler Bridge connects East Nashville neighborhoods with downtown. It's been frequently featured on the TV show *Nashville* because of its great views of the city, and many folks get their iconic Music City photos taken here. It is named after the civil rights crusader and journalist. At the base of the east side of the bridge is **Cumberland Park** (592 S. 1st St., 615/862-8508, http://nashville.gov/parks), and the East Bank Landing's kayak, canoe, and paddleboard launches.

MAP 1: Spanning the Cumberland River, one block south of Broadway; free

TENNESSEE SPORTS HALL OF FAME

Sports fans of all kinds will enjoy the Tennessee Sports Hall of Fame. Located in a state-of-the-art 7,500-square-foot exhibit space inside Bridgestone Arena, the hall chronicles the history of sports in Tennessee beginning in the 1800s. The hall is chock-full of photos and videos of players through the ages. Athletes honored include Jay Cutler (a Vanderbilt University graduate) and Peyton Manning. The aim of the museum is to emphasize athletics' high ideals of sportsmanship and teamwork and to honor the accomplishments of many.

MAP 1: Bridgestone Arena, 501 Broadway, 615/242-4750, http://tshf.net; 10am-5pm Tues.-Sat.; $3 adults, $2 children

Germantown and Capitol Hill

Map 2

★ BICENTENNIAL CAPITOL MALL STATE PARK

Tennessee celebrated its 100th anniversary in 1896 with the construction of the beloved Centennial Park, so it made sense to celebrate its 200th anniversary in much the same way. The Bicentennial Capitol Mall State Park occupies 19 acres on the north side of the capitol building and offers excellent views of the capitol, which towers over it. The mall and the capitol are separated by a steep hill and more than 200 steps, which may look daunting but are worth the climb for the views and access to downtown.

The mall has dozens of features that celebrate Tennessee and Tennesseans, including a 200-foot granite map of Tennessee embedded in concrete; a River Wall with 31 fountains, each representing one of Tennessee's rivers; and a timeline with Tennessee events, inscriptions, and notable quotes from 1796 to 1996. A one-mile path that circles the mall's

Nashville with Kids

The Adventure Science Center is an indoor playground for families.

Sure, Nashville is filled with beer, bourbon, and late-night carousing: That's the honky-tonk way. But there's no shortage of things for kids to do, see, and eat.

Animal lovers will adore the meerkat exhibit at the **Nashville Zoo at Grassmere,** as well as the zoo's Wild Animal Carousel. There's something new going on at the zoo almost every week.

The **Adventure Science Center** and its **Sudekum Planetarium** offer hands-on exhibits, education disguised as entertainment, and a great option for being indoor on rainy days. Clear nights call for a drive to the **Dyer Observatory.**

Nashville's many parks and open green spaces are perfect for getting kids moving. The **Centennial Sportsplex** offers ice-skating, tennis, and more. Hillsboro Village's **Fannie Mae Dee Park** is known as "the dragon park" because of a giant dragon sculpture that kids love to climb. **Cumberland Park** adds epic rivers and a little ecology education to the play experience. In warm-weather months, **Nashville Shores** and **Wave Country** are great cool-off spots.

Nashville Children's Theatre has been offering stage productions for little ones since 1931.

Hungry after all that play? Berry Hill's **The Pfunky Griddle** lets kids (and their parents) cook their own pancakes on a table-side grill, filling them with M&Ms, blueberries, or other toppings.

perimeter is popular with walkers and joggers, and a 2,000-seat amphitheater is used for special events. The park may be a civics lesson incarnate, but it is also a pleasant place to pass the time. Ninety-five carillon bells (for the state's 95 counties) play "The Tennessee Waltz," "Rocky Top," and other Tennessee-themed songs every hour on the hour.

To the west of the mall is the amazing **Nashville Farmers' Market** (900 Rosa Parks Blvd., 615/880-2001, http://nashvillefarmersmarket.org), where you can buy fresh produce, flowers, gourmet breakfasts and lunches, and locally made crafts. Locals often picnic in the mall with goodies from the market. There's plenty of free parking here, except when there's a Nashville Sounds baseball game at nearby **First Tennessee Park** (19 Junior Gillam Way, 615/690-4487, www.firsttennesseepark.com). Don't speed. Because this is a state park, tickets come from the state police, and they're pricier than Metro Nashville tickets.

MAP 2: 600 James Robertson Pkwy., 615/741-5280, http://tnstateparks.com; sunrise-sunset daily; free

MILITARY BRANCH MUSEUM

Associated with the **Tennessee State Museum** (505 Deaderick St., 615/741-2692, www.tnmuseum.org), the Military Branch Museum highlights the overseas conflicts of the United States, beginning with the Spanish-American War in 1989 and ending with World War II. The exhibits examine the beginnings of the wars, major battles, and outcomes. There is a special exhibit about Alvin C. York, the fascinating Tennessee native and World War I hero. The military museum is located in the War Memorial Auditorium on the south side of the capitol.

MAP 2: War Memorial Auditorium, 301 6th Ave. N., 615/741-2692, www.tnmuseum.org; 10am-5pm Tues.-Sat.; free

THE MUSICIANS HALL OF FAME & MUSEUM

Not to be confused with the Country Music Hall of Fame, The Musicians Hall of Fame & Museum (MHOF) honors the people who pick and strum—not necessarily the stars and not the songwriters, but the guitar players, drummers, and others who, regardless of genre or instrument, make a song something to which we want to tap our toes. The MHOF was displaced when the city built the mammoth Music City Center. Located inside **Municipal Auditorium**—once the city's leading concert venue—since 2013, the MHOF has memorabilia and instruments from the unsung heroes of the industry. Inductees are nominated by current members of the American Federation of Musicians and others. The 8,500-square-foot Grammy Museum Gallery explores the creative process behind making music, from songwriting to recording.

MAP 2: 401 Gay St., 615/244-3263, www.musicianshalloffame.com; 10am-5pm Mon.-Sat.; $24 adults, $20 seniors and military, $14 youth

TENNESSEE STATE CAPITOL

Set on the top of a hill and built with the formality and grace of classic Greek architecture, the capitol building of Tennessee strikes a commanding pose overlooking downtown Nashville and one unlike the traditional domed state capitol buildings. Construction of the capitol began in 1845; it took 14 years to finish the building. The capitol is constructed of limestone, much of it from a quarry located near present-day Charlotte and 13th Avenues. In the 1950s, extensive renovations were carried out, and some of the original limestone was replaced. The interior marble came from Rogersville and Knoxville, and the gasoliers were ordered from

Philadelphia. The capitol was designed by architect William Strickland, who considered it his crowning achievement and is buried in a courtyard on its north end. Ask at the information desk for a printed guide that identifies each of the rooms and many of the portraits and sculptures both inside and outside the building. If the legislature is not in session, you can go inside both the House and Senate chambers, which look much as they did back in the 19th century. In the 2nd-floor lobby, you can see two bronze reliefs depicting the 14th and 19th amendments to the U.S. Constitution, both of which were ratified by the state of Tennessee in votes held at the capitol. **Guided tours** (9am-3pm Mon.-Fri.) of the capitol depart hourly. Ask at the information desk inside for further details.

MAP 2: Charlotte Ave. between 6th and 7th Aves., 615/741-2692, http://capitol.tn.gov; 8am-4pm Mon.-Fri.; free

TENNESSEE STATE MUSEUM

The displays at the Tennessee State Museum are largely straightforward combinations of text and images, and they require visitors to read and examine on their own. (There are few video presentations.) For patrons with enough patience to give the displays their due, the museum offers an excellent overview of Tennessee history from Native Americans to the New South era of the 1880s. Exhibits detail the state's political development, explore the Revolutionary and Civil Wars, and profile famous Tennesseans including Andrew Jackson and Davy Crockett. They also cast a spotlight on the lifestyles and diversions of Tennesseans of various eras, from the early frontierspeople to a free African American family before Emancipation. Special artifacts include the top hat worn by Andrew Jackson at his presidential inauguration, a musket that belonged to Daniel Boone, and the jawbone of a mastodon that called Tennessee home some 10,000 years ago.

Plans to move the museum to a new building near the Nashville Farmers' Market in 2019 are underway.

MAP 2: 505 Deaderick St., 615/741-2692, www.tnmuseum.org; 10am-5pm Tues.-Sat., 1pm-5pm Sun.; free

WAR MEMORIAL PLAZA

This stone plaza on the south side of the capitol is an open space surrounded by Doric columns and tablets inscribed with the names of more than 3,000 Tennesseans who died in World War I. It's a lovely place to people-watch. A number of state office buildings are nearby, and state employees can be seen walking to and fro, particularly at lunchtime. The famous **War Memorial Auditorium** (301 6th Ave. N., 615/782-4040, www.wmarocks.com) is also located here.

MAP 2: Charlotte Ave. at 7th Ave. N.; dawn-dusk daily

★ PARTHENON

In 1893, funds began to be raised for a mighty exposition that would celebrate the 1896 centennial of the state of Tennessee. Though the exposition would start a year late, in 1897, it would exceed all expectations. The old West Side Race Track was converted to a little city with exhibit halls dedicated to transportation, agriculture, machinery, minerals, forestry, and African Americans, among other themes. It had Chinese, Cuban, and Egyptian villages; a midway; and an auditorium. The exposition attracted 1.7 million people between May 1 and October 31.

When the exposition closed in the fall of 1897, all the exhibit halls were torn down except for a life-size replica of the Greek Parthenon, which had housed an art exhibit during the centennial. The exposition grounds were made into a public park, aptly named Centennial Park, and Nashvillians continued to admire their Parthenon.

The Parthenon replica had been built out of wood and plaster, and it was designed only to last through the centennial. Remarkably, it survived well beyond that. But by the 1920s, the Parthenon was crumbling. City officials, responding to public outcry to save the Parthenon, agreed to restore it, and they hired a contractor to rebuild the replica. The contractor did so using tinted concrete. Today the Parthenon remains one of Nashville's most iconic landmarks. It is a monument to the creativity and energy of the New South and also to Nashville's distinction as the Athens of the South. You can see and walk around the Parthenon simply by visiting Centennial Park. It is, in many respects, most beautiful from the outside, particularly when lit dramatically at night.

As breathtaking as it is from the exterior, it is worth paying to go inside the Parthenon. The landmark has three gallery spaces; the largest is used to display works from its permanent collection of 63 pieces of American art. The other two galleries host interesting changing exhibits. But upstairs is the remarkable 42-foot statue of the goddess Athena by local sculptor Alan LeQuire. *Athena* is designed as a replica of what the statue would have looked like in ancient Greece. In ancient Greece the doors of the Parthenon would have been open, and she would have been seen from a distance. In Nashville her scale and gilded loins are front and center.

MAP 3: 2500 West End Ave., 615/862-8431, http://nashville.gov/parthenon; 9am-4:30pm Tues.-Sat., 12:30pm-4:30pm Sun.; $6 adults, $4 seniors and children

RCA STUDIO B

As a rule, the music labels in Music Row are open for business, not tours. The lone exception is RCA Studio B. The RCA studio was the second recording studio in Nashville and the place where artists including the Everly Brothers, Roy Orbison, Dolly Parton, Elvis Presley, and Hank Snow recorded hits. Also called the RCA Victor Studio, this nondescript studio operated from 1957 to 1977. Visitors on the one-hour tour, which departs from the Country Music Hall of Fame downtown, hear anecdotes about recording sessions at the studio and see rare footage of a 1960s Dottie West recording session. Tours can only be purchased in conjunction with admission to the Country Music Hall of Fame.

MAP 3: 1611 Roy Acuff Pl., 615/416-2001, http://studiob.org; tours hourly 10:30am-2:30pm daily; $40 adults, $30 youth

THE UPPER ROOM

Three million Christians around the world know the *Upper Room Daily Devotional Guide,* a page-a-day pocket devotional available in 106 countries and 40 languages. Headquartered in Nashville, the Upper Room Ministry has established a bookstore, museum, and chapel to welcome visitors. The Upper Room Chapel and Museum features a small museum of Christian-inspired art, including a wonderful collection of Nativity scenes from around the world made from materials ranging from needlepoint to camel bone. Visitors may also tour the chapel, with its 8- by 20-foot stained-glass window and 8- by 17-foot wood carving of Leonardo da Vinci's *Last Supper.* A 15-minute audio presentation discusses features of the carving and tells the history and mission of the Upper Room.

MAP 3: 1908 Grand Ave., 615/340-7207, http://chapel.upperroom.org; 8am-4:30pm Mon.-Fri.; $5 suggested donation

VANDERBILT UNIVERSITY

Named for philanthropist Commodore Cornelius Vanderbilt, who donated $1 million in 1873 to found a university that would "contribute to strengthening the ties which should exist between all sections of our common country," Vanderbilt University is now one of the region's most respected institutions of higher education. A private research university, Vanderbilt has an enrollment of 6,700 undergraduates and 5,200 graduate students. The university comprises 10 schools, a medical center, public policy center, and The Freedom Forum First Amendment Center. Vanderbilt's campus life is vibrant and includes a daily roll call of lectures, recitals, exhibits, and other special events for students, locals, and visitors alike. Check http://calendar.vanderbilt.edu for an up-to-date listing of all campus events. Vanderbilt offers a self-guided tour of the campus's trees, which form the Vanderbilt Arboretum. Most trees on the tour are native trees common to Nashville and Middle Tennessee. Download a podcast, print a copy of the tour from the website (http://vanderbilt.edu/trees/tours), or contact the university for more information.

Designated visitor parking is in several lots on the Vanderbilt campus. Look on the eastern edge of the sports facilities parking lot off Natchez Trace, in the Wesley Place parking lot off Scarritt Place, or in the Terrace Place parking lot between 20th and 21st Avenues north of Broadway. Pay attention to the signs, as the university parking monitors do ticket those who park in prohibited areas.

MAP 3: 2201 West End Ave., 615/322-7311, http://vanderbilt.edu

Midtown and 12 South

Map 4

BELMONT MANSION

Originally named Belle Monte, this elaborate summer home of Adelicia Acklen was constructed in 1853. Belmont Mansion, as it is known today, is a monument to the glories of the Victorian age. Adelicia was born to a wealthy Nashville family in 1817. When she was 22, she married Isaac Franklin, a wealthy bachelor 28 years her senior. When Franklin died seven years later, Adelicia inherited his substantial wealth. Adelicia re-married to Joseph Acklen, a young lawyer, and together they planned and built Belmont Mansion. The home was constructed in the Italian style, with touches of Egyptian revival style. It boasts 36 rooms and 16,000 square feet of space, including a grand gallery where the Acklens hosted elaborate balls and dinner parties. The property included a private art gallery, aviary, zoo, and conservatory, as well as a lake and acres of mani-cured gardens. After the Civil War, Adelicia traveled to Europe, where she purchased a number of paintings and sculptures that are now on dis-play in her restored mansion. Visitors to the mansion are given a 1-hour guided tour of the property, which includes the downstairs sitting and entertaining rooms and three of the upstairs bedrooms. Other specialty tours, including a gardens and grounds tour ($20) and an art tour ($23) are also available with advanced reservations. Note: Only the first floor is wheelchair accessible.

When entering the address in a GPS system, use 1700 Acklen Ave.

MAP 4: 1900 Belmont Blvd., 615/460-5459, www.belmontmansion.com; 10am-4pm Mon.-Sat., 11am-4pm Sun.; $15 adults, $14 seniors, $10 students, $5 children ages 6-12

BELMONT UNIVERSITY

The school for girls founded in the Belmont Mansion in 1890 evolved in 1913 to the Ward-Belmont School for Women and in 1951 to coed Belmont College. In 1991 it became Belmont University, a higher-education institu-tion with links to the Tennessee Baptist Convention. Today Belmont is a fast-growing university with highly respected music and music business programs. In 2011 the school opened the first new law school in the state in the last century. Belmont, which hosted one of the 2008 presidential de-bates, has a student enrollment of 6,400. Campus tours are available twice a day on weekdays. Several Belmont facilities are worth visiting, including the **Curb Event Center** (2002 Belmont Blvd., 615/460-8500), which hosts sporting events, concerts, and lectures.

MAP 4: 1900 Belmont Blvd., 615/460-6000, www.belmont.edu; 24 hours daily; free

The Jubilee Singers

In 1871, Fisk University needed money. Buildings at the school established in old Union army barracks in 1866 were decaying, while more and more African Americans came to seek education.

So in what might now be considered a very Nashville-style idea, the school choir withdrew all the money from the university's treasury and left on a world tour. The nine singers were Isaac Dickerson, Maggie Porter, Minnie Tate, Jennie Jackson, Benjamin Holmes, Thomas Rutling, Eliza Walker, Green Evans, and Ella Sheppard. Remembering a biblical reference to the Hebrew "year of the jubilee," Fisk treasurer and choir manager George White gave them their name, the Fisk Jubilee Singers.

The choir struggled at first, but before long audiences were singing their praises. They toured first the American South, then the North, and in 1873 sailed to England for a successful British tour. Their audiences included William Lloyd Garrison, Wendell Phillips, Ulysses S. Grant, William Gladstone, Mark Twain, Johann Strauss, and Queen Victoria. Songs like "Swing Low, Sweet Chariot" and "Nobody Knows the Trouble I've Seen" moved audiences to tears. The singers introduced the spiritual to mainstream audiences and erased negative misconceptions about African Americans and African American education.

In 1874 the singers returned to Nashville. They had raised enough money to pay off Fisk's debts and build the university's first permanent structure, an imposing Victorian Gothic six-story building now called Jubilee Hall. It was the first permanent structure built solely for the education of African Americans in the United States.

Every **October 6,** the day in 1871 that the singers departed Fisk, the university recalls their struggle and their triumph with a convocation featuring the modern-day Jubilee Singers. It's free and open to the public.

The singers—an always-impressive group of students—still perform regularly. If you have an opportunity to hear them, don't miss it.

FISK UNIVERSITY

Founded in 1866 to educate newly freed slaves, Fisk University has a long and proud history as one of the United States' foremost black colleges. W. E. B. Du Bois attended Fisk, graduating in 1888, and Booker T. Washington married a Fisk alumna and sent his own children to Fisk. In more modern times, Knoxville native and poet Nikki Giovanni attended Fisk. Fisk sits at the corner of Jefferson Street and Dr. D. B. Todd Jr. Boulevard, about 10 blocks west of downtown Nashville. The campus is a collection of elegant redbrick buildings set on wide green lawns, though a few more modern buildings, including the library, break up the classical feel. The oldest Fisk building is **Jubilee Hall,** on the north end of the campus, which was the first permanent building constructed for the education of African Americans in the country. It was built with money raised by the Fisk Jubilee Singers, who popularized the spiritual during a world tour 1871-1874. Another notable building is the **Little Theatre,** a white clapboard building that once served as a Union hospital during the Civil War.

McKissack and McKissack, Architects

The oldest African American architectural firm in Tennessee can trace its roots to Moses McKissack (1790-1865), a member of the West African Ashanti tribe. Sold into slavery to William McKissack of North Carolina and then Middle Tennessee, Moses became a master builder. He passed his knowledge on to his son, Gabriel Moses McKissack, born in 1840. Gabriel Moses passed his knowledge of the building trade to his own son, Moses McKissack III, born in 1879.

Moses McKissack III was born in Pulaski, where he received a basic education in the town's segregated schools. In 1890 he was hired by a local white architect. Until 1905, McKissack designed and built homes throughout the area, including many in Mount Pleasant in Maury County. He developed a reputation as an excellent architect and tradesman.

In 1905 McKissack moved to Nashville, where he started his own construction company. Within a few years, he was working on major projects. He built a home for the dean of architecture and engineering at Vanderbilt University and the Carnegie Library at Fisk University. In 1922, Moses's brother, Calvin, joined him, and they opened McKissack and McKissack, Tennessee's first African American architectural firm.

The McKissacks have continued to distinguish themselves in the building industry, and they have also kept the business in the family. Since 1991 the company has been led by Cheryl McKissack, a fifth-generation McKissack. The firm employs more than 100 people and has corporate offices across the country, including Washington DC and New York City.

The campus is beautiful from many approaches but is particularly striking if you enter on 17th Avenue North from the south, where you will be greeted by the big iron Fisk University gate. There is some metered and free street parking on the side streets in the neighborhood, and campus lots are well marked for visitors.

MAP 4: 1000 17th Ave. N., 615/329-8500, www.fisk.edu; daily 24 hours; free

MARATHON VILLAGE

This neighborhood dates back to 1881. A former auto factory, Marathon Village now houses sleek urban condos, restaurants, a tasting room for **Corsair Artisan Distillery** (1200 Clinton St., #110, 615/200-0321, www.corsairdistillery.com), **Bang Candy Company** (1300 Clinton St., 615/587-4819, www.bangcandycompany.com), and shops like **Antique Archaeology** (1300 Clinton St., 615/810-9906, www.antiquearchaeology.com), owned by Mike Wolfe of TV's *American Pickers* fame. Live music venue **Marathon Music Works** (1402 Clinton St., 615/891-1781, www.marathonmusicworks.com) brings out the locals, and architecture and history buffs love the buildings' bones.

MAP 4: Bordered by 12th Ave., Jo Johnston Ave., 16th Ave., and Clinton St., www.marathonvillage.com

Just across Dr. D. B. Todd Jr. Boulevard from Fisk University is Meharry Medical College, the largest private, comprehensive, historically black institution educating medical professionals. It was founded in 1876 as the Medical Department of the Central Tennessee College of Nashville, under the auspices of the Freeman's Aid Society of the Methodist Episcopal Church. At one time in its history, Meharry was responsible for graduating more than half of all African American doctors and nurses in the United States. Today it has an enrollment of almost 800 students.

MAP 4: 1005 Dr. D. B. Todd Jr. Blvd., 615/327-6000, http://home.mmc.edu

Music Valley

Map 6

COOTER'S

If you're game for Music Valley's signature camp, head straight for Cooter's, a gift shop and museum dedicated to the *Dukes of Hazzard* television show. The museum features a mind-boggling array of toys, ornaments, and model cars manufactured in the 1970s to profit off the Dukes' wild popularity. You can also see one of the bright-orange Dodge Chargers that became the Dukes' icon. In the gift shop, buy a pair of "official" Daisy Dukes or any number of General Lee souvenirs. Cooter's is operated by Ben Jones, who played Cooter, the affable sidekick mechanic, in the original television series. In recent years, Jones has been one of the forces behind DukeFest, a wildly popular annual celebration of fast cars and the General Lee held at the Nashville Motor Speedway.

MAP 6: 2613 McGavock Pike, 615/872-8358, http://cootersplace.com; 8:30am-9pm Sun.-Thurs., 8:30am-9pm Fri.-Sat; free

★ GRAND OLE OPRY HOUSE

Nashville's most famous broadcast can trace its roots to October 1925, when Nashville-based National Life and Accident Insurance Company opened a radio station in town. Its call letters (then and now), WSM, stood for "We Shield Millions," the company's motto.

WSM hired George D. "Judge" Hay, a radio announcer who had worked in Memphis and Chicago, to manage the station. Hay—who, while in Chicago, had announced one of the nation's first live country radio shows—planned to create a similar such program in Nashville.

On November 25, 1925, Hay invited a 78-year-old fiddler, Uncle Jimmy Thompson, to perform live on Saturday night over the radio waves. The response was electric, and WSM continued to broadcast live old-time music every Saturday night. In May 1927, the program developed the name the Grand Ole Opry, practically by chance. Hay was segueing from the previous program of classical opera to the barn dance. "For the past hour, we have been listening to music taken largely from Grand Opera. From now on, we will present the Grand Ole Opry," he said. The name stuck. By 1939, the Opry gained a slot on the nationwide NBC radio network, allowing it to reach a national audience every week.

Always a live audience show, the Opry was performed in several different venues over the years. It started in the WSM studio, then moved to the Hillsboro Theater (now the Belcourt), the Dixie Tabernacle on Fatherland Street, and the War Memorial Auditorium downtown. In 1943 it moved to the Ryman Auditorium, where it remained until 1974, when National Life built a new 5,000-seat auditorium in a rural area north of Nashville. The first show from the new Opry House in Music Valley was broadcast on March 16, 1974. After the 2010 Nashville flood, the Opry House was gutted and renovated.

The music that flows from the Opry's stage has changed over the years. Today it is a showcase for all types of country and country-inspired music, including bluegrass, gospel, honky-tonk, and zydeco. It remains, however, one of the most esteemed and celebrated institutions in American music.

The Opry performs at least two times a week, Friday and Saturday, with additional shows on Tuesday night most weeks. The Opry also offers a backstage tour. Daytime tour tickets go on sale two weeks in advance and are generally offered every 15 minutes; if you are buying tickets to a show, you can also purchase a post-concert backstage tour led by docents, where you'll get to see dressing rooms, learn lots of Opry history, and hear plenty of juicy stories about performers and their backstage behavior. One of the highlights of the guided tour is getting to go onstage and have your photo taken under the lights. If you book a postshow tour, you'll see a performer or two.

MAP 6: 2802 Opryland Dr., 615/871-6779, www.opry.com; daytime tour: times vary, check website; postshow backstage tour: 9:30pm Tues., Fri.-Sat.; VIP tour: 6:30pm Tues., Fri.-Sat.; Daytime tour: $26 adults, $21 children; postshow backstage tour: $29 adults, $24 children; VIP tour: $150

WILLIE NELSON AND FRIENDS MUSEUM

A few doors down from Cooter's, you will find Willie Nelson and Friends Museum, which looks like a roadside stand in the touristy Music Valley area. It's packed with memorabilia from Nelson's career, showcasing a number of things that once belonged to the artist, including his golf bag, a replica of his tour bus, and the guitar he played during his first performance on the Grand Ole Opry. Many of the Willie Nelson items were purchased by museum operators Jeannie and Frank Oakley at an IRS auction. The gift shop is popular for trip mementos, though few visitors think of this spot as a real "museum." A quick trip here is appreciated by true country fans, but it isn't a go-out-of-your-way destination.

MAP 6: 2613 McGavock Pike, 615/885-1515, http://willienelsongeneralstore.com; 8:30am-9pm daily; $10

Nashville on the Small Screen

It is perhaps the most meta of Music City's attractions: From 2012 to 2018, Nashville was the subject of a TV show called *Nashville.* The hour-long nighttime drama (which first aired on ABC and then moved to CMT) was filmed on location and many of the show's actors, who are also songwriters and singers, relocated to Music City to launch their music careers.

As the show grew more popular, the lines between the real Nashville and the one on TV blurred. Many of the actors have now appeared on the stage of the Grand Ole Opry both in character and as themselves. There are CDs and concert tours from the cast. The homes of the characters have been featured on HGTV. Eric Close, who played the mayor on the show, led the city's annual Christmas parade several times, instead of the city's actual mayor!

Part of the reason for the show's popularity is, for all its soap opera-ness, part of it feels authentic. Episode names use Hank Williams song titles, a hat tip to the man who made country music what it is. Backup musicians on the show are actual full-time, professional musicians who live and work in Nashville.

For fans, it is easy to take a tour of the sites of the show as part of a tour of Nashville. The most comprehensive is from **Gray Line:** a 3.5-hour tour showing off characters' homes and venues that pop up in the show (http://graylinetn.com/abcs-nashville, $52 adults, $26 children). **Grand Avenue** offers a custom *Nashville* tour; https://grandavenueworldwide.com/tours, prices vary). Many of the city's popular attractions, including **The Bluebird Cafe** and **Ryman Auditorium,** now have sections of their tours devoted to the TV show. Art imitates life.

South Nashville

Map 7

ADVENTURE SCIENCE CENTER

Children and grown-ups alike will enjoy the hands-on science education available at the Adventure Science Center. Interactive exhibits explore how the body works, the solar system, and other scientific areas. Perhaps the most popular attraction is the multistory climbing tower in the building's center, which features a giant guitar and other instruments and is always covered in enthusiastic visitors. The center's **Sudekum Planetarium** (http://sudekumplanetarium.com; additional $7 adults, $6 children) is the largest planetarium in Tennessee. It has 164 seats and offers a variety of space-themed shows. It also includes gravity-suspending rides and exhibits about spaceflight, the moon, and the solar system.

MAP 7: 800 Fort Negley Blvd., 615/862-5160, www.adventuresci.com; 10am-5pm daily; $16 adults, $12 children

CITY CEMETERY

Right next to Fort Negley Park, off Chestnut Street, is the old City Cemetery. Opened in 1822, City Cemetery was the final resting place of

Clockwise from top left: a tiger at Nashville Zoo at Grassmere; The Hermitage, the home of Andrew Jackson; Belle Meade Plantation.

many of Nashville's most prominent early citizens, including founder James Robertson; William Driver, the U.S. Navy captain who named the flag "Old Glory"; Mabel Lewis Imes and Ella Sheppard, members of the original Fisk Jubilee Singers; and 14 Nashville mayors. During the Civil War, the cemetery was contracted to bury more than 15,000 Union and Confederate dead, though they were later reinterred in different cemeteries.

Pamphlets and signage on-site will help you along a self-guided tour. Guided tours are available by appointment and tell the history of Nashvillians who are buried at this historical site.

MAP 7: 1001 4th Ave. S., http://thenashvillecitycemetery.org; dawn-dusk daily; guided tours by appointment; free

FORT NEGLEY PARK

Early in the Civil War, the Union army determined that taking and holding Nashville was a critical strategic link in their victory. So after Nashville fell in 1862, the Federals wasted no time fortifying the city against attacks. One of the city's forts was Fort Negley, built between August and December 1862 on St. Cloud Hill south of the city center.

Fort Negley owes its existence to the 2,768 men who were enrolled to build it. Most were black people, some free and some enslaved, who were pressed into service by the Union army. These men felled trees, hauled earth, and cut and laid limestone for the fort. They slept in the open and enjoyed few, if any, comforts while they labored. Between 600 and 800 men died while building the fort, and only 310 received payment.

When it was completed, Fort Negley was the largest inland masonry fortification in North America. It was never challenged. Fort Negley was abandoned by the military after the war, but it remained the cornerstone of one of Nashville's oldest African American communities, now known as Cameron-Trimble. During the New Deal, the Works Progress Administration rebuilt large sections of the crumbling fort, and it became a public park.

Explore the **visitors center** (noon-4pm Tues.-Thurs., 9am-4pm Fri.-Sat. June-Aug., noon-4pm Tues.-Fri., 9am-4pm Sat. Sept.-May, free) to learn the story of the fort. It includes a museum about the fort and Nashville's role in the Civil War. There is a short paved loop trail around the base of the fort, plus raised boardwalks through the fortifications themselves. Historical markers tell the story of the fort's construction and detail its military features. Fort Negley is one of the great places to take in a view of Music City.

MAP 7: 1100 Fort Negley Blvd., 615/862-8470, http://nashville.gov; dawn-dusk daily; free

LANE MOTOR MUSEUM

Kids and adults alike relish coming to this one-of-a-kind, off-the-beaten-track museum. Here you'll find all manner of automobiles, from early hybrids and steam engines to a car that's so small it can be "reversed" merely by picking it up with a lever and putting it down facing the other direction. The amphibious cars are always a delight, too.

The museum, based in the old Sunbeam Bakery, has the largest collection of European cars and motorcycles in the country. In fact, the collection is so big that not everything is on view at all times. There's a decent play area for kids who need a break.

MAP 7: 702 Murfreesboro Pike, 615/742-7445, www.lanemotormuseum.org; 10am-5pm Thurs.-Mon.; $12 adults, $8 seniors, $3 children

NASHVILLE ZOO AT GRASSMERE

See familiar and exotic animals at the Nashville Zoo at Grassmere. Many of the zoo's animals live in beautiful habitats like Lorikeet Landing, Gibbon Islands, and Bamboo Trail. The zoo's meerkat exhibit, featuring the famously quizzical animals, is one of its most popular. The Wild Animal Carousel is an old-time carousel with 39 different brightly painted wooden animals.

The zoo is located at Grassmere, the onetime home and farm of the Croft family. The historical Croft farmhouse has been preserved and is open for guided tours March through mid-October.

MAP 7: 3777 Nolensville Pike, 615/833-1534, www.nashvillezoo.org; 9am-6pm daily mid-Mar.-mid-Oct., 9am-4pm daily mid-Oct.-mid-Mar.; $16 adults, $14 seniors, $11 children ages 3-12, free to children under 3, free parking

TENNESSEE AGRICULTURAL MUSEUM

The Tennessee Agricultural Museum celebrates the ingenuity and dedicated labors of farm life from the 17th to the 20th centuries. Operated by the Tennessee Department of Agriculture and set on the department's pleasant South Nashville campus, the museum depicts various facets of Tennessee farm life. It has exhibits about clothes washing, blacksmithing, coopering, plowing, weaving, and more. Outside, there is a small kitchen garden with heirloom vegetables and replicas of a log cabin, one-room schoolhouse, and outdoor kitchen. A short self-guided nature trail illustrates the ways that settlers used various types of native Tennessee trees. Visitors can always see the historical exhibits on their own in this welcoming and educational space. Hands-on demonstrations are typically only offered on summer Saturdays and by advance appointment for groups with a small fee. The knowledgeable staff are available to answer any questions.

MAP 7: 440 Hogan Rd., 615/837-5197, http://tnagmuseum.org; 9am-4pm Mon.-Fri.; self-guided tour free

TENNESSEE CENTRAL RAILWAY MUSEUM

Railroad enthusiasts should make a detour to the Tennessee Central Railway Museum. This institution is best known for its special railroad excursions that are part tour, part performance. The museum houses a collection of railroad equipment and paraphernalia. Dedicated volunteers restore and care for the collection and are more than willing to chat about railways with interested visitors. The museum is located in a largely industrial area between the interstate and the railroad tracks, one block north of Hermitage Avenue and east of Fairfield Avenue. It's a quick drive from downtown or East Nashville. (For details on themed railway tours that depart from the museum, see page 162.)

MAP 7: 220 Willow St., 615/244-9001, www.tcry.org; 9am-3pm Tues., Thurs. and Sat.; free

TRAVELLERS REST PLANTATION AND MUSEUM

Travellers Rest was the home of John Overton, a Nashville lawyer who helped found Memphis, served on the first Tennessee Supreme Court, and was a trusted advisor to Andrew Jackson, the seventh U.S. president and the first from Tennessee. When workers were digging the cellar for the original home in 1799, they uncovered Native American skeletons and artifacts—Overton had chosen a Mississippian-era Indian mound for the site of his residence. But the archaeological finds did not stop Overton, who initially named his home Golgotha, or hill of skulls. The name did not stick, however; tradition has it that Overton later named the home Travellers Rest because it was his place of rest between long trips as a circuit judge in Middle and East Tennessee. Visitors to Travellers Rest may choose to skip the mansion tour. But to get the real story and flavor of the property, go for the full 45-minute guided tour.

MAP 7: 636 Farrell Pkwy., 615/832-8197, http://travellersrestplantation.org; 10am-4:30pm Mon.-Sat. (last tour leaves 4pm); $12 adults, $11 seniors, $10 children ages 7-11, free children 6 and under

Greater Nashville   Map 8

BELLE MEADE PLANTATION

The mansion at the former Belle Meade Plantation is the centerpiece of present-day Belle Meade Plantation and one of the finest old homes in the city. Its name means beautiful pasture, and indeed it was Belle Meade's pastures that gave rise to the plantation's fame as the home of a superb stock of horses. Purchased as 250 acres in 1807 by Virginia farmer John Harding and his wife, Susannah, the estate grew to 5,400 acres at its peak in the 1880s and 1890s.

Belle Meade was never a cotton plantation, though small amounts of the cash crop were grown here, along with fruits, vegetables, and tobacco. Instead it was the horses, including the racehorse Iroquois, that made Belle Meade famous. The mansion was built in 1820 and expanded in 1853. Its grand rooms are furnished with period antiques, more than 60 percent of which are original to the house. The estate also includes outbuildings, such as a smokehouse, dairy, and the original log cabin that Harding built for his family when they moved to Belle Meade in 1807.

The plantation also includes a slave cabin, which houses an exhibit on Belle Meade's enslaved population, which numbered more than 160 at its peak. Two of these slaves are described in detail. Susanna Carter was the

The Sculpture of William Edmondson

The first African American artist to have a one-man show at the Museum of Modern Art in New York was Nashville-born sculptor William Edmondson (1874-1951).

Edmondson was born in the Hillsboro area of Nashville. He worked for decades as a laborer on the railroads, a janitor at Women's Hospital, and in other similar jobs before discovering his talent for sculpture in 1929. Edmondson told *The Tennessean* that his talent and passion were God-given: "God appeared at the head of my bed and talked to me, like a natural man, concerning the talent of cutting stone He was about to bestow. He talked so loud He woke me up. He told me He had something for me."

A prolific sculptor, Edmondson worked exclusively with limestone, and he created angels, women, doves, turtles, rabbits, and other "varmints." He also made tombstones. Edmondson never learned to read or write, and he called many of his works "mirkels" because they were inspired by God.

In the 1930s, Louise Dahl-Wolfe, a photographer for *Harper's BAZAAR* magazine, brought Edmondson and his work to the attention of Alfred Barr, the director of the Museum of Modern Art. Barr and other trustees of the museum admired what they termed as Edmondson's "modern primitive" work, and they invited him to display a one-man show at the museum in 1938. In 1941, the Nashville Art Museum put on an exhibit of Edmondson's work.

Edmondson continued to work until the late 1940s, when he became ill with cancer. After his death in 1951 he was buried in an unmarked grave at Mount Ararat Cemetery in Nashville. The city park at 17th Avenue North and Charlotte Avenue is named in honor of Edmondson.

Some of Edmondson's work is on display at **Cheekwood** (page 56).

mansion's housekeeper for more than 30 years, and she remained with the family even after the end of slavery. On her deathbed, Selena Jackson, the mistress of Belle Meade for many years, called Susanna "one of the most faithful and trusted of my friends." The other African American who features prominently at the museum is Bob Green, whose skill and experience as a hostler earned him one of the highest salaries ever paid to a horse hand of the day. Visitors to Belle Meade are given a one-hour guided tour of the mansion and then visit the outbuildings and grounds on their own.

MAP 8: 110 Leake Ave., 615/356-0501, http://bellemeadeplantation.com; 9am-5pm daily; $24 adults, $20 seniors, $13 students, $10 children 6-12, children 5 and under free

CHEEKWOOD

Plan to spend a full morning or afternoon at Cheekwood, so you can experience the full scope of this magnificent art museum and botanical garden. Galleries in the Cheekwood mansion house the museum's American and European collections, including some excellent contemporary art. Cheekwood has the largest public collection of works by Nashville artist William Edmondson, the sculptor and stoneworker. The museum usually displays items from its permanent collection as well as traveling exhibitions from other museums. Many exhibits have special ties with Nashville.

But Cheekwood is far more than just an art museum. The mansion overlooks hundreds of acres of gardens and woods, and it is easy to forget that you are near a major American city when you're there. Walk the mile-long Carell Woodland Sculpture Trail past works by 15 internationally acclaimed artists, or stroll past the water garden to the Japanese garden. There are dogwood gardens, an herb garden, a delightful boxwood garden, and much more. Wear comfortable shoes and pack a bottle of water so that you can enjoy the grounds in comfort.

Cheekwood owes its existence to the success of the coffee brand Maxwell House. During the 1920s, Leslie Cheek and his wife, Mabel Wood, invested in the new coffee brand being developed by their cousin, Joel Cheek. Maxwell House proved to be a success and earned the Cheeks a fortune, which they used to buy 100 acres of land in West Nashville. The family hired New York residential and landscape architect Bryant Fleming to create a 30,000-square-foot mansion and neighboring gardens. Cheekwood was completed in 1933.

Leslie Cheek lived in the mansion just two years before he died, and Mabel lived there for another decade before deeding it to her daughter and son-in-law, who later offered it as a site for a museum and garden. Cheekwood opened to the public in 1960.

MAP 8: 1200 Forrest Park Dr., 615/356-8000, http://cheekwood.org; 9 am-4pm Tues.-Sun.; $20 adults, $18 seniors, $13-16 students and children, $5 parking

★ FONTANEL MANSION

The former estate of country music icon Barbara Mandrell, Fontanel Mansion has become a surprising draw for locals and tourists alike since it opened in 2010. These 136 acres include walking trails, an outdoor live music venue, a zipline course, a restaurant with its own live music, a hotel, an art gallery, and a gift shop. But the main attraction for visitors is the mansion, a 27,000-square-foot log cabin, which is the city's only country music mansion tour.

Fans get to see how the most famous of the Mandrell sisters lived before her retirement. Tours (1.25 hours; advanced reservations recommended) are sometimes given by Mandrell's daughter, who throws in lots of personal tidbits (such as stories of her brothers jumping from the second story into the pool). Even those who don't love "I Was Country When Country Wasn't Cool" will appreciate the music history, artifacts such as Gretchen Wilson's "Redneck Woman" Jeep, the former indoor shooting range, and the bucolic scenery and impressive architecture.

MAP 8: 4225 Whites Creek Pike, 615/727-0304, http://fontanel.com; 10am-4pm daily; $24 adults, $22 seniors, $14 children

Founded in 1912, Hadley Park is believed to be the oldest public park developed for African Americans in the South and, most likely, the United States. The park got its start when Fisk University president George Gates requested that the city buy land and create a park for its black citizens. This was in the era of segregation, so other city parks were not open to black people. The request was granted, and the park opened in July 1912. An old farmhouse was converted into a community center, and benches and a playground were installed. It is now home to a state-of-the-art gym and fitness center, computer labs, meeting rooms, and tennis courts.

MAP 8: 1037 28th Ave. N., 615/862-8451; 6am-8:30pm Mon.-Thurs., 6am-7:30pm Fri., 8am-noon Sat.; $3 adults, $1.50 seniors and children

★ THE HERMITAGE

Andrew Jackson's plantation home is Nashville's best historical tourist attraction, even though it's technically 16 miles east of the city. The Hermitage is where Jackson retired following his two terms as president of the United States, and it is where he and his beloved wife, Rachel, are buried. Following President Jackson's death, The Hermitage remained in family hands until 1853, when it was sold to the state of Tennessee to pay off the family's debts. It opened as a museum in 1889 and was restored largely because of the persistence of the Ladies Hermitage Association. Because the property never left family hands before it was sold to the state, many of the furnishings are original, and even the wallpaper in several rooms dates back to the years when Andrew Jackson called it home.

The Hermitage tour and museum focus not only on Jackson and the construction and decoration of the mansion, but also the African American slaves who worked at The Hermitage plantation. It makes no effort to gloss over some of Jackson's less favorable legacies. Curators and archaeologists have studied The Hermitage to learn about the hundreds of men and women who made The Hermitage profitable and successful for so many years. The tour of the grounds takes visitors to Alfred's Cabin, a slave cabin occupied until 1901 by former Hermitage slave Alfred Jackson. You also learn about the agriculture that took place on The Hermitage and can see cotton being cultivated during the summer months. To learn even more about The Hermitage's slaves, take an add-on **wagon tour** (Apr.-Oct., $11).

Visitors to The Hermitage first watch a video about Andrew Jackson and The Hermitage and then can continue on to a museum. Even if you are not typically an audio-tour-type person, consider the one of the grounds, which includes a kids' version narrated by Jackson's pet parrot. Guided tours of the mansion are included in admission. Plan on spending at least three hours here to make the most of your visit. Try to come when the weather is good, so you can take in the grounds and not just the residence.

MAP 8: 4580 Rachel's Ln., 615/889-2941, http://thehermitage.com; 9am-4pm daily mid-Oct.-mid-Mar.; 8:30am-5pm daily mid-Mar.-mid-Oct.; $20 adults, $17 seniors, $15 students, $10 children

African American Heritage

From the Civil War to civil rights, baseball to Oprah, the African American experience is part of what has made Nashville the city it is. Today Music City is home to four historically black colleges and universities, a number of African American churches, and historical and cultural sites.

Among the highlights:

- More than 2,700 men, most of them black, some free, some slaves, toiled to build **Fort Negley** (http://nashville.gov), what was then the largest inland masonry fortification and a crucial fort in the Civil War. As many as 800 people died while building the fort, and many more African American soldiers died during the Battle of Nashville. The Union army did not supply weapons to the black soldiers or slaves; they were forced to protect themselves with whatever tools they had.

- Head to the 2nd floor of **Nashville Public Library** downtown (http://library.nashville.org) to learn about the sit-ins that took place in Nashville and the progress they made to help desegregate public services nationwide.

- **First Tennessee Park**, the new home of the Nashville Sounds, was built on the site of **Sulphur Dell** (http://sulphurdell.com), which in the 1800s was baseball's home in Nashville. In the 1930s, it was the center of African American baseball in the South.

- The **Fisk Jubilee Singers** (www.fiskjubileesingers.org) were the first world-touring musical group and, thanks to Queen Victoria, the inspiration for the Music City moniker for Nashville. Today they continue the tradition of singing spirituals for audiences worldwide.

- Founded in 1912, **Tennessee State University** (www.tnstate.edu) has had many achievements; among them it has produced more Olympic gold medalists than any other university in the United States. Graduates include Olympic champion Wilma Rudolph and Oprah Winfrey.

- When the **Nashville Museum of African American Music** (www.nmaam.org) opens in 2019, it will be the first museum dedicated to recognizing and celebrating the musical accomplishments of African Americans. The space will feature five galleries covering more than 50 genres of music, including blues, hip-hop, and R&B.

TENNESSEE STATE UNIVERSITY

Founded in 1912 as the Agricultural and Industrial State Normal College for black students, Tennessee State University is now a comprehensive university with more than 9,000 students. In 1979, as a result of a court order to desegregate the state's universities, TSU merged with the Nashville campus of the University of Tennessee. Today TSU's student body is 75 percent African American.

Walking through the leafy, brick-building campus, which takes up more than 500 acres in North Nashville, you'll pass the historical President's Residence, the columned McWherter Administration Building, and the modern Lawson Hall. Campus tours are offered twice daily on weekdays during the school year.

MAP 8: 3500 John A. Merritt Blvd., 615/963-5000, www.tnstate.edu; 24 hours daily; campus tours 10am and 2pm Mon.-Fri. Sept.-Apr., 10am and 2pm Mon.-Thurs. May-Aug.; free

Restaurants

Look for ★ to find
recommended restaurants.

Highlights

★ **Best Meat-and-Three:** This iconic cafeteria style of eating is a Nashville way of life. **Arnold's Country Kitchen** is the essence of the experience (page 64).

★ **Best Place to See Southern Food Reinterpreted:** Sean Brock's **Husk Nashville** takes classic ingredients to new levels (page 66).

★ **Most Surprising Place to Find Southern Dishes:** Chinese street food meets the South at the unusual and elegant **Tansuo** (page 68).

★ **Best Food Theater:** Both **The Catbird Seat** and **Bastion** are about world-class dining experiences, not just what's on the plate (pages 76 and 90).

★ **Best Hamburger:** Locals love the better-than-anywhere burger, served on French bread at **Rotier's** (page 78).

★ **Best Way to Get a Cookie Before Bed: Jake's Bakes** will deliver warm cookies—and milk, if you like—to your hotel before your head hits the pillow (page 79).

★ **Most Transformative Dining Experience:** You'll feel like you've gone south of the border with the food, music, and spirit at **Plaza Mariachi** (page 91).

★ **Best Biscuit:** Lots of places are known for such flaky goodness, but since 1951 **The Loveless Cafe** is the one to beat (page 92).

★ **Late-Night Food Worth the Heartburn: Prince's Hot Chicken Shack** is open till 4am some nights. You may toss and turn, but the Nashville-style spice is worth the pain (page 92).

PRICE KEY

💲 Entrées less than $10

💲💲 Entrées $10–20

💲💲💲 Entrées more than $20

Nashville has been called "Nowville" by *GQ* magazine. Nowhere is its "nowness" more evident than in the culinary scene.

More than a few high-profile chefs—including *Chopped*'s Maneet Chauhan, RJ Cooper, and world-famous Jonathan Waxman, just to name three—have opened kitchens here, adding serious street cred to serious eats. You can find anything you want to eat here. The Catbird Seat has consistently been named one of the nation's best dining experiences. Farm-to-fork and Vietnamese cuisines shine here, too.

Of course, this is the South, and Southern food, in all its interpretations, still reigns supreme. It would be a mistake to dine your way through Nashville without indulging in spicy hot chicken, flaky biscuits, and buttery grits. Don't skip a stop at a **meat-and-three,** a Nashville-style cafeteria where you choose one meat dish (often pot roast or fried chicken) and up to three vegetables (macaroni and cheese counts as a vegetable in this context).

Different neighborhoods have their strengths and weaknesses. You're likely to have a more traditionally touristy experience in Music Valley or downtown, while the best ethnic eats are along Nolensville Pike and Charlotte Pike. East Nashville and Germantown have more than their fair share of small, chef-driven restaurants with seasonal menus. Because many of these spots have a limited number of tables, be flexible about your reservation time and plan ahead.

For all its culinary stars, Nashville is still a laid-back town, and that often means the service isn't to the level of the food, even in the fine-dining establishments. But remember to tip well—in all likelihood your server is an aspiring singer-songwriter.

Previous: freshly baked biscuits at Biscuit Love; Butcher & Bee.

BARBECUE AND SOUTHERN

THE SOUTHERN STEAK AND OYSTER 💲💲💲

When The Southern opened, it was as if a void was filled. Locals and visitors alike flocked to this sleek welcoming downtown bar and restaurant to eat oysters the likes of which are not typically found away from the coasts. In addition to the oysters, The Southern has a fun take on the classic Nashville hot chicken, gumbo, and an impressive cocktail list. Its location makes it a madhouse before the symphony or during conventions, but that buzz is part of its appeal. The Southernaire Market, around the corner, sells limited packaged grocery items, T-shirts, and other gift items perfect for bringing home to remember your trip.

MAP 1: 150 3rd Ave. S., 615/724-1762, www.thesouthernnashville.com; 7:30am-10pm Mon.-Thurs., 7:30am-11pm Fri., 10am-11pm Sat., 9:30am-10pm Sun.

THE STANDARD 💲💲💲

Located in the historic Smith House, The Standard is a restaurant of ages gone by. The service is to the standards (pun intended) of this Victorian home. You'll feel like a guest on *Downton Abbey* as your every need is attended to. Menu items include wedge salads, crab bisque, and "bacon-wrapped-bacon" (that's a pork chop wrapped in bacon). You'll need to forget your diet and bring a credit card, as dining at The Standard is neither healthy nor inexpensive. But it is a night on the town unlike any you've had in decades.

MAP 1: 167 Rosa L. Parks Blvd., 615/254-1277, www.smithhousenashville.com; 5pm-9pm Mon.-Thurs., 5pm-10pm Fri.-Sat.

PUCKETT'S GROCERY & RESTAURANT 💲💲

There's no shortage of fried chicken south of the Mason-Dixon. Even so, people often throng to one of Puckett's three locations for some of what folks say is among the area's best. The downtown outpost of this regional mainstay has classic Southern food (don't skip the fried green beans) in a casual, often crowded environment. There's live music many nights and a full bar, but the real appeal is stick-to-your-ribs comfort food in a restaurant that will get you in and out in time to see a show at the Ryman.

MAP 1: 500 Church St., 615/770-2772, www.puckettsgro.com; 7am-10pm Mon.-Thurs., 7am-11pm Fri.-Sat., 7am-9pm Sun.

★ ARNOLD'S COUNTRY KITCHEN 💲

Set in a red cinder-block building on the southern edge of downtown, Arnold's is a food lover's dream. No haute or fusion cuisine here—this is real food. It's set up cafeteria-style, so grab a tray while you peer at the wonders before you: chocolate pie, congealed salad (that's Jell-O to those who don't know), juicy sliced tomatoes, turnip greens, mashed potatoes, squash casserole, macaroni and cheese—and that's just the "vegetables." Choose a vegetable plate, with either three or four vegetables, or a meat-and-three for about a buck more. Meals come with your choice of pillowy yeast rolls or corn bread. The full lunch, plus a drink, will run you under $10. There will likely always be a line out the door at this popular spot.

MAP 1: 605 8th Ave. S., 615/256-4455, www.arnoldscountrykitchen.com; 10:30am-2:45pm Mon.-Fri.

BISCUIT LOVE $

This biscuit business started as a food truck and now has a location here in The Gulch (as well as one in Hillsboro Village). The kitchen crew here gets creative with its biscuit dough, frying it into doughnuts (aka "bonuts") and using it to make French toast served with fruit compote. Biscuits also make an appearance in myriad sandwiches, such as the East Nasty featuring signature Nashville hot chicken and cheddar. There are biscuit-less options to be had, including oatmeal, omelets and hash, but that's not why those long lines have formed out the door.

MAP 1: 316 11th Ave. S., 615-490-9584, http://biscuitlove.com; 7am-3pm daily

JACK'S BAR-B-QUE $

If you are downtown and craving barbecue, Jack's is your best option. It isn't the best in the city, but the location can't be beat. Choose from barbecue pork shoulder, brisket, turkey, ribs, or sausage, and pair it with classic Southern sides like green beans, macaroni and cheese, and fried apples. Jack's serves five types of barbecue sauce, including classic Tennessee, Texas, and Kansas City. Adding to the appeal of the decent, affordable food is the fact that Jack's service is fast and friendly. There's a second location (334 W. Trinity Ln., 615/228-9888) near East Nashville and a third location called **Jack Cawthon's Bar-B-Que** (1601 Charlotte Ave., 615/341-0517).

MAP 1: 416 Broadway, 615/254-5715, www.jacksbarbque.com; 10:30am-8pm Mon.-Thurs., 10:30am-10pm Fri.-Sat., 11am-6pm Sun.; hours may be extended during summer

HOT CHICKEN
PARTY FOWL $$

If you prefer your hot chicken joint to also have live music and a lengthy list of drinks, Party Fowl delivers with spiked slushies, a big beer list, and plenty of craft bourbon cocktails. Warm up for the main event (Nashville hot chicken, of course) with the piggy chips—bacon-fried potato chips with traditional Alabama white barbecue sauce for dipping. There's also a decent selection of salads and non-hot chicken options, including a burger, po' boys, and a whole beer can chicken. There's another location in suburban Donelson (close to Music Valley).

MAP 1: 719 8th Ave. S., 615/624-8255, http://partyfowlnashville.com; 11am-10pm Mon.-Thurs., 11am-11pm Fri., 10am-11pm Sat., 10am-10pm Sun.

NEW AMERICAN

CAPITOL GRILLE $$$

Rub elbows with legislators, lobbyists, and other members of the Music City jet set at the Capitol Grille. Located in the ground floor of the elegant Hermitage Hotel a stone's throw from the Tennessee State Capitol, this is the sort of restaurant where marriages are proposed and deals are done. The menu is fine dining at its best: choice cuts of meat prepared with exacting care and local ingredients. In fact, the ingredients are grown at the nearby Farm at Glen Leven, and this connection to the land has made the restaurant one of the leaders in the farm-to-fork movement. Dinner features rack of elk, sea bass, and pork chops; the provenance of each is noted on the menu. The lunch menu is more modest, including the Capitol Grille burger, a grilled pimento cheese sandwich, and meat entrées. Breakfast may be the most decadent of all, with cinnamon-swirl French toast, eggs Benedict, lobster and shirred eggs, and an array of fresh pastries and fruit. Adjacent to the Capitol Grille is the old-school **Oak Bar,** a wood-paneled and intimate bar for pre- or postdinner drinks and conversation.

MAP 1: Hermitage Hotel, 231 6th Ave. N., 615/345-7116, www.capitolgrillenashville.com; 6:30am-11am, 11:30am-2pm, and 5pm-10pm daily (brunch 11am-2pm Sat.-Sun.)

FIN & PEARL $$$

A relative newcomer to The Gulch, Fin & Pearl has quickly become the city's seafood star. The menu includes a large selection of raw oysters, braised and grilled octopus, a tapenade salad, and fried whole bronzini. The decor is sleek but not overly minimalist. This is one spot where you're likely to meet both locals and tourists.

MAP 1: 211 12th Ave. S., 615/577-6688, https://finandpearl.com; 7:30am-10pm Mon.-Thurs., 7:30am-11pm Fri., 10am-11pm Sat., 10am-10pm Sun.

GRAY & DUDLEY $$$

Named for the building's former identity as Gray & Dudley Hardware Company, this bar and restaurant is attached to the swanky 21c Museum Hotel. Expect trendy bar snacks, contemporary American entrées, and, for dessert, perhaps the most decadent cream puff you've ever laid eyes on. Also not to be missed: Some pretty incredible art, including ceramic sculptures from artist Beth Cavener Stichter. The cozy environment can be both date-night intimate or work-meeting appropriate.

MAP 1: 221 2nd Ave., 615/610-6460, www.grayanddudley.com; 7am-11am, 11:30am-3pm, and 5:30pm-10pm Mon.-Thurs., 7am-11am, 11:30am-3pm, and 5:30pm-11pm Fri., 7am-3pm and 5:30pm-11pm Sat., 7am-3pm and 5:30pm-10pm Sun. (lounge until midnight Sun.-Thurs., 1am Fri.-Sat.)

★ HUSK NASHVILLE $$$

Nestled in Rutledge Hill, in a historical former mayoral home, Husk Nashville was one of the most anticipated restaurants to open in 2013, and years later, it is still one of the city's most coveted tables. Owned by chef

Sean Brock, Husk relies on Southern ingredients, but not necessarily traditional Southern recipes. The menu changes daily, based on what is available locally and even from the restaurant's own garden. Attention to detail is tantamount at Husk: Order a steak and choose your own handcrafted knife; signage in front lists the source of ingredients. Service is attentive and the ambience welcoming.

MAP 1: 37 Rutledge St., 615/256-6565, www.husknashville.com; 11am-2pm and 5pm-10pm Mon.-Thurs., 11am-2pm and 5pm-11pm Fri., 10am-2pm and 5pm-11pm Sat., 10am-2pm and 5pm-10pm Sun.

MERCHANTS ⑤⑤⑤

Since 1892, Merchants has been a fixture in downtown Nashville, first as a hotel and then, beginning in 1988, as a restaurant. In the 1990s it was the go-to place for proms and parents' weekends, and as a result got a little sleepy. The current owners—the folks behind The Catbird Seat, Patterson House, Pinewood, and others—revitalized the joint. Now it is two distinct spaces—one upstairs, one down—that appeal to business diners, visitors, and the special-occasion crowd. The menu is classic: Cobb salads, burgers, fried green tomatoes, steaks, chops, and more.

MAP 1: 401 Broadway, 615/254-1892, www.merchantsrestaurant.com; downstairs 11am-11pm Mon.-Thurs., 11am-1am Fri., 10:30am-1am Sat., 10:30am-11pm Sun., upstairs 5pm-10pm daily

WATERMARK ⑤⑤⑤

With one of the first "modern Southern" menus in town, Watermark ushered in a new dining scene to Nashville. Many new restaurants have opened in Music City since, but Watermark has remained at the top of the culinary scene. Watermark creates European-influenced Southern dishes, with cream sauces and deconstructed approaches to traditional recipes. The wine list is ample. Service is professional and befitting of a fine-dining establishment.

MAP 1: 210 4th Ave. S., 615/254-2000, www.watermark-restaurant.com; 5:30pm-9:30pm Mon.-Thurs., 5:30pm-10pm Fri.-Sat.

ADELE'S ⑤⑤

In a former automobile garage in The Gulch, chef Jonathan Waxman brought Music City his signature clean California-inspired food. The menu is heavy on seasonal ingredients, and changes as a result, but not in a heavy-handed way. The JW chicken and JW potatoes are year-round favorites. The open kitchen and sleek design are welcoming, but not overly fussy, just like the food. Somehow Adele's, which was inspired by Waxman's mother, manages to be both somewhere you can take kids or go on a date night. The wine and cocktail lists are impressive.

MAP 1: 1210 McGavock St., 615/988-9700, www.adelesnashville.com; 5pm-10pm Mon.-Thurs., 11am-11pm Fri.-Sat., 10:30am-10pm Sun.

WHISKEY KITCHEN ❸❸

This restaurant/bar is one of The Gulch's many see-and-be-seen spots. Starting as soon as the office crowd shuts down their laptops, Whiskey Kitchen has a happening bar scene, with both indoor and outdoor space. The outdoor patios are heated so that they can corral the crowds even in cold-weather months. The menu is better than bar food, with good burgers, a variation of Nashville hot chicken, and lots of dishes made with—you guessed it—whiskey. The wine and cocktail list is creative.

MAP 1: 118 12th Ave. S., 615/254-3029, www.mstreetnashville.com/whiskey-kitchen; 11am-1am Sun.-Thurs., 11am-2am Fri.-Sat.

PINEWOOD ❸

Part coffee shop, part restaurant, and part adult playland, there's a little bit of something for everyone at indoor-outdoor Pinewood. It sounds like a disaster—upscale cocktails and bowling and smoked short ribs all together—but it is a delight. Don't miss the fried broccoli or the fried chicken. Cool off with frozen cocktails poolside—yes, there's an outdoor pool in summer, and also a bocce court, six bowling lanes, and a bar fashioned out of an Airstream trailer. Pinewood anchors a complex of businesses in renovated trolley barns looking at downtown, so the view from the parking lot shouldn't be missed either.

MAP 1: 33 Peabody St., 615/751-8111, www.pinewoodsocial.com; 7am-1am Mon.-Fri., 9am-1am Sat.-Sun., Airstream and patio 11am-11pm daily

ASIAN
★ TANSUO ❸❸❸

Owned by celebrity chef Maneet Chauhan, Tansuo is hard to describe. The kitchen is helmed by chef Chris Cheung, who riffs on Chinese cuisine and street fare for lunch, dinner, and Sunday brunch, with a twist of traditional Southern tastes, all inside a beautifully designed restaurant. Variations might include open-faced pork dumplings, wok-crisped fish, and a Peking duck that feeds two to four diners and requires a 48-hour preorder. The space is open, welcoming, and intimate, and the cocktails are delicious.

MAP 1: 121B 12th Ave. N., 615/782-6786, www.tansuonashville.com; 5pm-10pm Mon.-Thurs., 5pm-11pm Fri.-Sat., 10:30am-2:30pm, 5pm-10pm Sun.

DINERS AND COFFEE SHOPS
THE MOCKINGBIRD ❸❸

This self-professed "modern diner" serves cleverly named, beautifully plated dishes for sharing (or not). Seoul Purpose is bulgogi-style flank steak with a potato latke waffle and runny egg; Don't Worry, Brie Happy is a brie-packed grilled cheese with chimichurri and jalapeño jam; In Pie We Crust is the classic French dish coq au vin encased in a potpie. Prices are higher than at a traditional diner, but this is anything but traditional. The environment is that of a happening urban cocktail bar, which The

Top: array of dishes at Biscuit Love. Bottom: the menu board at Fin & Pearl.

Mockingbird also is, so the space is loud. The Mockingbird is in the same building as Tansuo and Chauhan Ale & Masala House.

MAP 1: 121 12th Ave. N., 615/741-9900, www.mockingbirdnashville.com; 4pm-10pm Sun.-Thurs., 4pm-11pm Fri.-Sat.

THE DINER $

Downtown Nashville has a lot going for it, but affordable, late-night eateries are not on that list. The Diner is a problem-solver of sorts, as, at least on some floors, the lights are always on. There are six levels, snazzy furniture and lighting, and stunning downtown views out the windows, especially from the top-floor oyster bar. The menu varies based on which floor you are seated (typical diner fare, American cuisine, or seafood), and all the dishes come from a centralized kitchen, so service can be slow. But there's free valet parking, round-the-clock service, and the location, in walking distance to lots of attractions and hotels, can't be beat.

MAP 1: 200 3rd Ave. S., 615/782-7150, www.thediner.com; 24 hours daily

FRIST CENTER CAFÉ $

Much more than the typical museum snack shop, the Frist Center Café is popular with downtown office workers and others for its fresh salads, wraps, and sandwiches. The restaurant is located at the rear of the Frist Center for the Visual Arts and has lovely outdoor seating in the warm-weather months. Sandwiches are available whole or half, and you can add a soup, salad, or fries for a well-rounded lunch. The café also has daily hot lunch entrées, plus a case of tempting desserts.

MAP 1: 919 Broadway, 615/244-3340, www.fristcenter.org; 10am-5:30pm Mon.-Wed., Sat., 10am-9pm Thurs.-Fri., noon-5:30pm Sun.

PROVENCE $

Provence, located inside the Nashville Public Library, serves excellent European-style pastries, breads, and salads, as well as coffee. Provence's signature sandwiches include creamy chicken salad and a turkey and brie version. Or you can try a sampler of the café's salads, including roasted-vegetable salad, lemon-dill potato salad, or pesto orzo salad. Save room for a decadent pastry, or at least a cookie, which come in varieties like raspberry shortbread, chocolate espresso, and ginger molasses. For breakfast, nothing beats a buttery croissant spread with jam. Provence also has locations at Iris Café at the Peabody College Library (1210 21st Ave. S., 615/322-8887) and in Hillsboro Village (1705 21st Ave. S., 615/386-0363).

MAP 1: 601 Church St., 615/664-1150, www.provencebreads.com; 7am-4pm Mon.-Fri., 9am-3pm Sat.-Sun.

SUN DINER $

Open 24 hours and just steps from The Johnny Cash Museum and the Lower Broad honky-tonks, the location and convenience of Sun Diner is hard to beat. The setup is a retro-style cafeteria counter, where you'll sit on stools and chat with the friendly staff. Hangover helpers include a break-fast burger served on a glazed doughnut, gravy-covered fried chicken and waffles, and the pork belly eggs Benedict.

MAP 1: 105 3rd St., 615/742-9099, http://sundinernashville.com; 24 hours daily

GREEK

THE GREEK TOUCH $

This small Greek eatery in the Arcade is a great Nashville find: It has rela-tively authentic Mediterranean food combined with that famous Southern hospitality. The food isn't anything unusual: spanakopita (spinach pie), baklava, gyros, and a Greek salad, plus specialties like a slow-cooked pork chop. The Greek Touch is a good choice for a quick, affordable meal down-town, plus an option for takeout.

MAP 1: 13 Arcade, 615/259-9493; 10:30am-2:30pm Mon.-Fri.

INDIAN

CHAUHAN ALE & MASALA HOUSE $$

Maneet Chauhan is known for appearing on *Iron Chef America*, *The Next Iron Chef*, and *Chopped* and now as the owner of three restaurants in Nashville. The eatery that bears her name brought Indian street food and a fusion of dishes and tastes to a city that wasn't known for its Indian cui-sine. The vibe is fun and friendly, the cocktails go down easy, and there is even an interpretation of a Nashville hot chicken dish.

MAP 1: 123 12th Ave. N., 615/242-8426, http://chauhannashville.com; 11am-2:30pm and 5pm-10pm Sun.-Thurs., 11am-2:30pm and 5pm-11pm Fri., 5pm-11pm Sat.

PIZZA

MANNY'S HOUSE OF PIZZA $

In the lower level of the downtown Arcade, Manny's House of Pizza serves up thick- and thin-crust varieties (both full pies and by the slice), massive stromboli, mighty lasagna, and huge meatball subs. The restaurant is small; eating in can be a challenge, particularly because Nashvillians flock here for the best slice in town. Manny's stays open later on the first Saturday of the month to accommodate hungry crowds at the downtown Art Crawl.

MAP 1: 15 Arcade Alley, 615/242-7144, www.mannyshouseofpizza.com; 10am-6pm Mon.-Fri., 11am-5pm Sat.

SWEETS

GOO GOO CLUSTER STORE $

Nashville's legendary candy company has been selling sweets for more than a century. In this flagship red, white, and blue shop it serves its full array of treats, plus some varieties only made in this open kitchen. Watch the dessert bar chef create something you'll love (even if your dentist doesn't), from floats to pies to cheesecake. Pick up a batch of Goo Goo Cluster candies, King Leo Peppermints, and other treats for folks

Clockwise from top left: Tansuo; Caviar & Bananas; a collection of hand mirrors decorating the wall at Henley.

at home. Goo Goo-branded hats, T-shirts, Hatch Show Print posters, and other goodies are also for sale. Don't miss the historical exhibit about the Goo Goo brand.

MAP 1: 116 3rd Ave. S., 615/490-6685, http://googoo.com; 10am-7pm daily (hours may change seasonally)

Germantown and Capitol Hill

Map 2

BARBECUE AND SOUTHERN

MONELL'S $$

Family-style dining is not for everyone. But if you know that your party wants to share platters of fried chicken and country ham, then you ought to consider doing so at Monell's. Located in a brick house in Germantown (with several other locations across the city, including one near the airport), Monell's is the local's go-to for a family brunch or celebratory Southern dinner out. Everything is all you can eat, and the menu changes based on the day of the week. Contributing to its family-friendly appeal: Kids under 3 eat free, and children 4-12 dine at a reduced price.

MAP 2: 1235 6th Ave. N., 615/248-4747, http://monellstn.com; 8am-3pm Mon., 8am-3pm and 5pm-8:30pm Tues.-Sat., 8am-4pm Sun.

BIG AL'S DELI $

More of a meat-and-three-style cafeteria than a deli, Big Al's serves up homemade Southern specialties from a modest house in Salemtown, just north of Germantown. The menu changes daily, but expect classics like pork chops and jerk chicken served with sweet tea. Whatever you do, don't skip the smashed potatoes.

MAP 2: 1827 4th Ave. N. 615/242-8118, www.bigalsdeliandcatering.com; 6am-2pm Mon.-Fri., 9am-1pm Sat.

MARY'S OLD FASHIONED PIT BAR-B-QUE $

When was the last time you were handed your food through a hole cut in the wall? That's the case at Mary's, a Memphis-style barbecue place that is long on flavor, but short on atmosphere. The pulled pork and ribs are locals' favorites, though there isn't much on the menu that isn't tasty. Mary's is best as a takeout stop, perhaps on your way to tour Fisk University, rather than a dine-in destination.

MAP 2: 1106 Jefferson St., 615/256-7696; 10am-10pm Mon.-Thurs., 10am-midnight Fri.-Sat.

NEW AMERICAN

BUTCHERTOWN HALL $$

Honoring the neighborhood's historic butcher shops, Butchertown Hall has a meat-centric menu that has fans clamoring for a seat at the Germantown table. The menu is ample, but most locals opt for either the street tacos or platters of meat. The interior is a buzzy, exciting space surrounded in subway tile and sleek, modern fixtures. As a result, the rooms inside can be loud; Butchertown isn't the place for an intimate conversation. Outside patio dining is a different decibel level. Parking is available in adjacent historical Morgan Park.

MAP 2: 1416 4th Ave. N., 615/454-3634; 11am-10pm Mon.-Thurs., 11am-11pm Fri., 10am-11pm Sat., 10am-10pm Sun.

GERMANTOWN CAFÉ $$

One of the first restaurants to embrace what eventually became the gentrified Germantown neighborhood, Germantown Café is as close to a patriarch as the area has. Some longtime residents complain that the menu hasn't changed in years and years. But others like that consistency. The menu is small but solid, with meat loaf, pork medallions, crab cakes, and salmon. Sunday brunch is very popular, particularly on holidays like Mother's Day. The lunch crowd tends to be spillover business folks from downtown. There's free valet parking at night; street parking is easy enough during the day.

MAP 2: 1200 5th Ave. N., 615/242-3226, www.germantowncafe.com; 11am-3pm and 5pm-close Mon.-Fri., 10am-2pm and 5pm-close Sat.-Sun.

HENRIETTA RED $$

From the team behind Pinewood and Bastion, along with Nashville native and chef Julia Sullivan, Henrietta Red is a seafood-friendly barroom, with an emphasis on seasonal contemporary cooking. The room is sleek and well-designed, and buzzing with activity, making for a space that's loud, but not overbearing. The marble-topped oyster bar is popular with locals from the surrounding Germantown neighborhood.

MAP 2: 1200 4th Ave. N., 615/490-8042, www.henriettared.com; 5:30pm-10pm Tues.-Fri., 10am-2pm and 5:30pm-10pm Sat.-Sun. (bar until midnight Tues.-Thurs., 1am Fri.-Sat.)

ROLF & DAUGHTERS $$

One of several farm-to-fork-focused restaurants in Germantown, Rolf & Daughters is a pasta-centric, rustic, contemporary restaurant with a killer cocktail list. The tables are communal, so you'll get to meet your neighbors as you sample from a menu that changes with the seasons. In addition to the pasta, the chicken liver and crostini is a local favorite, though some gripe about the small serving of bread that accompanies it (and an upcharge for extra bread). The restaurant is located in the century-old Werthan Factory

building. Parking is not an issue when you dine here; deciding what tasty
treat you want to order is.

MAP 2: 700 Taylor St., 615/866-9897, www.rolfanddaughters.com; 5:30pm-10pm daily

THE BAND BOX $

Located in right field of First Tennessee Park, this is a seriously hip place to
hang out during a Nashville Sounds game. You'll find gourmet spins on the
classic burgers and dogs, plus options like a quinoa chopped salad and glob-
ally inspired snacks such as empanadas and jalapeño corn fritters. Cocktails
include fun frozen options, fizzy palms, and local craft brews. Don't worry,
you can still get soft-serve ice cream in a souvenir helmet, but your focus
should be on the better-than-ballpark food. The owners operate several of
Nashville's best restaurants (including Pinewood and Bastion). There are
also board games and other diversions. If you want to eat here while the
Sounds are playing, you'll need to have tickets to the game.

MAP 2: First Tennessee Park, 401 Jackson St., one hour prior to first pitch-midnight
Thurs.-Sat. during home games

ITALIAN
CITY HOUSE $$$

One of Nashville's most acclaimed restaurants, City House is nestled in
a brick building on an unassuming block of Germantown. Chef Tandy
Wilson has received many of the nation's important culinary accolades,
including being named one of the best chefs in the South by the James
Beard Foundation. The menu is modern Italian, often heavy on the pork,
with inventive pizzas and cocktails. Service can be slow, particularly if you
come with large groups, and the space is loud, so don't expect an intimate
conversation. It is always an option to eat at the bar, which is a fun choice
if you want to chat with locals.

MAP 2: 1222 4th Ave. N., 615/736-5838, http://cityhousenashville.com; 5pm-10pm Mon.,
Wed.-Sat., 5pm-9pm Sun.

PIZZA
SLIM & HUSKY'S $

Perhaps the cornerstone of the burgeoning Buchanan Street district, this
North Nashville pizzeria (named for the respective builds of its owners)
bakes up über-popular signature pies and design-it-yourself options, plus
local beer. Pizzas come in either slim (10-inch) or husky (14-inch) sizes.
Novel options include a pizza with three kinds of pepperoni and a vegan
option with dairy-free cheese. Expect long lines if you come at peak times.

MAP 2: 911 Buchanan St., 615/647-7017, www.slimandhuskys.com; 10:30am-11pm
Mon.-Sat.

MEXICAN
LITTLE DONKEY $$

This modern taqueria in Germantown makes its own tortillas from hand-ground corn and smokes its own meats for tacos and other treats, including bowls, tortas (Mexican sandwiches), burritos, and platters. Some dishes take that Mexican cuisine and combine it with Southern traditions, resulting in a fried chicken dinner served with beans and queso fresco. The grass-fed burger topped with green chile is a favorite. Margaritas are served by the glass or pitcher.

MAP 2: 1120 4th Ave. N., #103, 615/567-5886, www.thelittledonkey.com; 11am-9:30pm Sun.-Thurs., 11am-10:30pm Fri.-Sat.

Music Row  Map 3

BARBECUE AND SOUTHERN
HOG HEAVEN $

Near Centennial Park and the Vanderbilt campus, Hog Heaven is a nondescript yet well-known landmark for barbecue. Pulled-pork sandwiches and beef brisket are among the most popular menu items at this mostly takeout eatery. What distinguishes it from other barbecue spots is a good cross section of non-pork offerings. Locals like the Alabama-style white barbecue sauce. Seating is essentially in a screened-in porch: Don't expect climate control.

MAP 3: 115 27th Ave. N., 615/329-1234, www.hogheavenbbq.com; 10am-7pm Mon.-Sat.

HOT CHICKEN
HATTIE B'S HOT CHICKEN $

For some people, Nashville-style hot chicken, that spicy, local delicacy, is only authentic if it is served panfried in a shack without AC or adequate seating. If that's your criteria, then this is not the spot for you. But for many people Hattie B's is the answer to their hot chicken prayers. The recipes are delicious, with options for everyone ranging from mild to Shut the Cluck Up, with all the amenities of a traditional restaurant, including beer and some vegetarian-friendly side dishes. There are also locations in West Nashville (5209 Charlotte Ave., 615/712-7137) and Melrose (2222 8th Ave. S.), with the same hours, more parking, and frequently shorter lines.

MAP 3: 112 19th Ave. S., 615/678-4794, http://hattieb.com; 11am-10pm Mon.-Thurs., 11am-midnight Fri.-Sat., 11am-4pm Sun.

NEW AMERICAN
★ THE CATBIRD SEAT $$$

To describe The Catbird Seat as a restaurant is a bit of a misnomer. It is a culinary performance that happens to include dinner. There are just 22 seats in this U-shaped space. Once you get a coveted reservation (available online only), you'll be treated to three hours of wines paired with a seasonal meal made before your eyes by Chef Ryan Poli. Some of the ingredients sound odd, but most of them will blow your mind. Reservations are opened 30 days in advance. The 9- to 11-course tasting menu is $115 without drinks. The nonalcoholic pairings are as inventive as the wines.

MAP 3: 1711 Division St., 615/810-8200, www.thecatbirdseatrestaurant.com; 5:30pm-9pm Wed.-Sat.

HENLEY ⑤⑤⑤

This sleek American brasserie inside the shiny new Kimpton Aertson Hotel in Midtown has James Beard Award-winning chef RJ Cooper at the helm. It's a full-service hotel restaurant, so expect breakfast, brunch, lunch, and dinner, plus an impressive lineup of signature cocktails. The cuisine is seasonal, and dishes are meant for sharing, which is easy to do from a comfy back-room leather bench or up front at the gleaming popular bar.

MAP 3: 2023 Broadway, 615/340-6378, www.henleynashville.com; 7am-10am and 5pm-10pm Mon.-Wed., 7am-10am and 5pm-11pm Thurs.-Fri., 7am-10:30am and 5pm-1am Sat., 7am-10:30am and 5pm-10pm Sun.

TIN ANGEL ⑤⑤

A neighborhood joint near the Vanderbilt campus, Tin Angel is housed in a historical building with, appropriately, tin ceilings. Described as an "American bistro," Tin Angel has solid soups, salads, and entrées, including some that are inspired by other now-shuttered favorite Nashville restaurants. Popular menu items include crab cakes, pasta dishes, and a burger made with grass-fed beef and bacon. The bar is hopping in the evenings.

MAP 3: 3201 West End Ave., 615/298-3444, www.tinangel.net; 4:30pm-10pm Mon.-Sat., 4:30pm-9pm Sun.

ASIAN

SUZY WONG'S HOUSE OF YUM ⑤⑤

The name of this restaurant reveals that it is not your average Chinese food joint. Owned by *Top Chef* alumnus Arnold Myint, Suzy Wong's has a menu of shared plates with an Asian fusion spirit. Combined with an inventive cocktail menu and a high-energy soundtrack, this is a great place to go and paint the town red with friends. The food is fun—think Asian nachos—rather than authentic, and this is not a place for kids or those who don't want to have to speak over a din. There are plenty of vegetarian and gluten-free options on the menu, too. On the weekends, come by for **Drag'n Brunch** (10am-3pm Sat.-Sun.) complete with drag performances.

MAP 3: 1515 Church St., 615/329-2913, www.suzywongsnashville.com; 5pm-10pm Tues.-Thurs., 5pm-11pm Fri.-Sat., 10am-3pm and 5pm-11pm Sun.

DINERS AND COFFEE SHOPS

CAVIAR & BANANAS 💲💲

Part café, part coffee shop, and part market, Caviar & Bananas is a Charleston-based restaurant with a location near the Vanderbilt campus. The light and bright takeout mecca is on the ground level of the Kimpton Aertson Hotel, where you'll find a glass case filled with prepared foods to eat in or take away, plus a wine and small plates menu, breakfast sandwiches, brunch bowls, sandwiches and salads, bakery goodies, and plenty of coffee and tea. Outdoor dining is offered on a street-side patio.

MAP 3: 2031 Broadway, 615/340-9005, www.caviarandbananas.com; 7am-8:30pm Mon.-Thurs., 7am-9pm Fri., 8am-9pm Sat., 8am-8pm Sun.

ELLISTON PLACE SODA SHOP 💲

In today's retro-happy world, it isn't too hard to find an old-fashioned soda shop. But how many of them are the real thing? Elliston Place Soda Shop, near Centennial Park and Vanderbilt, is one of those rare holdovers from the past, and it's proud of it. The black-and-white tile floors, lunch counter, and Purity Milk advertisements may have been here for decades, but the food is consistently fresh and good. Choose between a sandwich or a plate lunch, but be sure to save room for a classic milk shake or slice of hot pie with ice cream on top.

MAP 3: 111 Elliston Pl., 615/327-1090, www.ellistonplacesodashop.com; 7am-8pm Mon.-Thurs., 7am-10pm Fri.-Sat.

FIDO 💲

Fido is more than a coffee shop. It is a place to get work done, watch deals being made, and see and be seen. Take a seat along the front plate-glass windows to watch the pretty people as they stroll by the upscale clothing boutiques of Hillsboro Village. Don't let the laid-back vibe fool you; you can get a real meal here. In addition to coffee, the menu also features solid entrées, sandwiches, salads, and tempting baked goods.

MAP 3: 1812 21st Ave. S., 615/777-3436, www.bongojava.com; 7am-11pm daily (kitchen closes 9pm Mon., 10pm Tues.-Sun.)

★ ROTIER'S 💲

Said to have the best burger in Nashville, Rotier's is also a respected meat-and-three diner. It may look like a dive (okay, maybe it is a dive), but the food lives up to the hype. Choose from classic sandwiches or comfort-food dinners. The Saturday breakfast will fuel you all day long. Ask about the milk shake, a city favorite that appears nowhere on the menu. Whatever you order, don't miss the hash brown casserole. One of the best things about Rotier's is that it is one of the few places in Nashville where everyone goes. City politicians, Vanderbilt professors, music stars, tourists, and locals all come here for a burger, a bargain, and a blast from the past.

MAP 3: 2413 Elliston Pl., 615/327-9892, www.rotiersrestaurant.com; 10:30am-9:30pm Mon.-Tues., 10:30am-10pm Wed.-Fri., 9am-10pm Sat.

PANCAKE PANTRY ⑤

There's a lot of hype surrounding Nashville's favorite breakfast restaurant, the Pancake Pantry. Founded in 1961 and still family owned, the Pantry serves some of the best pancakes in the city. Owner David Baldwin says that the secret is in the ingredients, which are fresh and homemade. Many of the flours come from Tennessee, and the syrup is made right at the restaurant. The Pantry proves that a pancake can be much more than plain. The menu offers no fewer than 20 varieties, and that doesn't include the waffles. Try the fluffy buckwheat cakes, savory cornmeal cakes, sweet blintzes, or the old standby buttermilk pancakes. And if you decide to order eggs instead, the good news is that most of the other breakfast platters on offer come with a short stack of pancakes, too. The Pantry offers egg-white omelets for the health-conscious, and it's very kid-friendly as well, except for the fact that on weekend mornings, and many weekdays, the line for a seat at the Pantry goes out the door.

MAP 3: 1796 21st Ave. S., 615/383-9333, www.thepancakepantry.com; 6am-3pm Mon.-Fri., 6am-4pm Sat.-Sun.

INTERNATIONAL
AMERICANO ⑤⑤

Mediterranean- and Spanish-inspired tapas are the name of the game at this lively restaurant near the Vanderbilt campus. Some dishes feature Asian flavors as well, such as the spicy tuna guacamole. The Nashville hot cauliflower is an innovative veggie-centric (and relatively healthy) take on the local classic. Check the daily happy hour specials for discounted cocktails and snacks.

MAP 3: 1720 West End Ave., 615/321-2209, www.americanonashville.com; 11am-9pm Mon.-Thurs., 11am-10pm Fri., 10am-10pm Sat., 10am-9pm Sun.

MEXICAN
SAN ANTONIO TACO CO. ⑤

This Tex-Mex joint has an obsessive fan base among Vanderbilt students and alumni, who spend hours here downing tacos, soda, and oddly addictive queso dip served with light, crunchy chips. The soundtrack has literally not changed in 25 years, nor has the decor. But the real appeal of SATCO, as locals call it, is the deck, which is perfect for people-watching while drinking from a bucket of beer.

MAP 3: 416 21st Ave. S., 615/327-4322, www.thesatco.com; 11am-midnight Sun.-Thurs., 11am-1am Fri.-Sat.

SWEETS
★ JAKE'S BAKES ⑤

Need to satisfy your sweet tooth, call Jake's Bakes and within 30 minutes warm cookies will be delivered to your hotel room, conference center, meeting room, or college dorm room (you can add milk to your order, of course). Some varieties are seasonal, but Jake's has perfected its own recipes of classics such as chocolate chip and snickerdoodle. If you don't want a full dozen, you can swing by to get a single cookie to go.

MAP 3: 2422 Elliston Pl., 616/645-5916, www.jakesbakesnashville.com; 10am-11:30pm Mon.-Fri., noon-11:30pm Sat.-Sun.

Midtown and 12 South   Map 4

BARBECUE AND SOUTHERN
SWETT'S $$

One of Nashville's most beloved meat-and-threes is Swett's, family owned and operated since 1954. People come from all over the city to eat at this Nashville institution, which combines soul food and Southern cooking with great results (and in 2012 they added barbecue to their offerings). The food here is homemade and authentic, down to the real mashed potatoes, the vinegary greens, and the yeast rolls. Swett's is set up cafeteria-style. Start by grabbing dessert—the pies are excellent—and then move on to the good stuff: Country-fried steak, pork chops, meat loaf, fried catfish, and ham are a few of the usual suspects. A standard plate comes with one meat, two sides, and a serving of either yeast roll or corn bread, but you can add more sides if you like. Draw your own iced tea—sweet or unsweet—at the end of the line, and then find a seat.

MAP 4: 2725 Clifton Ave., 615/329-4418, www.swettsrestaurant.com; 11am-8pm daily

NEW AMERICAN
SLOCO $

Founded by Jeremy Barlow, Sloco is a little sandwich shop with a big idea. This is a sustainable spot, meaning ingredients are local and seasonal. If you visit Nashville in December, you won't find a tomato on your sandwich here. A percentage of proceeds are donated to local food charities. Because of the ingredients and concept, prices are higher than your typical sandwich shop. The adjacent bar Meet Room serves beer and wine with charcuterie plates.

MAP 4: 2905 12th Ave. S., 615/499-4793, www.slocolocal.com; 9am-5pm Sun.-Tues., 9am-8pm Wed.-Sat.

ASIAN
PM $$

One of the restaurants owned by *Top Chef* contestant and local celeb Arnold Myint, PM is a fun Asian eatery with an indulgent cocktail and sake list. The restaurant knows its audience, as it is smack-dab in the center of the Belmont University neighborhood. The staff are fun and energetic and know they will see most of their clients the later it gets at night. Parking can be tricky depending on the day and time you are trying to dine.

MAP 4: 2017 Belmont Blvd., 615/297-2070, www.pmnashville.com; 11am-1am daily (sushi service stops at midnight; bar open until 2am)

ATHENS FAMILY ⑤

In cities like Chicago, Greek diners like this are a dime a dozen. In Nashville, Athens is one of the only 24-hour (at least on weekends) places to get an omelet after your late-night honky-tonking. All the classic diner dishes are served here, in a bright, clean space with friendly waitstaff. There's ample parking, and prices are decent. Come on a weekend morning and expect a wait. The bacon lamb burger has been featured on national TV and is a local legend.

MAP 4: 2526 Franklin Pike, 615/383-2848, www.athensfamilyrestaurant.com; 7am-10pm Mon.-Sat., 7am-9pm Sun.

BONGO JAVA ⑤

Nashville's original coffee shop, Bongo Java is still one of its most popular. Located near Belmont University, Bongo Java is regularly full of students chatting, texting, and surfing the web thanks to free wireless internet. Set in an old house with a huge front porch, Bongo feels homey, welcoming, and perhaps a bit more on the hippie side than other Nashville coffee shops. Breakfast, including Bongo French toast, is served all day. There are other Bongo Java locations, including one in East Nashville (107 S. 11th St., 615/777-3278).

MAP 4: 2007 Belmont Blvd., 615/385-5282, www.bongojava.com; 7am-9pm daily

INTERNATIONAL

INTERNATIONAL MARKET AND RESTAURANT ⑤

The venerable International Market and Restaurant, near Belmont University and Hillsboro Village, is a time-honored choice for a cheap lunch in Nashville. The cafeteria serves lots of vegetable, noodle, and rice dishes, many of them Thai in origin, at prices that seem not to have risen much since the restaurant was established in 1975. If you want to splurge, order a "from the kitchen" special of pad Thai or another dish, which will be made from scratch just for you. Owner Patti Myint is the mother of *Top Chef* contestant and local restaurateur Arnold Myint.

MAP 4: 2010 Belmont Blvd., 615/297-4453, www.internationalnashville.com; 11am-9:30pm daily

PIZZA

MAFIAOZA'S PIZZERIA AND NEIGHBORHOOD PUB ⑤⑤

This is a busy pizza spot with beer on tap and an open kitchen where you can see your pizza slide into the oven. In an effort to keep little ones entertained, kids are welcome to roll out their own dough at the counter, then their pizzas are put in the oven first, while mom and dad have a drink or an appetizer and everyone is happy. The patio is popular on warm summer nights. Some people quibble that the pizza is not New York-style authentic, as advertised.

MAP 4: 2400 12th Ave. S., 615/269-4646, www.mafiaozas.com; 4pm-3am Tues.-Fri., 11am-3am Sat.-Sun.

SWEETS
LAS PALETAS ⑤

For years there was no sign on the door, and the only way to find Las Paletas's amazing, inventive popsicles was to follow the long line of people waiting to get in. There is now a sign (and posted hours) and, of course, still lines of locals waiting to get a perfect grapefruit paleta to cool the heat of summer or a tasty Mexican caramel treat after lunch at nearby Burger Up. The frozen treats are also sold at **Bongo East** (107 S. 11th St., 615/777-3278, www.bongojava.com) in East Nashville.

MAP 4: 2911 12th Ave. S., 615/386-2101; 11am-8pm Tues.-Sat., 11am-6pm Sun.-Mon.

East Nashville   Map 5

HOT CHICKEN
BOLTON'S SPICY CHICKEN & FISH ⑤

It is a matter of local debate whether it is Prince's or Bolton's that serves up the city's most authentic culinary specialties. Hot chicken here is served bone-in, on a piece of white bread (soaking up the heat), with a pickle on top. And it is really spicy. It's made to order and panfrying takes time, so plan for a 20-minute wait. As its name suggests, Bolton's also serves spicy fish. Bolton's has a second location (2309A Franklin Pike, 615/383-1421).

MAP 5: 624 Main St., 615/254-8015, www.boltonsspicy.com; 11am-9pm Mon.-Sat.

PEPPERFIRE ⑤

Like many things in East Nashville, the hot chicken experience at Pepperfire is a little nontraditional. Spice levels at Pepperfire range from "light mild" to "XX hot," and while the XX is hot, it has lots of flavor, not just fire. There are vegetarian-friendly options, such as a spicy grilled cheese, and chicken tenders for those who don't want the bone-in option. The long communal tables are favorites of bachelor parties in town for the weekend. Pro tip: Avoid the wait by calling in your order ahead of time so it's ready when you arrive.

MAP 5: 1000 Gallatin Ave., Ste. C, 615/582-4824, www.pepperfirehotchicken.com; 11am-9pm Mon.-Wed., 11am-10pm Thurs.-Sat.

NEW AMERICAN
MARGOT CAFÉ AND BAR ⑤⑤⑤

This small East Nashville bistro has been serving European-style food for special-occasion diners since before the neighborhood was hip. Other restaurants have more notoriety these days (and many of Margot Café's alumni have gone on to helm other restaurants), but Margot Café is still a reliable option for a nice dinner out. The menu is well edited, the service attentive, and the space cozy. The Sunday brunch, with seasonal options such as eggs and duck hash, is popular and crowded.

MAP 5: 1017 Woodland St., 615/227-4668, www.margotcafe.com; 5:30pm-10pm Tues.-Sat., 11am-2pm Sun.

BUTCHER & BEE $$

A Nashville outpost of the Charleston original, Butcher & Bee serves seasonal, shareable new American fare with global influences, including a heavy dose of Mediterranean flavors. Starters (called *mezze*) are the stars here, and the whipped feta with pita is a local obsession. The menu is heavily influenced by what's in season and inspired by chefs from around the world. Reservations are recommended for tables, but it is usually easy to grab a seat at the counter.

MAP 5: 902 Main St., 615/226-3322, https://butcherandbee.com; 11am-2pm and 5pm-10pm Mon.-Tues., 11am-2pm and 5pm-11pm Wed.-Thurs., 11am-2pm and 5pm-midnight Fri., 10am-2pm and 5pm-midnight Sat., 10am-2pm and 5pm-10pm Sun.

EASTLAND CAFE $$

Eastland was one of East Nashville's stalwart upscale dining spots before anyone else bothered to try to put a good restaurant on this side of the river. The place remains solid and cozy, with a nice menu of fish, pasta, and meat. The patio is romantic and comfortable in the summer. But it is the impressive happy hour, with specials on both food and drinks, that draws in the locals.

MAP 5: 97 Chapel Ave., 615/627-1088, www.eastlandcafe.com; 5pm-10pm Mon.-Thurs., 5pm-11pm Fri.-Sat.

THE FAMILY WASH $$

Named for the former Laundromat in which it was located when it first opened, The Family Wash is part live music listening room, part bar, part restaurant, part neighborhood gathering place. It captures the offbeat energy that so well defines Nashville. Come here to hear local musicians of all stripes (definitely not just country) and eat supper that is better than average bar food. Locals love the shepherd's pie. There's also a small takeout coffee area for that early-morning caffeine fix.

MAP 5: 626A Main St., 615/645-9930, www.familywash.com; 8am-midnight Mon.-Sat., 9am-9pm Sun.

FORT LOUISE $$

This little blue house in Inglewood has been a number of shops and restaurants over the years, but when Chicago chef Greg Biggers joined the team at this local-focused restaurant, those in the neighborhood had the feeling they finally had something that would stick around for a while. Enjoy the fun, funky dining room or the popular back patio as you sample curry-fried chicken with local honey, coconut barbecue baby back ribs with pineapple fried rice, house-made potato chips with blue cheese, or Thai chili chicken wings. Don't skip the soft serve ice cream for dessert.

MAP 5: 1304 McGavock Pike, 615/730-6273, http://hungrylikefort.com; 5pm-10pm Tues.-Fri., 10am-2pm and 5pm-10pm Sat.-Sun.

LOCKELAND TABLE ⑤⑤

Lockeland Table is one of several small farm-to-fork restaurants in Nashville. The cozy eatery is great for dining with friends or on a date, and the menu takes a creative direction on Southern specialties. Check out the chowchow, mac and cheese, and the fried green tomato salad. The space itself has a city-meets-farm vibe, but is small and therefore often crowded. Make reservations before you head over.

MAP 5: 1520 Woodland St., 615/228-4864, www.lockelandtable.com; 5pm-10pm Mon.-Sat.

MARCHÉ ARTISAN FOODS ⑤⑤

Known mostly as a brunch place, Marché is a solid East Nashville breakfast, brunch, and lunch joint, with a tiny grocery section to boot. The menu is bistro inspired, with seasonal salads and entrées, plus homemade baked goods and a decent wine list. The window-filled room looks out on busy Gallatin Pike and during the day is buzzing with good energy. You are guaranteed a long wait for weekend brunches.

MAP 5: 1000 Main St., 615/262-1111, www.marcheartisanfoods.com; 8am-4pm Tues.-Sun.

RUMOUR'S EAST ⑤⑤

Situated in an old house in the heart of East Nashville, Rumour's East is a cozy local eatery with a decent fresh menu and an impressive wine list. Dishes change seasonally but are likely to include a vegetarian option or two, salads, pizza, and entrées like meatballs or a grilled fish. Don't miss taking a peek at the beautiful curved wooden bar, even if you are seated in another room. The patio is a lovely place for alfresco dining.

MAP 5: 1112 Woodland St., 615/262-5346, http://rumourseast.com; 5pm-10pm Sun., Tues.-Thurs., 5pm-11pm Fri.-Sat.

THE PHARMACY BURGER PARLOR & BEER GARDEN ⑤

The Pharmacy is a beer garden and burger joint that has been popular beyond anyone's expectation. In addition to an in-depth beer and burger menu, the team at The Pharmacy makes sodas by hand. The big grassy backyard beer garden is packed anytime the outdoor temperatures rise. Expect long waits on weekend nights. Park in a monitored lot or a well-lit spot, as break-ins are not uncommon in the area.

MAP 5: 731 McFerrin Ave., 615/712-9527, www.thepharmacynashville.com; 11am-10pm Sun.-Thurs., 11am-11pm Fri.-Sat.

Sky Blue looks like a coffee shop, and the coffee and bagels are good, but this restaurant is a full-service option for breakfast and lunch. Breakfast is served all day and one of the reasons locals love it here, particularly the biscuit bowl, with eggs and sausage gravy. The armadillo grilled cheese sandwich has cheese on both the outside and the inside. The space is sweet and cozy, with vintage tablecloths on each table and the work of local artists on the walls. The space is small and waits can be long as locals have discovered how tasty it is—and since it appeared on the TV show *Nashville.*

MAP 5: 700 Fatherland St., 615/770-7097, www.skybluecoffee.com; 7pm-3pm daily

DINERS AND COFFEE SHOPS
BARISTA PARLOR $

To call Barista Parlor a coffee shop is a gross understatement. It is more an art gallery where the coffee is the star. A renovated auto shop, this is a big, well-designed space with great signage from local artists, uniforms from local designers, interesting furniture, and attentive servers. They take coffee very seriously here and are happy to answer your questions about their pour-over style and different blends. Be patient as your caffeine fix is prepared. The folks behind Barista also have a location in Germantown (1230 4th Ave. N., 615/401-9144), as well as one in The Gulch, called **Barista Parlor Golden Sound** (610 Magazine St., 615/227-4782). Both have essentially the same feel and vibe as the original outpost.

MAP 5: 519B Gallatin Ave., 615/712-9766, http://baristaparlor.com; 8am-8pm daily

FOOD STANDS
I DREAM OF WEENIE $

Long before there was a food truck craze, a nonmobile renovated VW bus captured the hearts of East Nashvillians. The lines continue, with people waiting for specialty hot dogs, chips, and drinks. There are a number of hot dog varieties offered on a regular basis, such as the Kraut Dog (served with sauerkraut), as well as some that are offered as specials, such as the Pizza Dog. There is a grassy area where you can sit and eat your dog, but most people take their dogs to go.

MAP 5: 113 S. 11th St., 615/226-2622; 11am-5pm Mon.-Thurs., 11am-6pm Fri.-Sun., hours vary seasonally

MEXICAN
MAS TACOS POR FAVOR $

Mas Tacos was known and loved just for its food truck, but its physical restaurant and bar where fans can go for the tasty tacos, soups, and other Mexican delights, has surpassed the truck in popularity. The menu is bigger than seems possible given the tiny kitchen, and specials change throughout the week. You order at a window, and there's almost always a line, but it moves quickly. The patio provides great East Nashville people-watching.

MAP 5: 732 McFerrin Ave., 615/543-6271; 11am-9pm Mon.-Fri., 10am-9pm Sat.

Follow That Food Truck!

Like every big city with a hipster population worth its salt, Nashville has scores of food trucks driving to and fro, selling gourmet delicacies from their wheel-based restaurants. These snack masters tend to show up at places with big lunch crowds, late night after concerts, and at large public events, so you may just run into them. **Centennial Park** is a popular stop for the trucks at lunchtime, but they also make it to many neighborhoods (and suburbs) at some point during the week. The trucks also congregate at **Nissan Stadium** three hours before Tennessee Titan home games.

Nashville Food Truck Association (http://foodtrucksnash.org) lists menus and upcoming planned stops for more than 60 trucks. If you prefer your meals alfresco, check out this list.

- One of Nashville's first food trucks, **The Grilled Cheeserie** (http://grilledcheeserie.com/truck) serves delicious grilled cheese sandwiches and tomato soup. It travels all over the city, particularly to farmers markets in the summer (and, in fact, became so popular, there's also now a shop in Hillsboro Village, 2003 Belcourt Ave.). Track it via Twitter (@GrilldCheeserie), or text CHEESE in a message to 88000.

- It is hard to miss the bright pink presence that is **Barbie Burgers.** To find their tasty burgers and sweet potato fries, check their Twitter (@BarbieBurgers).

- Twitter is the best way to find acai bowls, juices, and other healthy options from **Don Miguel** (@DMJuicery).

- **Boheme's Banana Boat** (@bohemes_banana_boat) sails into late-night spots in a boat on wheels.

- **Bao Down** (@baodownTN) uses local meats to fill its authentic Chinese steamed buns for a Tennessee take on a traditional food.

PIZZA

FINE POINTS PIZZA $

This East Nashville pizzeria doles out the closet thing Nashville has to New York-style pizza. Stop by to grab it by the slice (cut from 20-inch pies) or choose a traditional stromboli or garlic knots. Whole pies feature inventive toppings such as habanero cream sauce, sliced meatballs, or vegan cheese. The kitchen staff toss the dough in the air just like pizza makers did when you were a kid … and it is still fun to watch.

MAP 5: 1012 Woodland St., 615/915-4174, www.fivepointspizza.com; 11am-11pm Sun.-Thurs., 11am-midnight Fri.-Sat., late-night window 11pm-1am Sun.-Thurs., midnight-3am Fri.-Sat.

SANDWICHES

MITCHELL DELICATESSEN $

Not a deli in the traditional sense, Mitchell Delicatessen is one of the most creative sandwich shops in town. Order the roasted lamb and raita; a Vietnamese-style creation with pork, liver pâté, and veggies; or a BLT fit for a king. Breakfast is served until 11am, and there is also a daily menu of soups and hot plate specials. Stop here for top-notch bread, cheese, and meats for your own sandwiches, too.

MAP 5: 1306 McGavock Pike, 615/262-9862, http://mitchelldeli.com; 7am-10pm Mon.-Sat., 8am-4pm Sun.

SWEETS

THE SODA PARLOR $

Come to this retro-inspired East Nashville sweets shop for gourmet milk shakes, floats, waffle sundaes, and free arcade games. If you're in the mood for shopping, there's also a retail section with retro/hipster clothing and souvenir-type goodies. The family-friendliness of the place makes it good for sweets lovers of all ages.

MAP 5: 966 Woodland St., 615/678-7275, www.thesodaparlor.com; 11am-10pm Mon.-Sat., 11am-8pm Sun.

Music Valley Map 6

BARBECUE AND SOUTHERN

OPRY BACKSTAGE GRILL $$

Located at the Inn at Opryland, Opry Backstage Grill is the first of what may (or may not) eventually become a chain of Opry-themed restaurants. The menu is filled with family-friendly Southern dishes, such as a brisket sandwich, fried green tomatoes, and shrimp and grits. More authentic meat-and-threes can be found around town, but in the Music Valley neighborhood, this is the best choice. The decor is Opry-themed, and servers often jump up on stage to perform a quick number.

MAP 6: 2401 Music Valley Dr., 615/231-8854; 11am-10pm Mon.-Thurs., 11am-11pm Sat.-Sun.

HOT CHICKEN

SCOREBOARD BAR & GRILL $$

If you're in Music Valley and craving hot chicken, this sports bar and eatery is a solid option. Besides the usual pub grub, there are barbecued meat salads, burgers, catfish and steak dinners, and, while Scoreboard is no traditional chicken shack, many locals swear by the hot chicken, in the form of bites, tenders, or bone-in breast on Texas toast.

MAP 6: 2408 Music Valley Dr., 615/883-3866; 11am-3am daily

Top: Mexican marketplace Plaza Mariachi. **Bottom:** a burger at Butcher & Bee.

NEW AMERICAN

CASCADES AMERICAN CAFÉ $$

One of a number of restaurants inside the Gaylord Opryland Resort, Cascades is situated in the atrium, alongside an indoor waterfall (hence the name). The menu is heavy on the seafood, with Gulf fish, crab cakes, and other specialties, but there are also plenty of vegetarian options. Some decently priced lunch combos are offered, too. For breakfast, there's a buffet with an omelet and waffle station, plus breakfast meats, pastries, and fruit.

MAP 6: 2800 Opryland Dr., 615/458-6848; 6:30am-10pm daily

STEAK HOUSES

OLD HICKORY STEAKHOUSE $$$

Steak houses are not traditionally bargain dining experiences, nor are resort restaurants. So knowing that this is a one-two punch on your wallet is good preparation. Once you're committed to spending cash on your tab, you'll be pleasantly surprised. This is Opryland's highest-end restaurant, and the food and service live up to that billing. The restaurant serves all the steak house staples, many made with herbs grown on-site. Other menu items that earn acclaim include the cheese plates, Maine diver scallops, and foie gras. The restaurant's herb garden surrounds it in the hotel atrium, and patio seating lets you enjoy the atrium's views. Validated hotel parking is available.

MAP 6: 2800 Opryland Dr., 615/458-6848; 5pm-10pm Sun.-Thurs., 5pm-11pm Fri.-Sat.

THAI

SUKHO THAI RESTAURANT $

When's the last time you dined at a restaurant encircled by a go-kart track? Welcome to Music Valley, where such contradictions are par for the course. This Thai restaurant has a nice ambience that is a complete departure from the go-kart track that surrounds it. It isn't the most authentic Thai kitchen in the city, but in Music Valley, it is one of the only solid international cuisine options. The pepper steak is excellent, and the red and green curries are very good and scorching hot (but you can ask for either to be served mild). Takeout is available if you want to head back to the hotel after a long day of sightseeing.

MAP 6: 2450 Music Valley Dr., 615/883-6050, www.sukhothainashville.com; 11am-2pm and 4pm-9pm Mon.-Thurs., 11am-2pm and 4:30pm-10pm Fri., 4pm-10pm Sat.

NEW AMERICAN

★ BASTION ⑤⑤

The first thing to know about Bastion is that it's divided into two spaces. The left side is the bar, which is an offbeat, hip, popular people-watching spot with nice art, good nachos, and great drinks. The right side is the 24-seat restaurant, tables at which are at a premium as the restaurant has repeatedly made best-of lists across the country. When you arrive, you'll be given a piece of paper with an à la carte list of dishes made from fresh ingredients. Part of the experience that Chef Josh Habiger created is watching the food being prepared, and getting to talk to the staff about the concepts behind the food. The room is designed to feel like you are in someone's living room, complete with a turntable playing music. Allow enough time to fully engage in the experience of eating here. Make reservations (up to four weeks in advance).

MAP 7: 434 Houston St., Ste. 110, 615/490-8434, www.bastionnashville.com; 5:30pm-9:30pm Wed.-Sat.; bar 5pm-2am Tues.-Sat.

THE YELLOW PORCH ⑤⑤

People who like Berry Hill's Yellow Porch are incredibly loyal. Located in a cute, comfortable house, The Yellow Porch serves solid American cuisine, with good salads, appetizers, and entrées, not to mention a quality wine list and killer desserts. There is a small porch that is nice for dining in the summer, but it looks out on a traffic-heavy street.

MAP 7: 734 Thompson Ln., 615/386-0260, www.theyellowporch.com; 11am-3pm, 5pm-10pm Mon.-Sat.

CUBAN

BACK TO CUBA CAFÉ ⑤

Nolensville Pike is Nashville's ethnic food mecca, so it stands to reason that Back to Cuba opened its doors here. On the menu are traditional Cuban favorites: giant grilled sandwiches of pork, ham, and cheese; empanadas; and arroz con pollo. For dinner, try the roast pork or grilled shrimp, and don't skip the lacy fried plantains and spicy black beans. It ain't Miami, but this is the closest you'll get to authentic Cuban food in these parts.

MAP 7: 4683 Trousdale Dr., 615/837-6711; 11am-9pm Tues.-Sat.

DINERS AND COFFEE SHOPS

GABBY'S BURGERS & FRIES ⑤

Gabby's is largely a lunch spot in the gentrifying Wedgewood/Houston neighborhood (dinner service is only on Friday). Locals love this tiny place thanks to the grass-fed beef patties, handmade black bean burgers, and sweet potato fries. Expect a wait, as the place is small, and more likely than not you'll sit at the counter to eat. Police officers, active military, and fire-fighters receive 20 percent off their bills.

MAP 7: 493 Humphreys St., 615/733-3119, http://gabbysburgersandfries.com; 10:30am-2:30pm Mon.-Thurs., 10:30am-7:30pm Fri., 11am-2:30pm Sat.

THE PFUNKY GRIDDLE $

This Berry Hill restaurant has a gimmick. The tables are outfitted with hibachi-type grills. You order pancakes, eggs, or breakfast potatoes, and you're served the ingredients to cook on your own. The potatoes are particularly well-seasoned, and pancakes are all you can eat with your choice of toppings and two kinds of batter. There are sandwiches and other dishes prepared in the kitchen, should you not want to make your own food. The menu includes many gluten-free options. Waits for a table can be long on the weekend.

MAP 7: 2800 Bransford Ave., 615/298-2088, www.thepfunkygriddle.com; 8am-2pm Tues.-Fri., 7am-2pm Sat.-Sun.

KURDISH

DUNYA KABOB $

Nashville has a large Kurdish immigrant population, with plenty of authentic eateries dotting busy Nolensville Pike. If you haven't before, this is the place to try the cuisine. Kurdish specialties of chicken, lamb, beef, and seafood kabobs, grilled vegetables, and gyro sandwiches fill the menu. A buffet includes tabouleh, plus soups and salads. The surroundings are strictly no-frills, with both tables and booths, and a TV showing the news. There's ample parking in the back.

MAP 7: 2521 Nolensville Pike, 615/242-6664; 11am-9pm daily

MEXICAN

★ PLAZA MARIACHI $

This Mexican marketplace features a number of restaurants mixed with grocery stores, clothes shops, and other services. Dining highlights include Argentinean steak house Tres Gauchos, sweets shop Ninas Nieves De Garrafa, and a walk-up ceviche bar called El Ceviche Loco. Come at night and you can take free dance lessons, and even during the day there's often live music. The atmosphere can seem a little like a cruise ship—lots of flashing lights and faux scenic backdrops—but the food is fun, affordable, and festive.

MAP 7: 3955 Nolensville Pike, 615/373-9292, www.plazamariachi.com; 10am-9pm Mon.-Wed., 10am-11pm Thurs.-Sat., 10am-10pm Sun.

BARBECUE AND SOUTHERN
★ THE LOVELESS CAFE ❺❺

The Loveless Cafe is an institution, and some may argue it's a state of mind. But this little café-that-could is increasingly a destination, too, not only for Nashville visitors but also for those touring the heartland of Tennessee. The Loveless got its start in 1951 when Lon and Annie Loveless started to serve good country cooking to travelers on Highway 100. Over the years the restaurant changed hands, but Annie's biscuit recipe remained the same, and it was the biscuits that kept Nashvillians, including many famous ones, coming back for more. In 1982, then owner George McCabe started the Hams & Jams mail-order business, and in 2003 the Loveless underwent a major renovation that expanded the kitchen and dining rooms and added additional shops in the rear. The food at the Loveless is good, no doubt about it. The biscuits are fluffy and buttery, the ham salty, and the eggs, bacon, and sausage will hit the spot. The supper and lunch menu has expanded to include Southern standards like fried catfish and chicken, pit-cooked pork barbecue, pork chops, and meat loaf, as well as a few salads. Loveless is located about 20 miles from downtown Nashville; plan on a 30-minute drive out Highway 100. Once you get out of the congestion of the West End, it's a pretty trip.

MAP 8: 8400 Hwy. 100, 615/646-9700, www.lovelesscafe.com; 7am-9pm daily

JIM 'N NICK'S BAR-B-Q ❺

Another barbecue chain, Jim 'N Nick's is popular with Vanderbilt students and other west-siders who like the standards, such as pulled pork, ribs, and brisket, as well as the unusual, such as barbecue nachos. Unlike a lot of other barbecue places, Jim 'N Nick's is not a hole-in-the-wall. It has seating, a drive-through, and a wine and cocktail menu. Try the cheese biscuits.

MAP 8: 7004 Charlotte Pike, 615/352-5777, www.jimnnicks.com; 11am-9:30pm Sun.-Thurs., 11am-10:30 pm Fri.-Sat.

HOT CHICKEN
★ PRINCE'S HOT CHICKEN SHACK ❺

Out of all the food that you eat in Music City, you'll likely still be dreaming about Prince's Hot Chicken when you get home. "Hot chicken" is panfried chicken that is also spicy, and it is special to Music City. Prince's serves three varieties: mild, hot, and extra hot. Most uninitiated will find the mild variety plenty spicy, so beware. It is served with slices of white bread—perfect for soaking up that spicy chicken juice—and a pickle slice. You can add a cup of creamy potato salad, coleslaw, or baked beans if you like. When you walk into Prince's, head to the back, where you'll place your order at the window, pay, and be given a number. Then take a seat, if you can find one, while you wait for your food. You can order to go or eat in. Your food is made to order, and Prince's is very popular, so the wait often exceeds 30 minutes. Take heart, though—Prince's chicken is worth it.

MAP 8: 123 Ewing Dr., 615/226-9442; 11:30am-10:30pm Tues.-Thurs., 11:30am-4am Fri., 2pm-4am Sat.

NEW AMERICAN

SALT & VINE 🌑🌑

With its sleek subway tile and open-concept design, this West Nashville wine bar is an unexpected modern oasis. It is open for both lunch and dinner, but dinner is the draw, with options ranging from cheese and meat boards to salads, sliders, and other snacks. Mediterranean, Latin, and American flavors are all in the mix here. For wine deals, come during weekday happy hour. There's an adjacent wineshop if you'd like a bottle to go.

MAP 8: 4001 Charlotte Ave., 615/800-8517; 10am-10pm Mon.-Sat.

FRENCH

TABLE 3 🌑🌑

Amid the chains that surround the Mall at Green Hills is a surprising French food gem. The European-style bistro has solid steak frites, soups, salads, and omelets, the likes of which you'd find across the pond. Service is polite and accurate, if not speedy, and a small grocery offers to-go items if that works better for your schedule. The mall has ample parking but can be a zoo on weekend nights.

MAP 8: 3821 Green Hills Village Dr., 615/739-6900, http://table3nashville.com; 11:30am-9pm Mon., 11:30am-10pm Tues.-Thurs., 11:30am-11pm Fri.-Sat., 10:30am-9pm Sun.

ITALIAN

CAFFE NONNA 🌑🌑🌑

For some of the best Italian food in Nashville, head west to the neighborhood of Sylvan Park, where you'll find Caffe Nonna. Inspired by Chef Daniel Maggipinto's own *nonna* (grandmother), the café serves rustic Italian fare. Appetizers include salads and bruschetta, and entrées include the divine Lasagne Nonna, made with butternut squash, ricotta cheese, spinach, and sage. The service at Caffe Nonna is friendly and attentive, and the atmosphere is cozy, but the space is small. Call ahead for a table.

MAP 8: 4427 Murphy Rd., 615/463-0133, www.caffenonna.com; 11am-2pm and 5pm-9pm Mon.-Thurs., 11am-2pm and 5pm-10pm Fri., 5pm-10pm Sat.

CAFÉ FONTANELLA 🌑🌑

Café Fontanella is an Italian eatery that would not be a destination in and of itself, if not for its location. As the restaurant for the Fontanel Mansion complex, it is the best place to eat before a concert at the Carl Black Chevy Woods Amphitheater at Fontanel or before or after touring the mansion. The barnlike space that houses the restaurant is pleasant and welcoming, parking is easy, and the porch has rocking chairs when you have to wait

Top: Salt & Vine. **Bottom:** The Loveless Cafe, one of Nashville's most iconic stops.

Hot Chicken!

Nashville's most sublime food experience is not to be found in a fine restaurant or even at a standard meat-and-three cafeteria. It is served on a plate with a slice of Wonder bread and a pickle chip. It is hot chicken, a very spicy panfried delicacy, made with bone-in breast and secret spices.

Legend goes that in the 1930s a woman made an extra spicy dish to punish her philandering boyfriend. But it turned out that he *liked* it extra hot, and Prince's Hot Chicken Shack was born.

A growing number of shops specialize in this regional treat: **Hattie B's Hot Chicken** (112 19th Ave. S., 615/678-4794, www.hattieb.com); **400 Degrees** (3704 Clarksville Pike, 615/244-4467, www.400degreeshotchicken.com); **Pepperfire** (1000 Gallatin Ave., Ste. C, 615/582-4824, www.pepperfirehotchicken.com), which allows you to call in your order so it is ready for pickup by the time you arrive; **Prince's Hot Chicken Shack** (123 Ewing Dr., 615/226-9442), the most famous hot chicken shack, which has the longest lines; and **Bolton's Spicy Chicken & Fish** (624 Main St., 615/254-8015 and 2309A Franklin Pike, 615/383-1421). Each has its special spices, but the basic idea is the same. Order it as spicy as you can take it, but not so hot that you can't enjoy the flavor. Panfrying takes time, so you're likely to wait wherever you go. **Party Fowl** (719 8th Ave. S., 615/624-8255) is a good choice for a group who wants to drink with their spicy food, while **Scoreboard Bar & Grill** (2408 Music Valley Dr., 615/883-3866) is your best bet for hot chicken near the Gaylord Opryland.

If you want perks like indoor seating, air-conditioning, or other menu choices with your hot chicken, you have some options. Many local chefs like to play with the idea of hot chicken in their menus, so don't be surprised to see it pop up in unexpected places. **The Southern Steak and Oyster** (150 3rd Ave. S., 615/724-1762, www.thesouthernnashville.com) has a hot chicken salad, for example, while **Americano** (1720 West End Ave., 615/321-2209, www.americanonashville.com) uses the spices on cauliflower.

for a table. There's often live music, and the service is pleasant. The food is average traditional (think red sauce) Italian.

MAP 8: 4125 Whites Creek Pike, 615/724-1601, http://fontanel.com; 11am-9pm Mon.-Fri., 10am-10pm Sat., 10am-9pm Sun.

MEXICAN

PARK CAFE ⑤⑤⑤

Park Cafe is Sylvan Park's reliable upscale dinner-out spot, with a small but solid menu of meats and poultry. Typically at least one vegetarian-friendly item is on the menu. Like its sister restaurants **Eastland Cafe** (97 Chapel Ave., 615/627-1088, www.eastlandcafe.com) and **Pomodoro East** (701 Porter Rd., 615/873-4978, www.pomodoroeast.com), Park Cafe offers an impressive happy hour with specials on both food and drinks that draws in the locals. The space is dark in a cozy way, great for a date or an intimate chat. Parking can be challenging on Murphy Road on the weekends.

MAP 8: 4403 Murphy Rd., 615/383-4409, http://parkcafenashville.com; 5pm-10pm Mon.-Thurs., 5pm-11pm Fri.-Sat.

LOCAL TACO $

Sylvan Park's Local Taco is a small taco shop with a big patio. The taco varieties change often, and are as likely to be Korean or California-inspired as much as Mexican or Tex-Mex. There are also offbeat choices like a taco filled with Nashville hot chicken, poblano cream, and pickles. Prices are low, the margaritas are plentiful, and the joint is often jumping. Other locations are in East Nashville (100 Fatherland St., 615/454-6892) and suburban Brentwood. Parking can be a challenge.

MAP 8: 4501 Murphy Rd., 615/891-3271, www.thelocaltaco.com; 11am-9pm Sun.-Thurs., 11am-10pm Fri.-Sat.

VIETNAMESE

KIEN GIANG $

Just west of the Kroger grocery store, in a strip mall near the K&S World Market, is one of Nashville's favorite Vietnamese restaurants. The ambience is not fancy, and the service can be slow, but the spring rolls, phô, and other dishes are flavorful and authentic. Bring cash: Kien Giang does not accept plastic. (Note: Using the address "5300 Charlotte Pike" may work better in some GPS systems.)

MAP 8: 5845 Charlotte Pike, 615/353-1250; 11am-9pm daily

MISS SAIGON $

A renovation made Miss Saigon seem swanky in comparison to its neighbors, all of whom are authentic Vietnamese eateries in this area of town. Miss Saigon is in a strip mall on a hill off Charlotte Avenue; it can be easy to miss the driveway. But when you arrive, you'll find more than ample parking, friendly staff, and a fresh menu with tasty spring rolls, banh mi sandwiches, and many types of phô. Miss Saigon is usually buzzing, but there's rarely a wait for a table.

MAP 8: 5847 Charlotte Pike, 615/354-1351, www.misssaigontn.com; 10am-9pm Wed.-Mon.

SWEETS

BOBBIE'S DAIRY DIP $

Go back in time to this old-fashioned burger and ice cream shop. You park and walk up to the window. Order and then sit at one of the few picnic tables until your shake or sundae is ready. On summer nights the place is packed with families, couples on date night, and others enjoying the simplest of pleasures. Hours vary based on the weather. A hot spell may encourage them to open their doors (er, windows) in early March.

MAP 8: 5301 Charlotte Ave., 615/463-8088; 11am-7pm Mon.-Sat., noon-5pm Sun. spring-fall

FOX'S DONUT DEN $

In general, eating at a joint that is known for its signage as much as it is for its food is a bad idea. But at Fox's Donut Den, you get to take in the old-time

Not Just for Vegetarians

Nashville, with its hot chicken and its meat-and-threes, isn't known as a vegetarian paradise. But as its food scene in general has become more varied, so have the vegetarian options. Here's a look at some of the more interesting options for those looking for a plant-based meal (or two). Don't worry, omnivores, everyone will find something to eat at these spots:

- **AVO** (3 City Ave., #200, 615/329-2377): The entire menu at this quirky local favorite is plant-based, raw, and gluten-free. The AVOcado margarita (made with avocado, aged tequila, cilantro, and lime) is the talk of the town.

- **EIO & The Hive** (5304 Charlotte Ave., 615/203-0433, www.eioandthehive.com): This thoughtful restaurant in West Nashville is all about serving fare made with organic and local (the name is an acronym for Everything Is Organic), sustainably sourced ingredients. Dale Levitski, once of *Top Chef* fame, presides over the kitchen, which churns out creative dishes such as breakfast bruschetta, a tabouleh hoagie, and broth bowls.

- **Graze** (1888 Eastland Ave., 615/686-1060, www.grazenashville.com): This "plant-based bistro and bar" is at home in hip East Nashville, serving dinner as well as weekend brunch. Here, the cheese is made from cashews, the hot chicken sandwich is made with meat-free tempeh, and the banh mi is filled with seitan. There are also a handful of juices and smoothies for those looking for sustenance in liquid form.

- **Wild Cow** (1896 Eastland Ave., 615/262-2717, http://thewildcow.com): Despite the perhaps misleading name, this East Nashville joint is all about vegetarian and vegan fare made with organic and locally sourced ingredients when possible. Choose from salads, tacos, and bowls filled with grains or greens.

- **The Post East** (1701 Fatherland St., 615/457-2920, www.theposteast.com): This coffee shop and café focuses on meals for vegetarians, vegans, and gluten-free folks. The menu features breakfast classics, sandwiches, and salads, most made with organic ingredients. For a quick drink, there's a coffee bar, smoothies, and juices.

- **Sunflower Cafe** (2834 Azalea Pl., 615/457-2568, www.sunflowercafenashville.com): This Berry Hill house is home to a vegetarian cafeteria-style restaurant with a changing selection of entrées and sides served in meat-and-three style, albeit without the meat. Many of the offerings are vegan and gluten-free as well.

neon sign that graces Hillsboro Pike (and was part of a rezoning debate in Green Hills) and eat a tasty doughnut at the same time. The sweet breakfast treat of your choice is a matter of personal preference, but the apple fritters are a local favorite.

MAP 8: 3900 Hillsboro Pike, 615/385-1021; 5am-10pm Sun.-Thurs., 6am-midnight Fri.-Sat.

LA HISPANA PANADERIA ⑤

La Hispana Panaderia is one of the city's great bakery bargains. People flock here from across town for inexpensive bread and pastries that are as good as at the finest European bakery. Favorites include the crunchy white bread and their dense cookies and sweet tres leches cakes, craved by the most ardent sweet tooth.

MAP 8: 6208 Charlotte Pike, 615/352-3798; 6am-9pm daily

Nightlife

Look for ★ to find recommended nightlife.

Highlights

★ **Best Honky-Tonk:** Boot-scooting and toe-tapping are an essential part of the Nashville experience. Do it at **Robert's Western World** (page 102).

★ **Best Outdoor Music Venue:** The **Ascend Amphitheater** provides that open-air concert experience, in the heart of downtown (page 104).

★ **Bluegrass Best Bet:** For more than four decades good bluegrass has been played at **The Station Inn.** Don't miss it (page 104).

★ **Best Karaoke Joint:** Wanna pretend that you can sing like a local? Head to **Lonnie's Western Room** to belt 'em out (page 109).

★ **Best Place to Sip the Signature Drink:** There are lots of places that make Tennessee whiskey in Music City, but **Corsair Artisan Distillery** is one that is lauded by hipsters, bartenders, and other cocktail connoisseurs (page 117).

★ **Most In-Demand Venue:** The **Grand Ole Opry** is still the venue up-and-coming and veteran musicians want to play, and it still sells out many nights (page 123).

★ **Most Authentic Nashville Sound:** Whether you come for Midnite Jamboree, Cowboy Church, or something else, the **Texas Troubadour Theatre** is your best bet for a real Music City experience (page 123).

★ **Best Listening Room:** Go to **The Bluebird Cafe** if you want to hear the people who write the songs, not just those who sing them (page 124).

F rom concerts to theater, Music City earns its nickname with plenty of entertaining diversions. No trip to Nashville is complete without hearing live music.

Music City overflows with musicians and songwriters and opportunities to hear them. So whether you love to two-step or you prefer something with a different kind of beat, be sure to make time for music during your visit. (Honestly, it will be hard to ignore the sounds of music, no matter where you are in Nashville or why you came here.)

Even before you arrive in the city, you can plan out your nights thanks to the **Nashville Convention and Visitors Corporation** (www.visitmusiccity.com). Through a handy feature on their website, you can check out upcoming concerts a month or more in advance. Many venues will let you buy tickets in advance over the phone or online. **Now Playing Nashville** (www.nowplayingnashville.com) is a great resource for entertainment listings and discounted tickets. Now Playing Nashville also has a kiosk in the Nashville airport.

But don't panic if you can't plan ahead. One of the attractions of Music City is that there is always a show worth seeing somewhere. And because there are so many, there's always something that hasn't sold out.

While you're here, you must experience two of the city's most iconic venue types. The **honky-tonk** is a loud, dance-friendly home to Western swing. **Listening rooms** are quiet spots where songwriters shine.

Clubs listed in this chapter are categorized by their predominant music type, but keep in mind that variety is the name of the game. Most bars and clubs (except for honky-tonks) charge a cover when there is a band or performer, but songwriter nights and open mics are usually free.

Previous: AJ's Good Time Bar; Ascend Amphitheater.

HONKY-TONKS

AJ'S GOOD TIME BAR

Country megastar Alan Jackson bought one of Lower Broad's longtime honky-tonks, then called The Wheel, and opened AJ's Good Time Bar in 2016. The honky-tonk, named after one of Jackson's most popular songs, features a focus on country music, an increasingly rare occurrence on Broadway.

MAP 1: 421 Broadway, 615/678-4808, www.ajsgoodtimebar.com; 11am-3am daily; no cover

LAYLA'S

A cozy, dark dance hall, Layla's offers that honky-tonk trifecta: cheap beer, a hot dog cart, and no cover. It is often standing room only on Friday and Saturday nights, but that's not the only time to hear good music. Almost any time the lights are on, it's worth stepping inside. Head to the back entrance or the upper floor for more space.

MAP 1: 418 Broadway, 615/726-2799, www.laylasnashville.com; noon-midnight Sun.-Mon., noon-1am Tues., noon-2am Wed.-Sat., ages 21 and older after 6pm; no cover, donations to band encouraged

LEGENDS CORNER

Memorabilia of Nashville's past adorns the walls at Legends Corner, as you might expect from its name. This corner spot is smaller than some of the other honky-tonks, but it has the same all-day live music without some of the megacrowds that the others attract.

MAP 1: 428 Broadway, 615/248-6334, www.legendscorner.com; 10am-3am daily, ages 21 and older after 6pm; no cover, donations to band encouraged

NUDIE'S HONKY TONK

This is one of the newer honky-tonks on Lower Broad, but it has a serious connection to the past. Owned by the same folks who opened The Johnny Cash Museum, this bar celebrates all things Nudie Cohn. Nudie was the tailor who made suits for Johnny Cash and Elvis, among others. The bar is also a museum, with many of Nudie's famous works behind glass and one of his ostentatious cars, a $400,000 Cadillac El Dorado, hanging from the wall.

MAP 1: 409 Broadway, www.nudieshonkytonk.com; 11am-3am daily; no cover

★ ROBERT'S WESTERN WORLD

Robert's Western World is often voted the city's best honky-tonk by locals. Originally a store selling boots, cowboy hats, and other country music regalia, Robert's morphed into a bar and nightclub with a good gift shop and even a Sunday morning church service with gospel music. Many of the honky-tonks have similar acts playing similar music, but there's

Let's Go Honky-Tonkin'

It may be known locally as honkytonk, honky tonk, or honky-tonk, and it may be used as a noun (a bar that plays Western swing, where people dance), a verb (dancing to Western swing), or an adjective (a descriptor of the type of music), but one thing is for sure, in Nashville the honky-tonk is what makes Music City sing.

The main strip of these bars is found along Lower Broadway in the heart of downtown. They play a specific strain of country and western swing music, with a live band. Small or large, these venues all have some empty space to cut the rug because dancing is an essential part of Nashville honky-tonk.

The best places to go honky-tonking include **Tootsie's, Layla's, Legends Corner,** and **Robert's Western World.** Most of these establishments are open to all ages during the day, but convert to 21 and up after 6pm. They typically don't have a cover charge, though when the cowboy hat is passed for the band, don't forget to drop a few dollars in.

something about the energy of Robert's that makes it feel different from the rest. Hungry? Try the Recession Special, a fried bologna sandwich with chips and a PBR for five bucks.

MAP 1: 416 Broadway, 615/244-9552, http://robertswesternworld.com; 11am-3am Mon.-Sat., noon-3am Sun.; ages 21 and older after 6pm; no cover, donations to band encouraged

THE STAGE ON BROADWAY

The Stage is a honky-tonk that often plays second fiddle to the holy trinity—Robert's, Tootsie's, and Layla's—but gets its fair share of movie and TV cameo appearances. It has a large dance floor and music seven nights a week. Those under 21 are welcome before 6pm.

MAP 1: 412 Broadway, 615/726-0504, www.thestageonbroadway.com; 11am-3am daily, ages 21 and older after 6pm; no cover, donations to band encouraged

TOOTSIE'S ORCHID LOUNGE

The bright purple exterior of Tootsie's Orchid Lounge makes it hard to miss, and so it has been since 1960. This Lower Broad mainstay exudes classic country every day of the week, beginning as early as 10am. On weekend nights there are typically bands playing both upstairs and downstairs, and folks clamoring to get in and out. Tootsie's has a back door that opens onto the alley next to the Ryman. This is how Opry stars could make it from the bar to the stage in time for their curtain call. In town mid-October? Check out the annual Tootsie's birthday bash, a mammoth event. There's also a Tootsie's in the airport. It's not as fun as on Broadway, but it beats most airport bars.

MAP 1: 422 Broadway, 615/299-1585, www.tootsies.net; 10am-3am daily; no cover, donations to band encouraged

LIVE MUSIC

★ ASCEND AMPHITHEATER

This open-air concert venue offers the chance to rock out by the river in Metro Riverfront Park. Between folding seats, box seats, and the lawn, it can hold 6,800 concertgoers, all of whom get a view of the skyline and great sight lines to the stage. Almost immediately after opening in 2015, this became the place to see a big show, with well-known national acts on the schedule as well as the Nashville Symphony. Locals have been known to picnic nearby (or paddleboard or kayak on the river) during shows to hear the music being played.

MAP 1: 301 1st Ave. S., 615/999-9000, www.ascendamphitheater.com; hours vary by event; cost varies by event

Country and Bluegrass

COUNTRY MUSIC HALL OF FAME AND MUSEUM

The Country Music Hall of Fame and Museum hosts concerts, readings, and musical discussions regularly in an auditorium located inside the hall. These daytime events are often aimed at highlighting one type of country music or another, often in conjunction with a themed exhibit. The Hall of Fame is well respected, and often you'll find big names playing. Admission to concerts is free with your paid admission to the hall, so it is a good idea to plan your trip on a day when there's a concert scheduled (separate admission to concerts is not available). Check the website for a listing of upcoming events. Museum members get access to small concerts as well.

MAP 1: 222 5th Ave. S., 615/416-2001, http://countrymusichalloffame.com; 9am-5pm daily; free with museum admission or museum membership

★ THE STATION INN

It doesn't look like much (or anything) from the outside, but inside this cinder-block box is the city's most popular venue for bluegrass and roots music. The Station Inn is perhaps the country's best bluegrass club, and it showcases fine artists every night of the week. This homey and casual club opens nightly two hours before the music begins, typically at 7pm or 9pm. This is a 21-and-up club, unless you come with a parent or guardian. There is no cover for the Sunday-night bluegrass jam, at which almost everyone who is anyone picks up an instrument and plays. On Tuesday nights the beloved **Doyle & Debbie Show** (615/999-9244, www.doyleanddebbie. com; $20) offers its send-up of the music scene through live musical satire. Tickets must be purchased in advance. This cheeky show often sells out.

MAP 1: 402 12th Ave. S., 615/255-3307, http://stationinn.com; doors open 7pm daily, showtimes vary; $10-20, donations to band encouraged

WILDHORSE SALOON

The Wildhorse Saloon is a boot-scootin', beer-drinkin' place to see and be seen, though almost exclusively by tourists. When the Wildhorse opened in 1994, promoters drove a herd of cattle through the streets of downtown

Nashville. The huge dance floor is often packed with cowboys and cow-girls line dancing to the greatest country hits. Free dance lessons are of-fered every day (times vary per season). The Wildhorse books big-name acts many nights of the week, including country music, roots rock, and classic rock stars. The establishment is owned by Gaylord, the same folks who own the Ryman, Opryland, and the Opry, and it often offers deals for hotel guests. There is a shuttle (with a charge) back to the Opryland Resort for folks staying there.

MAP 1: 120 2nd Ave. N., 615/902-8200, http://wildhorsesaloon.com; 4:30pm-midnight Mon., 11am-midnight Tues.-Thurs., 11am-3am Fri.-Sun, hours may vary depending on show; cover varies based on show, typically $6 for ages 21 and older

Listening Rooms
THE LISTENING ROOM CAFÉ
This venue aims to be the best sound in town—a tall order in Nashville. Some would say that they've come pretty close. Musical offerings include up-and-coming singer-songwriters, local bands, and the occasional na-tional act. Unlike at other listening rooms, there are no rules against con-versation, but the idea is to come to hear the songwriters, not your friends. The Listening Room Café has a full menu and bar.

MAP 1: 217 2nd Ave. S., 615/259-3600, www.listeningroomcafe.com; 4pm-11pm Mon.-Fri., 10am-3pm and 4pm-11pm Sat., 10am-3pm Sun.; $5-10; $7 food/drink minimum pp per show when seated

Jazz and Blues
B. B. KING'S BLUES CLUB
If you need to get that country twang out of your head, a good dose of the Memphis blues will do it. B. B. King's Blues Club is a good place to start for a night of the blues. The club is a satellite of King's original Beale Street club, and it books live blues every night. The cover charge is usually under $10.

MAP 1: 152 2nd Ave. N., 615/256-2727, http://bbkings.com; 11am-midnight Sun.-Thurs., 11am-2am Fri.-Sat.; $5 after 7pm Sun.-Thurs., $10 after 9pm Fri.-Sat.

BOURBON STREET BLUES AND BOOGIE BAR
Located in the nightlife strip of Printers Alley, the Bourbon Street Blues and Boogie Bar is a club that is nothing fancy, but it is where to go if you your taste leans toward New Orleans-style jazz and blues. This is a small live music venue, so you get to be up close with the act on stage. Drink prices are reasonable, and the menu, with fried green tomato BLTs, po' boys, and alligator bites, fit the NOLA vibe.

MAP 1: 220 Printers Alley, 615/242-5837, www.bourbonstreetbluesandboogiebar.com; 11am-3am daily; no cover, donations to band encouraged

NIGHTLIFE DOWNTOWN

Yes, Music City Has More Than Country

It's true: Nashville is known for its country music. But Jack White relocated here. The Kings of Leon live here. The Black Keys are here. Robert Plant is often seen in 12 South. Ben Folds. Bob Dylan. The local list goes on. There is plenty of music being played, made, and heard in Music City that doesn't have a single note of twang (not that there's anything wrong with that).

If you're looking for jazz, blues, and rock music, you have lots of options. For the best and most innovative in the rock music scene, start at **Third Man Records** (623 7th Ave. S., 615/891-4393, http://thirdmanrecords.com), the music store/music venue owned by Jack White. Many of the employees are in bands themselves and can tell you what's going on around town.

Other good noncountry venues include **The Family Wash/Garage Coffee** (626A Main St., 615/645-9930, www.familywash.com), **Marathon Music Works** (1402 Clinton St., 615/891-1781, www.marathonmusicworks. com), and **The 5 Spot** (1006 Forrest Ave., 615/650-9333, www.the5spot. club).

Eclectic

3RD AND LINDSLEY

The neighborhood bar and grill 3rd and Lindsley showcases rock, alternative, progressive, Americana, soul, and R&B music. Over the years, they have developed a reputation for solid bookings, though if you were just driving down the street you wouldn't think a place that rocks could reside inside. Monday nights feature The Time Jumpers, a world-class Western swing jam band. The 3rd and Lindsley grill serves a full lunch and dinner menu, the bar is well stocked, and the club offers good sound quality and an adequate dance floor and seating. The atmosphere isn't particularly quirky or welcoming, but you came here for music, not decor.

MAP 1: 816 3rd Ave. S., 615/259-9891, www.3rdandlindsley.com; hours and cover cost vary based on event

CANNERY BALLROOM

Housed in an old warehouse that has been home to a flour mill, jam factory, and country music concert hall, Cannery Ballroom and its sisters **Mercy Lounge** and **The High Watt** are cool venues for live music. Cannery Ballroom is a large, somewhat cavernous space with lots of nice cherry-red touches, hardwood floors, and a shiny red bar. It can hold up to 1,000 people. Mercy Lounge upstairs is a bit more intimate, with a capacity of up to 500 people. The High Watt, also upstairs, holds similarly small shows. Mercy hosts 8 off 8th on Monday nights, a no-cover open mic where eight different bands each perform three songs. All three venues book rock, country, soul, and all sorts of other acts.

MAP 1: 1 Cannery Row, 615/251-3020, www.mercylounge.com; hours and cover cost vary based on event

Yes, this restaurant/wine bar/live music venue is a chain (it has locations in Chicago and New York, among others). But this chain is the brainchild of Michael Dorf, who created the iconic Knitting Factory club earlier in his career. That means even in a city like Nashville, where everyone is a musician or knows a musician, the musical lineup is impressive. Tickets typically include seating, so you can eat and drink and not crane your neck to see the act. This isn't a place where people generally get up and dance.

MAP 1: 609 Lafayette St., 615/324/1010, www.citywinery.com/nashville; 11am-2pm and 5pm-10pm Mon.-Thurs., 11am-2pm and 5pm-11pm Fri., 10:30am-2am Sat., 10:30am-2pm and 5pm-10pm Sun.; ticket prices vary

RYMAN AUDITORIUM

The most famous music venue in Nashville, the historic Ryman Auditorium continues to book some of the best acts in town, from just about every genre you can imagine. The hall also boasts some of the best acoustics around, and musicians love to show that off, often playing a song or two without a mic. It is a pleasure to watch artists' reverence for the space. (The church pew-style seats aren't particularly comfortable, but that's part of the experience.) Exhibits chronicle the auditorium's history, including a 100-seat theater experience called Soul of Nashville. Cafe Lula is the on-site restaurant.

MAP 1: 116 5th Ave. N., 615/889-3060, http://ryman.com; showtimes vary; box office and tours 9am-4pm daily; self-guided tour $20 adults, $15 children ages 4-11; backstage tour $30 adults, $25 children ages 4-11

PUBS

FLYING SAUCER

A few blocks from downtown, behind the Frist Center for the Visual Arts and Union Station, you'll find one of the city's most popular beer bars. The selection is huge, with imports, local brews, and everything in between. Monday is pint night, when you can get $3 pints of just about any of the beers on the wall. Weekday volume is manageable, but this place is packed on weekends.

MAP 1: 111 10th Ave. S., 615/259-3039, www.beerknurd.com; 11am-midnight Sun.-Thurs., 11am-2am Fri.-Sat.; no cover

BREWERIES, DISTILLERIES, AND TASTING ROOMS

JACKALOPE BREWING COMPANY

Nashville's third-oldest brewery, Jackalope offers tastings of its craft brews and tours of its small taproom. The beer selection changes monthly, so there's always an excuse to go back and try another. Jackalope's beers include Rompo Red Rye Ale, Thunder Ann American Pale Ale, and Bearwalker Maple Brown Ale. Growlers are available for purchase as well.

Celebrity Bars

What's next after you become a big country music artist? Open your own bar and music venue on Broadway, of course. Here's a quick overview of which bars might result in a megastar sighting:

· Alan Jackson bought former honky-tonk The Wheel and turned it into **AJ's Good Time Bar** (421 Broadway, 615/678-4808, www.ajsgoodtime-bar.com).

· Country megastar and Nashville local Dierks Bentley opened **Whiskey Row** (400 Broadway, http://dierkswhiskeyrow.com) in late 2017.

· *The Voice* judge and country music hottie Blake Shelton teamed up with Roman Hospitality to open **Ole Red** (300 Broadway, www.olered.com) in 2018.

· The initials at **FGL House** (120 3rd Ave. S., 615/961-5460, http://fglhouse.com) stand for Florida Georgia Line, the band that owns this multi-level bar.

· Famous duo Big & Rich are behind **Redneck Riviera** (208-210 Broadway, http://redneckrivieranashville.com), which opened in late 2017.

· Singer Gavin DeGraw and his brother are behind **Nashville Underground** (105 Broadway, 615/454-4431, www.nashunderground.com).

They offer 45-minute **tours** (Fri.-Sat.; $7, book online) which include a tasting and a souvenir pint glass.

MAP 1: 701 8th Ave. S., 615/873-4313, http://jackalopebrew.com; 3pm-8pm Mon.-Wed., 3pm-10pm Thurs., noon-8pm Fri.-Sat., noon-6pm Sun.; no cover

TENNESSEE BREW WORKS

At this taproom, you can taste the latest brews in pints, pitchers, and five-sample flights, plus order from a menu of elevated bar food, such as a pork belly BLT, an artisanal cheese board, and Nashville hot frog legs. There's live music nightly from Wednesday through Saturday, while Sunday is vinyl record day (BYO favorite to play). **Tours** (3pm, 4pm, and 5pm Sat., $7) include a 16-ounce pint of your choice.

MAP 1: 809 Ewing Ave., 615/436-0050, www.tnbrew.com; 11am-10pm Mon.-Sat., 11am-8pm Sun.

YAZOO TAP ROOM

Yazoo is the local craft beer of choice, and it can be found in most bars around town. Other bars, however, do not have the selection of the tap-room. Beer connoisseurs are very happy here. Hours change with the season, so check the website for updates. The taproom also fills growlers in case you want to take something to a party. If you're hungry, local food trucks like to park outside. **Tours** (Thurs.-Sat.; $8) of the brewery are offered, last about 45 minutes, and include beer tastings and a souvenir glass.

MAP 1: 910 Division St., 615/891-4649, http://yazoobrew.com; 3pm-9pm Wed.-Fri., 11am-9pm Sat.; no cover

BARS

ACME FEED & SEED

In the center of the city, where Broadway meets the Cumberland River, this historical building has been brought back to life. The multilevel bar, restaurant, and event space always has something going on in its 22,000 square feet of space, from trivia nights hosted by Geeks Who Drink to Americana music showcases to rooftop yoga and soul brunch. While the location screams "tourist," the combination of good views, cocktails, and events attracts plenty of locals, too.

MAP 1: 101 Broadway, 615/915-0888, http://theacmenashville.com; 11am-midnight Mon.-Thurs., 11am-3am Fri., 10am-3am Sat.; 10am-midnight Sun.; closing times can vary; no cover

★ LONNIE'S WESTERN ROOM

If you think your karaoke skills can keep up with all the Music City pros, head to Lonnie's Western Room. For 27 years this was the staple of Printers Alley. Development in the area forced Lonnie's to move around the corner, but it is still the city's number one spot for singing your heart out to prerecorded tracks. It is standing room only on the weekends; weeknights you can slip in and get a seat. Despite the name, folks do play things other than country music here.

MAP 1: 308 Church St., 615/828-7971, http://lonnieswesternroom.com; 6pm-3am daily; two-drink minimum; no cover

OAK BAR

The basement of the historical Hermitage Hotel is home to the swanky Oak Bar, a practically perfect place to have a drink before going out on the town or to the theater at TPAC. It's also great if you're just looking for something to do downtown. The cocktails are well crafted but not overly complicated and the service attentive. It can be hard to get a seat when the legislature is in session, but pretheater on weekends you might have the place to yourself. Happy hour runs daily 4:30pm to 6:30pm and features discounted drinks and snacks.

MAP 1: 231 6th Ave. N., 615/345-7116, www.capitolgrillenashville.com; 11am-11pm Sun.-Thurs., 11am-midnight Fri.-Sat.; no cover

SKULL'S RAINBOW ROOM

This historical venue originally opened in 1948. A classic cocktail from the dark wood-paneled bar is a must-have if you're on a sipping tour of downtown. Owned by Bill Miller (the brains behind Nudie's Honky Tonk

Drinks with a View

If you want evidence of Nashville's growth, look up. Music City's newest batch of hotels and high-rises brought with it a new rooftop bar scene. Want to take in the view while you sip and socialize? Try these favorites:

- Swanky **L27** (807 Clark Pl., 629/800-5070, http://l27nashville.com) atop the Westin, has an outdoor pool and two levels of city views, with food and drink. For the VIP experience, rent a cabana.

- The hip **L.A. Jackson** (401 11th Ave. S., 615/262-6007, www.lajacksonbar.com) at the Thompson hotel features DJ action from Third Man Records.

- The country-themed **UP** (901 Division St., 615/690-1722, http://uprooftoplounge.com) in The Gulch's Fairfield Inn & Suites serves disco-spiked punch and a Music City Sour (with apricot liqueur, lemon juice, and fresh rosemary) to sip while you take in the scene.

- River views are the attraction at **The George Jones** (128 2nd Ave. N., 615/818-0128, http://georgejones.com/rooftop-bar), the rooftop bar at the George Jones Museum. Look out at the Cumberland River and Nissan Stadium while enjoying the band.

- One of the four levels at Lower Broad's **The Valentine** (312 Broadway, 629/202-6979) is a stunning rooftop space.

- While **Nudie's Honky Tonk** (409 Broadway, www.nudieshonkytonk.com) boasts about its mega-long indoor bar, its rooftop deck is also a scene-stealer.

- Once you've checked out the three stages for live music, six bars, and two patios at **Crazy Town** (308 Broadway, 615/254-5460, http://crazytown-nashville.com), be sure to experience the rooftop deck.

- Open-air imbibing and dancing are on the menu at **The Stage on Broadway** (412 Broadway, 615/726-0504, www.thestageonbroadway.com).

- Live music, yoga classes, private parties, and more take place on the top of **Acme Feed & Seed** (101 Broadway, 615/915-0888, http://theacme-nashville.com), which has some of the best river views in the city.

and the Johnny Cash and Patsy Cline Museums), Skull's hosts burlesque shows seven days a week.

MAP 1: 222 Printers Alley, 615/810-9621, http://skullsrainbowroom.com; 11am-2am daily; no cover

PARADISE PARK TRAILER RESORT

Paradise Park Trailer Resort is divided into two spaces: The restaurant is on the right as you enter, the bar to your left. As the name suggests, it is decorated to look like a trailer park. Belly up to the bar to grab your drink, and stroll back to the dance floor, all the while feeling like you are outside. There are a few standard bar booths, but on Friday and Saturday nights, everyone is on the dance floor. The music is loud and generally includes bands playing covers of popular country songs. Paradise Park is a quintessential part of a downtown pub crawl. At some point, you're going to get hungry after (or while) drinking all that beer. This place can keep the beer parade going, but also claims to have the best burger in town, and you can still order it at 3am. The rest of the menu reflects the trailer resort theme with kitschy dishes like corn dogs, tater tots, and chili cheese fries.

MAP 1: 411 Broadway, 615/251-1515, http://paradiseparkonline.com; 11am-3am (bar), 10:30am-4:30am (kitchen) daily; no cover

WHISKEY KITCHEN
Sip your choice of bourbon, scotch, or whiskey neat or in cocktails at this hip hangout. The food menu features funky pub grub (think jalapeño fried pickles, yam fries, and calamari with smoked tomato dipping sauce), salads, sandwiches, burgers, and brick oven pizza. Tuesdays, order two-for-one cocktails 2pm-10pm.

MAP 1: 118 12th Ave. S., 615/254-3029, www.mstreetnashville.com/whiskey-kitchen; 11am-1am Sun.-Thurs., 11am-2am Fri.-Sat.

Germantown and Capitol Hill
Map 2

LIVE MUSIC
Jazz and Blues
NASHVILLE JAZZ WORKSHOP
The Nashville Jazz Workshop is more than a venue—it is the musical heartbeat of the city's jazz scene. Locals come here for classes, lessons, and lectures. But if you just want to listen, no worries. This is a great venue for jazz in all its definitions, from New Orleans sound to contemporary, performed by big names and serious students.

MAP 2: 1319 Adams St., 615/242-5299, www.nashvillejazz.org; hours and cover cost vary based on show

BREWERIES, DISTILLERIES, AND TASTING ROOMS
LITTLE HARPETH BREWING
German lagers are the name of the game at this brewery, named after a local waterway and located on the eastern bank of the Cumberland. The taproom also regularly hosts live music. **Tours** (6pm Fri., 5pm Sat., 4pm

Sun.; $20, book online ahead of time) of the brewery include a tasting and a glass to take home.

MAP 2: 30 Oldham St., 615/922-2690, http://littleharpethbrewing.com; 5pm-9pm Thurs.-Fri., 2pm-7pm Sat., 2pm-6pm Sun.

Music Row

Map 3

LIVE MUSIC
Listening Rooms
COMMODORE GRILLE

Commodore Grille is nestled inside the Holiday Inn near the Vanderbilt campus. Nothing about that makes it sound like a local hangout. But this has become a favorite listening room for Nashville singer-songwriters who want to perform in a quiet place with a good vibe. Their fans and friends appreciate the low-key nature and relatively easy parking. Call ahead to get info on songwriters' nights.

MAP 3: 2613 West End Ave., 615/327-4707; 5pm-10pm daily; no cover

Eclectic
CAFÉ COCO

Coffee shop by day, bar and live music venue by night. That describes Elliston Place's Café Coco, and frankly, Nashville as a whole. The space is small, but it offers a wide cross section of live music. Tuesday and Thursday are open-mic nights for songwriters, and Thursday through Saturday, it's open 24 hours. Metal and rock bands and hip-hop groups play other nights, when the cover is typically $10 or less.

MAP 3: 210 Louise Ave., 615/321-2626, http://cafecoco.com; 7am-midnight Sun.-Wed., 24 hours Thurs.-Sat.; cover cost varies by event

THE END

Proof that Nashville isn't all country and blues, this venue, close to the Vanderbilt University campus, thrives on indie rock. It is found at the end of an alley and has a dive-y feel, and people like it like that. It hosts events such as The Nashville Battle of the Bands. Most shows are 18 and older; the bar only sells beer, and the staff have been known to be as crusty as whatever is on the floor—but you come to The End for music.

MAP 3: 2219 Elliston Pl., 615/321-4457, http://endnashville.com; doors open an hour before shows, typically 8pm or 9pm; cover $5-10

EXIT/IN

For decades the Exit/In has been a favorite rock music venue, booking alternative country, blues, and reggae. The club is convenient to the Vanderbilt campus and therefore draws many Vanderbilt students. The venue is a little

worn around the edges. Grab a beer before the show at sibling bar **Hurry**
Back (2212 Elliston Pl., 615/915-0764, www.hurry-back.com).

MAP 3: 2208 Elliston Pl., 615/891-1781, www.exitin.com; hours and cover cost vary by event

PUBS

THE GOLD RUSH

Since 1974 The Gold Rush has been the place to go for a beer on Elliston Place. It remains a beloved late-night mellow hangout. The barbecue is better than you might expect, and the beer is cheap. Billiards, darts, and football on the TV round out the classic bar amenities. Brunch is served 11am-3pm on weekends with $3 Bloody Marys and mimosas.

MAP 3: 2205 Elliston Pl., 615/321-1160, www.goldrushnashville.com; 11am-3am daily; no cover

BARS

CABANA

In Hillsboro Village, Cabana is a popular place to people-watch and un-wind. It is a bar/restaurant/late-night hangout that attracts a youthful and well-dressed crowd from local universities, plus old-timers who are loyal to Cabana's longtime devotion to the neighborhood. Lounge at the bar or in the expansive backyard or reserve one of the semiprivate cabanas for your party of 2-12. Choose from dozens of beers, wines, and excellent martinis. The happy hour specials are some of the best in town.

MAP 3: 1910 Belcourt Ave., 615/577-2262, www.cabananashville.com; 4pm-10pm Sun.-Thurs., 4pm-midnight Fri.-Sat.; no cover

THE COUNTRY NASHVILLE

Equal parts bar, restaurant, and music venue, The Country draws folks for its 24 beer taps (many local), short but varied food menu (think Korean tacos, a pimento cheese-topped burger, and a daily offering of pie), and live music (despite the name, they play blues and rock as well as country here), most every night of the week.

MAP 3: 110 28th Ave. N., 615/320-4339, http://thecountrynashville.com; 4pm-midnight Sun.-Thurs., 4pm-2am Fri.-Sat.; no cover

OLD GLORY

A variety of things bring Nashvillians to this Edgehill Village bar, whether it be the airy, industrial interior (it was a boiler room in the '20s), the sea-sonal cocktails, or the DJ sets. You won't find a flashy entrance or even a sign. Get to the entrance (marked by a single gold triangle painted over the brick exterior) in the alley behind nearby restaurant Taco Mamacita. Prepare to be dazzled by the staircase as you descend.

MAP 3: 1200 Villa Pl., #103, 615/679-0509; 4pm-1am Mon.-Thurs., 4pm-2am Fri., noon-2am Sat., 4pm-1am Sun.; no cover

PATTERSON HOUSE

There's no sign on the exterior, but that hasn't kept people from across the country from discovering Patterson House. Cocktails here are mixed with care, and there's no standing room. You must have a seat in order to be served. This contributes to a civilized cocktail hour, but also means long waits. This is not a pickup scene, but a place to savor your cocktail, from its creation to its last drop. Above Patterson House is acclaimed restaurant The Catbird Seat.

MAP 3: 1711 Division St., 615/636-7724, http://thepattersonnashville.com; 5pm-1am Sun.-Wed., 5pm-3am Thurs.-Sat.; no cover

SPRINGWATER

There are basically three things you need to know about Springwater: It's a dive bar. The beer is cheap. It's cash only. All of the other details derive from these three. It's an actual dive bar, not a hip bar trying to be a dive, although somehow it has become hip, either because of this or in spite of it. The acts here are the very definition of eclectic. People-watching is especially entertaining, and more so after a few cheap beers.

MAP 3: 115 27th Ave. N., 615/320-0345, http://thespringwater.com; noon-3am daily; cover cost varies by event

GAY AND LESBIAN CLUBS

PLAY

Right next door to the club Tribe is Play, the city's highest-energy gay club, with drag shows and performances by adult-film stars. Although it is a gay bar, everyone is welcome as long as they're happy to be here. The drag shows are high-quality, but it is the dance floor (right next to the stage) that draws people in. On weekends that dance floor is packed. If you want more room to get your groove on, come on weeknights without drag shows.

MAP 3: 1519 Church St., 615/322-9627, www.playdancebar.com; 9pm-3am Wed.-Sun.; cover cost varies by event

TRIBE

You don't have to be gay to enjoy Tribe, but it helps to be beautiful or at least well dressed. The dance floor here is one of the best in the city, and the atmosphere is hip. Classic cocktails and other specialty drinks are the poison of choice at this Midtown club, which stays open until the wee hours. It has changed names and owners over the years, but has basically been the go-to gay dance spot for decades.

MAP 3: 1517 Church St., 615/329-2912, www.tribenashville.com;.5pm-1am Mon.-Thurs., 5pm-3am Fri., 11am-3am Sat., 11am-1am Sun.; no cover

COMEDY

THIRD COAST COMEDY CLUB

Founders Scott Field (founder of Improv Nashville) and Luke Watson (founder of LOL Nashville and Third Coast Improv Fest) are

established Nashville comedians who created a space just for comedy **115**
in a city where comedians were used to having to perform in music
venues. Choose from ongoing performances such as the namesake improv show Third Coast Comedy Show and the Roast the Host Open
Mic Night, plus shows from local troupes including LOL Nashville,
Music City Improv, Infinity Etc., and others. This venue, inside historical Marathon Village, is dedicated to comedy in all its forms, from
improv to sketch to stand-up.

MAP 3: 1310 Clinton St., 615/745-1009, www.thirdcoastcomedy.club; ticket prices vary,
generally $10-12

Midtown and 12 South Map 4

LIVE MUSIC
Listening Rooms
DOUGLAS CORNER CAFÉ

The Douglas Corner Café offers open mic on Tuesday nights and country and other acts the rest of the week. It's known as a listening room
where singer-songwriters show off their skills, and it's laid-back in
both attitude and ambience. An intimate setting, full menu, and decent acoustics make this a popular choice. Several live albums have
been recorded here.

MAP 4: 2106 8th Ave. S., 615/298-1688, http://douglascorner.com; 6pm-midnight
Mon.-Sat.; cover cost varies by event

Eclectic
THE BASEMENT

The Basement calls itself a cellar full of noise, but it's a good kind of noise.
Indie rock is the most common art form here, but they book other acts,
too. Admission is 21 and older, unless accompanied by a parent or guardian. The brick walls and subterranean feel give The Basement its cool atmosphere. It is nestled under Grimey's New and Preloved Music, one of
the city's best record stores. Parking is available behind the club and on
side streets.

MAP 4: 1604 8th Ave. S., 615/254-8006, http://thebasementnashville.com; showtimes
and cover cost vary; doors open one hour before showtime

MARATHON MUSIC WORKS

Housed in Marathon Village, the home of the former Marathon Motor
Works, this venue brings a modern take to an old space. This brick-lined
warehouse has two bars, a fun loftlike VIP space, and plenty of room to cut
a rug when the acts warrant it. An eclectic cross section of acts are booked
here; this is definitely not a country-music-only club. There's a parking
lot in the back, and sometimes free parking is available on the street. For

NIGHTLIFE MIDTOWN AND 12 SOUTH

Top: Jackalope Brewing Company is one of the brewers that makes Music City a beer town.
Bottom: Nudie's Honky Tonk, home to the longest bar in Nashville.

a preshow drink, stop in **William Collier's Room** (www.william-colliers.
com), a bar located inside Marathon that's open before, during, and after
shows.

MAP 4: 1402 Clinton St., 615/891-1781, www.marathonmusicworks.com; showtimes and

cover cost vary by event; box office 10am-4pm Fri. and one hour before showtime

PUBS

12 SOUTH TAPROOM AND GRILL

The extensive list of brews on tap has earned 12 South Taproom and Grill
a loyal local following. The above-average bar food includes several vegetarian-friendly options, but people come here because of the beer. Expect
a crowd—in all likelihood it will be standing room only on weekends. The
staff know their stuff and can help direct you to the right brew for your
tastes.

MAP 4: 2318 12th Ave. S., 615/463-7552, http://12southtaproom.com; 11am-midnight

daily; no cover

THE SUTLER SALOON

In the 1970s The Sutler was a dive bar/restaurant owned by country music
personality Johnny Potts. In 2014 it was reopened in the same, albeit revitalized, Melrose Theater location. It was immediately embraced by locals who remembered it (as well as those who didn't live in Music City
back in the day). The new Sutler has an impressive craft cocktail menu,
full food menu, an upstairs saloon, lower-level cellar, and a definite see-
and-be-seen vibe.

MAP 4: 2600 8th Ave. S., 615/840-6124, www.thesutler.com; saloon 11am-midnight

Mon.-Wed., 11am-2am Thurs.-Fri., 10am-2am Sat., 10am-3pm Sun.; cellar 5pm-midnight

Wed., 5pm-2am Thurs.-Sat.

BREWERIES, DISTILLERIES, AND TASTING ROOMS

★ CORSAIR ARTISAN DISTILLERY

This local distillery and brewery (they call it a "brewstillery") makes high-
end spirits, including rum, whiskey, moonshine, and vodka, plus high-
gravity beers. The team has won industry awards around the globe for
offbeat and limited-edition beverages. You can take a tour of the distillery to see how the whole thing works and then sample up to five of these
creations. Weekend tours sell out, so book in advance. Corsair also has a
location in **Wedgewood Houston** (601 Merritt Ave.).

MAP 4: 1200 Clinton St., #110, 615/200-0321, www.corsairdistillery.com; 11am-8pm

Tues.-Fri., noon-7pm Sat., noon-6pm Sun.; $8 tour and tasting, $2 tour only

COMEDY

ZANIES

Zanies books big stand-up comedy acts. Think national names, like TV
stars and stand-up comedians. Go wanting to laugh, and you will likely get

Tennessee Whiskey (And Where to Drink It)

When in Rome, do as the Romans do. When in Tennessee, drink Tennessee whiskey. Bourbon whiskey made here is considered Tennessee whiskey, and there is no shortage of different whiskeys to sip (or places to sip them).

By definition, a Tennessee whiskey must be aged for two years in new oak barrels and made from at least 51 percent corn. They are made with charcoal, a process that mellows them after distilling. As its name suggests, it must also be made in the state. The **Tennessee Whiskey Trail** (www. tennesseewhiskeytrail.com) is an organized itinerary to the state's signature distilleries. If you are up for a road trip, look at the different distilleries across the state, like the world-famous **Jack Daniel's Distillery** (visitors center 133 Lynchburg Hwy./Hwy. 55, 931/759-6357, www.jackdaniels.com), and go. Or just pick a few that are in the city limits:

- Tours and tastings are available at **Corsair Artisan Distillery** (1200 Clinton St., #110, 615/200-0321, www.corsairdistillery.com) locations in both Marathon Village and Wedgewood/Houston. Corsair is one of the area's award-winning small-batch distilleries.

- Nelson's **Green Brier Distillery** (1414 Clinton St., 615/913-8800, www. greenbrierdistillery.com) brought back a local brand, Belle Meade Bourbon, that was popular in the 1800s.

- **Pritchard's Distillery** (4105 Whites Creek Pike, 615/454-5991, http:// prichardsdistillery.com) first opened in Kelso, Tennessee, in 1997, though its recipes and name go back to the 1800s. Tour the location at Fontanel, Barbara Mandrell's former mansion, and sip samples of its small batches while enjoying the scenery.

- For a whiskey cocktail at a bar, belly up to **No. 308** (407 Gallatin Ave., 615/650-7344) or **Patterson House** (1711 Division St., 615/636-7724, http://thepattersonnashville.com).

what you paid for. There's a two-item minimum of drinks or food, neither of which is particularly remarkable. But you're there for the act, not the menu. Parking for the later weekend shows can be tricky.

MAP 4: 2025 8th Ave. S., 615/269-0221, http://nashville.zanies.com; showtimes 7:30pm Wed.-Thurs. and Sun., 7:30pm and 9:45pm Fri., 7pm, 9:15pm, and 11:30pm Sat., hours may vary; $15-25, plus a two-item minimum

LIVE MUSIC
Eclectic
THE BASEMENT EAST

A sibling venue to The Basement, this club hosts music acts of all genres several nights a week in East Nashville. New Faces Night on Tuesday is a popular place to hear singer-songwriters and artists presented by East Nashville Songwriter's Club. The original Basement's street cred and connections instantly made this venue a go-to for locals wanting to hear cutting-edge music of all kinds.

MAP 5: 917 Woodland Ave., 615/645-9174, http://thebasementnashville.com; showtimes and cover cost vary; doors open one hour before showtime

THE EAST ROOM

The East Room has high ceilings, comfy couches, and plenty of room to see the eclectic artists who perform here. Other events include midnight shows, open-mic comedy on Tuesdays, and even movie screenings. For a show schedule, check out The East Room's Facebook page.

MAP 5: 2412 Gallatin Ave., 615/335-3137; hours and cover cost vary by event

THE 5 SPOT

Fans of the television show *Nashville* know The 5 Spot as the grungy (in terms of both decor and sound) home to indie rock wannabes. With its heavy red curtains and eclectic mix, The 5 Spot has earned the title as the go-to venue on Mondays with two-for-one drinks, and its über-popular Keep on Movin' dance party featuring '50s and '60s rock, soul, and doo-wop. The crowd is equally diverse and changes depending on the night's theme.

MAP 5: 1006 Forrest Ave., 615/650-9333, www.the5spot.club; hours and cover cost vary

PUBS
SOUTHERN GRIST BREWING COMPANY

Seasonal brews at this outfit—started by three beer-loving Nashville transplants in 2017—range from Save Play, a saison with lemongrass and orange peel, to Underbite, an imperial cream ale. Munch on thin-crust pizza from 312 Pizza Company, soft pretzels with mustard, or beer cheese and truffles from Tempered Cafe & Chocolate.

MAP 5: 1201 Porter Rd., 615/727-1201, www.southerngristbrewing.com; 4pm-10pm Tues.-Fri., noon-11pm Sat., noon-8pm Sun.

Clockwise from top left: the stage at City Winery; the Doyle & Debbie Show, as seen at The Station Inn; the bar of The Listening Room Café.

SMITH & LENTZ BREWING

This brewery's list of 14-16 lagers and ales is constantly rotating. Repeat visitors will always find something new to taste, from the California Orange Imperial IPA to the Sock Tan Pale Ale. The brewery is named for its owners, Kurt Smith and Adler Lentz, who met in Texas before moving to Nashville to go into business together. Look for taproom events such as open-mic comedy and "brew and view" movie nights.

MAP 5: 903 Main St., no phone, www.smithandlentz.com; 4pm-10pm Mon.-Wed., 4pm-11pm Thurs., noon-11pm Fri.-Sat., noon-8pm Sun.; no cover

BARS

3 CROW BAR

Friendly and eclectic, with local eccentrics and possibly rock stars, 3 Crow Bar is the epitome of East Nashville. It is a particularly nice place to be on a sunny day when the garage door goes up and East Nashville in all its quirkiness walks by. This is also a great time to get the bushwhacker, a Southern concoction of rum, crème de cacao, and other secret ingredients, fed through a slushy machine. Need a place to lubricate work with a little lunch beer (open at 11am) and wireless internet? You won't be alone.

MAP 5: 1024 Woodland St., 615-262-3345, http://3crowbar.com; 11am-3am daily; no cover

THE EDGEFIELD SPORTS BAR & GRILL

The Edgefield Sports Bar & Grill is a no-frills watering hole that caters to East Nashville residents. This small neighborhood joint has the classic amenities: pool, darts, foosball, Skee-Ball, and backgammon. Locals love the burgers, but it is the no-pressure vibe that keeps them coming back.

MAP 5: 921 Woodland St., 615/228-6422; 11am-2am Mon.-Sat., 11 am-midnight Sun.; no cover

NO. 308

No. 308 is a sleek, mod hangout with handcrafted drinks. Come during happy hour (5pm-7pm Sun.-Fri.), when these custom cocktails are more budget-friendly. This spot is the definition of a hipster hangout, with its unassuming entrance nestled next to a paint store. But for all the retro furniture, the funky themed nights, and the skinny jeans, No. 308 is a friendly neighborhood bar that happens to be better looking and serves better drinks and bar food. The vibe changes as the night goes on; Friday and Saturday late nights morph into a dance party thanks to a DJ.

MAP 5: 407 Gallatin Ave., 615/650-7344, http://bar308.com; 5pm-3am daily; no cover

URBAN COWBOY PUBLIC HOUSE

This bar in the stable house behind the hipster-chic B&B of the same name serves craft cocktails and seasonal fare. Folks gather 'round the campfire

Tennessee Waltzing

In Nashville you hardly need to find a dance club to boogie. There is (quite literally) music in the streets; people will start moving whenever the mood strikes. The carillon bells play "The Tennessee Waltz" every hour on the hour at Bicentennial Mall, and it can be hard to resist the urge to start waltzing right there in public, whether you have a partner or not.

But if you want a more structured dance environ, no worries. There are dance floors, lessons, and places to cut the rug all over town. Downtown's **Wildhorse Saloon** (120 2nd Ave. N., 615/902-8200, www.wildhorsesaloon. com) offers dance lessons every single day of the week. This stop isn't considered particularly authentic by locals, but the lessons are free, the music is loud, and there's usually a good crowd.

Monday nights transform East Nashville's **The 5 Spot** (1006 Forrest Ave., 615/650-9333, www.the5spot.club) into a throwback party with swing dancing and Motown tunes. Despite taking place on a school night, it is regularly packed and lasts into the wee hours.

Nashville Palace (2611 McGavock Pike, 615/889-1540, www.nashville-palace.com) near Opryland is a good bet for line dancing without the downtown hubbub. **Plaza Mariachi** (3955 Nolensville Pike, 615/373-9292, www. plazamariachi.com) offers free salsa dancing classes many nights of the week.

for stories and delicious cocktails and food. On the weekends, brunch is served (11am-3pm).

MAP 5: 103 N. 16th St., 347/840-0525, www.urbancowboybnb.com/public-house; 4pm-11pm Tues.-Thurs., 4pm-midnight Fri., 11am-midnight Sat., 11am-11pm Sun.

GAY AND LESBIAN BARS

THE LIPSTICK LOUNGE

Women outnumber men at The Lipstick Lounge, a lesbian bar in East Nashville. This is a laid-back club with a better-than-average sound system and karaoke selection. Live music, pool, and great Tex-Mex-inspired food for brunch and dinner attract a crowd nearly every night. The crowds are more mixed during the week than on the weekends, when it is mostly gay and lesbian patrons.

MAP 5: 1400 Woodland St., 615/226-6343, http://thelipsticklounge.com; 5pm-1am Tues.-Fri., 10am-3am Sat.-Sun.; $5-10 on nights with entertainment

LIVE MUSIC
Country and Bluegrass
THE NASHVILLE PALACE

The Nashville Palace is an old-school restaurant, nightclub, and dance floor across from the Gaylord Opryland Resort. If your image of Nashville is line dancing and whatever you've seen in movies, this place is more likely to meet your mental image than anywhere on Lower Broad. Live music is on tap daily with start times for scheduled acts ranging from 5pm to 10pm. The patio makes for a good hybrid spot, if you want to hear music but not be right in the center of it all.

MAP 6: 2611 McGavock Pike, 615/889-1540, www.nashville-palace.com; 11am-2am daily; cover cost varies by event

★ GRAND OLE OPRY

If there's any one thing you really must do while in Nashville, it's go to see the Grand Ole Opry. Really. Even if you think you don't like country music, you need to give it a try. For more than 90 years, this weekly radio showcase of country music has drawn crowds to Nashville. Every show at the Opry is still broadcast live on WSM, a Nashville AM radio station. Shows are also streamed online, and some are televised on cable. But nothing beats the experience of being there. Often there is an additional Tuesday evening show.

Since this is a radio broadcast, shows start and end right on time. Every Opry show is divided into 30-minute segments, each of which is hosted by a different member of the Opry. This elite country music fraternity includes dozens of stars that you've heard of and others you haven't. The host performs two songs; one at the beginning of that half-hour segment and one at the end. In between they will introduce two or three other performers, each of whom will sing about two songs. In between segments, the announcers read radio commercials and stagehands change around the stage set.

MAP 6: 2804 Opryland Dr., 615/871-6779, www.opry.com; shows Tues., Fri., and Sat.; prices vary, typically $38-95

★ TEXAS TROUBADOUR THEATRE

The Texas Troubadour Theatre is home to a number of classic events, including the weekly Midnite Jamboree and Nashville Cowboy Church, as well as other events. The theater is nicer than you might expect, being in a strip mall, with roomy pew seating, good views of the stage, and a fun concessions stand. Every Sunday morning at 10am, locals and tourists dressed in anything from shorts to Stetsons gather here for a lively praise-and-worship country gospel church service.

MAP 6: 2416 Music Valley Dr., 615/585-9301, www.texastroubadourtheatre.com; hours and cover cost vary by event

BREWERIES, DISTILLERIES, AND TASTING ROOMS
THE BLACK ABBEY BREWING COMPANY

Three Nashville home brewers founded this brewery in 2013 to focus on Belgian-inspired ales that are both unique and accessible. **Tours** (1pm-4pm Sat., $10, book online or at the brewery) of the brewing operation include a pint glass and a 16-ounce pour of one beer. The interior has a monastery-like vibe, where arched wooden insets showcase brewery merch. Food trucks often visit on the weekends, making it a fine spot to grab a snack with your beer.

MAP 7: 2952 Sidco Dr., 615/755-0070, www.blackabbeybrewing.com; 3:30pm-8pm Mon.-Thurs., 2pm-9pm Fri., noon-9pm Sat., noon-6pm Sun.

GAY AND LESBIAN BARS
TRAX

For a low-key evening of shooting pool or a happy hour stop before dinner, TRAX is the place to go. The patio is a nice place to sit in warm weather. There is wireless internet and big-screen televisions, but little in the way of ambience. The back parking lot is well lit, a perk when leaving in the wee hours.

MAP 7: 1501 Ensley Blvd., 615/742-8856; noon-3am daily; no cover

Greater Nashville Map 8

LIVE MUSIC
Listening Rooms
★ THE BLUEBIRD CAFE

The Bluebird Cafe is where Nashville's real music magic happens. It's an unassuming room, small and, depending on the night, a bit cramped, but when people talk about how they heard so-and-so play in Nashville, odds are pretty good that it was here. The Bluebird is famous for its songwriters' nights, open mics, and performances in the round. Musicians aren't up on a stage, they are right there, with you. Since it is a small room, reservations are required, and this is not the place to plan to talk to your neighbor while the music plays. You will be shushed. Not every performer on the calendar is someone recognizable, but odds are they've written something that is. It's worth the risk to find out. Lines have always been long, but since Bluebird's appearance on the TV show *Nashville*, they're even longer. The Bluebird is all ages, except for its 10 bar seats, which are only for 21 and older.

MAP 8: 4104 Hillsboro Pike, 615/383-1461, http://bluebirdcafe.com; 5:30pm-midnight Mon. and Fri.-Sat., 5pm-midnight Tues.-Thurs. and Sun.; cover varies

Nashville's Craft Brewery Scene

No, it's not Portland or Milwaukee or other towns whose histories are steeped in beer. But Music City has seen its craft beer scene grow into something interesting in recent years. Here's a list of places to stop for a local ale (and in some cases, a taproom tour) if you crave a beer while in town:

- **Bearded Iris Brewing** (101 Van Buren St., 615/928-7988, www.beardedirisbrewing.com)

- **The Black Abbey Brewing Company** (2952 Sidco Dr., 615/755-0070, www.blackabbeybrewing.com)

- **Czann's Brewing Company** (505 Lea Ave., 615/748-1399, www.czanns.com)

- **Fat Bottom Brewing** (800 44th Ave., 615/678-5895, http://fatbottom-brewing.com)

- **Jackalope Brewing Company** (701 8th Ave. S., 615/873-4313, http://jackalopebrew.com)

- **Little Harpeth Brewing** (30 Oldham St., 615/922-2690, https://little-harpethbrewing.com)

- **New Heights Brewing Company** (927 5th Ave. S., 615/490-6901, www.newheightsbrewing.com)

- **Rock Bottom Brewery** (111 Broadway, 615/251-4677, www.rockbottom.com)

- **Southern Grist Brewing Company** (1201 Porter Rd., 615/727-1201, www.southerngristbrewing.com)

- **Smith & Lentz Brewing** (903 Main St., no phone, www.smithandlentz.com)

- **Tennessee Brew Works** (809 Ewing Ave., 615/436-0050, www.tnbrew.com)

- **Yazoo Tap Room** (910 Division St., 615/891-4649, http://yazoobrew.com)

NIGHTLIFE
GREATER NASHVILLE

RI'CHARD'S LOUISIANA CAFÉ

Ri'chard's is off the beaten track, but it's well-loved by locals craving a good listening room environment where they can hear their favorite songwriters without distractions. Don't miss the opportunity to order some great Cajun cooking while you listen.

MAP 8: 4420 Whites Creek Pike, 615/299-9590, www.richardscafe.com; 5pm-9pm Wed.-Sat., 11am-3pm Sun.; no cover

Eclectic

CARL BLACK CHEVY WOODS AMPHITHEATER

Opened in 2010, this 4,500-seat outdoor concert venue is nestled, as its name suggests, in the woods at Fontanel, a spot that used to be the home of country star Barbara Mandrell. The Carl Black Chevy Woods Amphitheater has space for picnicking on the lawn during a concert, as well as VIP boxes and folding chairs for a more traditional concert experience. This is an idyllic place to see a show, with the sunset over the city's horizon.

MAP 8: 4225 Whites Creek Pike, 615/724-1600, www.fontanel.com; hours and price vary based on event, box office 9am-5pm daily

BREWERIES, DISTILLERIES, AND TASTING ROOMS

FAT BOTTOM BREWING

This brewery focuses on beer, but it's also a spot for great food. Seasonal salads, good burgers, a cheese and charcuterie plate, and other better than bar-fare options make up the menu here, making Fat Bottom a good destination for a meal with your beer. Each of the flagship beers has a Vargus-girl style icon to distinguish it. The brewery also houses The Reserve, a 3,000-square-foot event space. The 45-minute brewery **tour** (6pm Fri., 2pm and 3pm Sat.; $10, book online) includes four beer tastes and a souvenir glass to take home.

MAP 8: 800 44th Ave., 615/678-5895, http://fatbottombrewing.com; 4pm-10pm Mon.-Thurs., 11am-midnight Fri., 10am-midnight Sat.-Sun.

BARS

GREENHOUSE BAR

Near the Mall at Green Hills, Greenhouse Bar offers specialty drinks, beers, and lots of hanging plants. To find it, look for the Green Hills Kroger and take a left. Its location means you'll find more locals than tourists. The two-story restaurant and bar has a nice patio in warm weather and plenty of TVs for the big game. The back parking lot is tiny, but there are others nearby and Uber and Lyft are always good options for a night out on the town.

MAP 8: 2211 Bandywood Dr., 615/385-4311, www.thefoodcompanynashville.com; 4pm-3am daily; no cover

Arts and Culture

Look for ★ to find
recommended arts and culture listings.

Highlights

★ **Where to Go Old School:** The annual summer **Bluegrass Nights at the Ryman** series brings the authentic bluegrass sound into Nashville's most hallowed halls (page 130).

★ **Most Unexpected Place to Admire Art:** The **21c Museum Hotel Nashville** is known for its contemporary art collection, which is free and open to the public (page 132).

★ **Best Place to See the Stage with the Little Ones: Nashville Children's Theatre** is the country's oldest children's

theater company, but the performances are anything but stodgy (page 132).

★ **Most Unexpected World-Class Art Collection:** Fisk University's **Carl Van Vechten Gallery** houses an impressive exhibit of the work and personal collection of Georgia O'Keeffe's husband, Alfred Stieglitz (page 137).

★ **Best Place to Hear the Bard:** The monthly **Shakespeare Allowed!** series from **Nashville Shakespeare** allows you to hear (and read) the plays aloud (get it?) without sets, actors, or costumes (page 143).

Long before Nashville was Music City, it was the Athens of the South, renowned for its cultural, academic, and artistic life. Universities, museums, and public arts facilities created an environment for unparalleled artistic expression.

Nashville has an opera company of its own (even if it doesn't get the attention of the Opry), not to mention an award-winning symphony (and symphony center), an innovative and growing visual arts scene, and ample opportunities to sample contemporary and classic music, film, and theater.

In the past, most of the city's arts attractions were concentrated downtown, with blocks of galleries clustered together. Even as art spreads out, this area remains bustling and interesting; it really comes alive during the **First Saturday Art Crawl** (www.nashvilledowntown.com), which takes place on the first Saturday of each month. There are free shuttles to take art lovers from gallery to gallery. Downtown is also dotted with public art projects, including the iconic red *Ghost Ballet* sculpture on the banks of the Cumberland River.

And now the neighborhood arts scene—always there, but not as publicized—is more accessible. The **East Side Art Stumble** on the second Saturday of the month gives a glimpse into East Nashville's growing, offbeat art scene and **Wedgewood/Houston's Art Night** (http://am-wh.com) does the same for its South Nashville neighborhood on the first Saturday of the month.

Previous: a dancer in Nashville Ballet's production of *Peter Pan;* 21c Museum Hotel brings contemporary art to Nashville.

CONCERT SERIES

★ BLUEGRASS NIGHTS AT THE RYMAN

In 1945 Earl Scruggs brought his banjo to the stage of the Ryman Auditorium—and with that, bluegrass became a vital part of the Grand Ole Opry. This summer series, which takes place on Thursday nights, honors that legacy. Bluegrass features some of the best pickers in the country. Starting in June and ending in July, this Ryman Auditorium series is always popular. Season passes are available, and many locals take advantage of that because they don't want to miss even one of these shows.

MAP 1: 116 5th Ave. N., 615/889-3060, http://ryman.com/bluegrass; 7:30pm Thurs. late June-late July; $30

MUSIC CITY ROOTS

In 2018 this weekly live Americana show moved downtown from nearby Franklin. The two-plus-hour multiple-act show includes live interview segments with the musical guests and on-air commercials, playing to an audience that often gets up and dances. Stay till the very end for the jam, when all the night's performers cram onstage for one last song. The show takes place on Wednesday evenings. It's a good idea to buy your tickets online in advance.

MAP 1: 423 6th Ave., no phone, http://musiccityroots.com; 7pm Wed.; $10-15

GALLERIES

THE ARCADE

If the 2nd floor of the Arcade looks locked up, it's because a number of small galleries and artists have spaces here, and their public hours are erratic at best. During the monthly **First Saturday Art Crawl** (www.nashvilledowntown.com, free), however, all the doors are open and the lights are on. This is the best place and time to see innovative and affordable art in the city, when the energy is high and the wine flows. Galleries feature artwork in media like sculpture, photography, painting, and printmaking. If you see something you like, buy it. Many of these galleries are essentially pop-up shops, and it may be hard to find the works again next month.

MAP 1: 244 5th Ave. N.; hours vary by gallery, 6pm-9pm first Sat. of the month; free

THE ARTS COMPANY

One of downtown's most accessible and eclectic galleries, The Arts Company offers exhibits of the works of local and national artists, with contemporary works ranging from the avant-garde to the everyday. The works are shown in a gallery space in an inviting historical building. Unlike

some other galleries, The Arts Company, one of the area's first galleries, **131**
typically works with a wide range of prices.

MAP 1: 215 5th Ave. N., 615/254-2040, www.theartscompany.com; 11am-5pm Tues.-Sat.;
free

HALEY GALLERY

A small gallery inside the mammoth Country Music Hall of Fame complex, Haley offers historical restrikes of original posters from the Hatch Show Print collection, as well as monoprints from Hatch master printer Jim Sherraden. The contemporary works here are interpretations of the Hatch Show Print style of classic prints; usually works on paper, but sometimes jewelry and decorative objects, too.

MAP 1: 224 5th Ave. S., 615/577-7711, http://hatchshowprint.com/haley-gallery;
9:30am-6pm Sun.-Wed., 9:30am-8pm Thurs.-Sat.; free

HERB WILLIAMS STUDIO

Herb Williams creates sculptures from Crayola crayons—not drawing with them, but using the waxy tools as ways to build his three-dimensional objects. His pieces are both whimsical and thought-provoking and increasingly well known around the globe (his work was on display in the White House). Once a curator at the Rymer Gallery, Williams is one of Music City's best-loved artists. He is willing to show off his process; just call in advance to make sure it is convenient.

MAP 1: 216 3rd Ave. N., 615/739-2449, http://herbwilliamsart.com; by appointment; free

THE RYMER GALLERY

Perhaps the most cosmopolitan of all Nashville's galleries, The Rymer Gallery installs thought-provoking exhibits with works from artists of national renown. With 3,000 square feet of exhibition space, this is often the center of activity for art crawls and other art community events, and the work shown here is typically high caliber. The Rymer also has a satellite space on Third Avenue, just a few blocks away.

MAP 1: 233 5th Ave. N., 615/752-6030, http://therymergallery.com; 11am-5pm Tues.-Sat.;
free

TINNEY CONTEMPORARY

Susan Tinney and Sarah Wilson bring some of the most challenging contemporary works to Nashville's walls. The gallery displays the works of local, regional, national, and international artists. Its welcoming space provides one of the best gathering places to sip wine and debate art during the monthly art crawls.

MAP 1: 237 5th Ave. N., 615/255-7816, http://tinneycontemporary.com; 11am-5pm
Tues.-Sat.; free

ARTS AND CULTURE DOWNTOWN

MUSEUMS

★ **21C MUSEUM HOTEL NASHVILLE**

The 21c Museum Hotel Nashville is, yes, a hotel, but it also houses a 10,500-square-foot contemporary art museum that is free and open to the public and unlike anything else in Nashville. The collection, like all of those in 21c hotels, is focused on art of the 21st century (hence the name) and tends to be fairly provocative work, including many interactive pieces. Exhibits change about once a year and rotate through the hotel chain's locations (which include Louisville and Cincinnati). The public art spaces, which are on the entry and lower levels, are free and open 24 hours a day.

MAP 1: 223 3rd Ave. N., 615/610-6400, www.21cnashville.com/museum; 24 hours daily; free

CHILDREN'S THEATER

★ **NASHVILLE CHILDREN'S THEATRE**

Nashville Children's Theatre is the oldest children's theater company in the United States. During the school year, the company puts on plays for children from preschool to elementary-school age in its colorful theater, a space that rivals a theater for grown-ups. In the summer there are drama classes for youngsters, plus lots of activities that include Mom and Dad. Recent years have included original NCT productions as well as nationally recognized plays.

MAP 1: 25 Middleton St., tickets: 615/252-4675, office: 615/254-9103, http://nashvillechildrenstheatre.org; box office 8:30am-4pm Tues.-Fri., 10am-2pm Sat. Sept.-May; showtimes generally 10am and 11:45am Tues.-Fri., 11am Sat., 2pm Sun.; $20 adults, $15 children ages 2-17

WISHING CHAIR PRODUCTIONS

Neither adults nor kids should miss the marionette shows at the Nashville Public Library. Using marionettes from the collection of former library puppeteer Tom Tichenor (dating back to the 1940s), plus others acquired from Chicago's Peekaboo Puppet Productions, the library's children's room staff put on excellent one-of-a-kind family entertainment. The group also partners with the Nashville Symphony and the Nashville Jazz Workshop, among other local institutions. Schoolchildren sometimes get to see the Wishing Chair Puppet Truck in their school parking lots.

MAP 1: 615 Church St., 615/862-5800, http://nashvillepubliclibrary.org/wishingchair; showtimes typically 9:30am, 10:30am, and 11:30am Tues.-Wed., but may vary; free

CLASSICAL MUSIC

NASHVILLE SYMPHONY ORCHESTRA

The Nashville Symphony Orchestra is housed in the remarkable Schermerhorn Symphony Center next to the Country Music Hall of Fame, one of the downtown buildings that was renovated as a result of 2010 flood damage. Nominated for 20 Grammies and selling more recordings than any other American orchestra, the symphony is a source of pride for Music City. Costa Rican conductor Giancarlo Guerrero is the symphony's seventh music director. The symphony puts on more than 200 performances each year, including classical, pops, and children's concerts. Its season spans September-May. Buying tickets online is a breeze, especially since you can easily choose where you want to sit. Discounted parking for symphony-goers is in the Pinnacle at Symphony Place, across the street from the Schermerhorn. During the summer, the symphony plays its Community Concerts series at locations across the city.

MAP 1: Schermerhorn Symphony Center, One Symphony Pl., 615/687-6400, http://nashvillesymphony.org; showtimes and ticket prices vary

Germantown and Capitol Hill

Map 2

CONCERT SERIES
LIVE ON THE GREEN

During Thursday nights in late summer, Public Square Park transforms for Live on the Green. The outdoor concert series tends to attract a lot of indie rock acts, and in recent years the names have gotten bigger, with performances from Alabama Shakes, Sheryl Crow, and Shakey Graves, among others. Live on the Green's audience is young, cool, and socially aware. Food and arts and crafts vendors line the sidewalks under tents.

MAP 2: 10 Public Sq., Public Square Park, 615/242-5600, www.liveonthegreen.com; 5pm Thurs. Aug.-early Sept., with some selected weekends; free general admission, $80-150 VIP tickets

PERFORMANCE VENUES
WAR MEMORIAL AUDITORIUM

Built in 1925 to honor Tennesseans who died in World War I, the War Memorial Auditorium is one of several live music venues that was once the home of the Grand Ole Opry (in this case 1939-1943). After the floods of 2010, it again hosted the Opry while the Opry House was under renovation. The space has a crescent-shaped stage and is known for having good acoustics, which attracts a wide variety of acts. Today the venue welcomes live musical acts, comedians, and others, including live public radio tapings, The Avett Brothers, Martina McBride, and Macklemore.

MAP 2: 301 6th Ave. N., 615/782-4030, http://wmarocks.com; varies by show

BALLET
NASHVILLE BALLET

Founded in 1981 as a civic dance company, the Nashville Ballet became a professional dance company in 1986. Entertaining more than 40,000

Top: The Nashville Symphony Orchestra plays at the Schermerhorn Symphony Center.
Bottom: Nashville Shakespeare's production of *A Midsummer Nights' Dream*.

patrons each year, the ballet performs both classical and contemporary pieces. The 22-person company often performs at the Tennessee Performing Arts Center in the James K. Polk Cultural Center downtown. Productions have included traditional story ballets such as *Romeo and Juliet*, *The Nutcracker*, and *Sleeping Beauty* as well as more modern-minded works from choreographers such as George Balanchine and Jiri Kylian.

MAP 2: Andrew Jackson Hall, 505 Deaderick St., 615/782-4040, http://nashvilleballet.com; box office 10am-5pm Mon.-Fri., and 90 minutes prior to any performance; showtimes and ticket prices vary

OPERA
NASHVILLE OPERA ASSOCIATION

Middle Tennessee's only opera association, the Nashville Opera Association puts on an average of four mainstage performances per season (Oct.-Apr.) and does a six-week tour to area schools. The opera performances typically take place at the Tennessee Performing Arts Center in the James K. Polk Cultural Center downtown. The opera's headquarters, the **Noah Liff Opera Center** (3622 Redmon St., 615/832-5242) hosts private events and some smaller performances.

MAP 2: Andrew Jackson Hall, 505 Deaderick St., 615/832-5242, http://nashvilleopera.org; box office 9am-5pm Mon.-Thurs. June-July, 9am-5pm Mon.-Fri. Aug.-May; showtimes and ticket cost vary

THEATER
NASHVILLE REPERTORY THEATRE

The Nashville Repertory Theatre is Tennessee's largest professional theater company. It stages a number of big-name shows and off-Broadway productions annually. The Rep performs in the Tennessee Performing Arts Center inside the James K. Polk Cultural Center in downtown Nashville. This is the same building that houses the Tennessee State Museum, plus some Nashville Opera performances and the Nashville Ballet. Some of their productions have included *Sense and Sensibility*, *A Christmas Story*, *Sweeney Todd*, *The Whipping Man*, *The Crucible*, *I Hate Hamlet*, and *Doubt*. The season runs October-May.

MAP 2: Andrew Johnson Theater, 505 Deaderick St., 615/782-4000, http://tennesseerep. org; box office 9am-5pm Mon.-Fri., performance times and ticket prices vary

CONCERT SERIES
MUSICIANS CORNER

Held in early summer and early fall, Musicians Corner is a concert series in its own location inside Centennial Park. There's some permanent seating in the form of stone benches, but most people bring blankets and camp chairs and hang for the day. Since 2010, more than 1,000 artists of all genres have graced this stage. Food trucks and kids' activities are on-site, but the focus is the music.

MAP 3: 2500 West End Ave., http://musicianscornernashville.com; noon-6pm Sat. May-June and Sept.-Oct., free

PERFORMANCE VENUES
BLAIR SCHOOL OF MUSIC

The Blair School of Music presents student, faculty, and visiting artist recitals frequently during the school year. Blair's ensembles include woodwind, string, brass, and big band. As Vanderbilt University's music school, Blair addresses music through academic, pedagogical, and performing activities.

MAP 3: 2400 Blakemore Ave., 615/322-7651, http://blair.vanderbilt.edu; showtimes and ticket cost varies by event

GALLERIES
SARRATT GALLERY

The Sarratt Gallery is housed in the main student center on the Vanderbilt campus, which has a more contemporary bent than the other on-campus gallery, the **Vanderbilt Fine Arts Gallery** (1220 21st Ave. S., 615/343-1702). The Sarratt frequently exhibits the work of alumni and students and kicks off the shows with popular opening receptions. The annual holiday sale is one of the best places to shop for artisan crafts in the city. The tall space is in a well-trafficked lobby of the student center, alongside a small courtyard with a fountain.

MAP 3: Vanderbilt University, 2301 Vanderbilt Pl., 615/322-2471, http://vanderbilt.edu/sarrattgallery; 9am-9pm Mon.-Fri., 10am-10pm Sat.-Sun. Sept.-mid-May, 8:30am-4:30pm Mon.-Fri. mid-May-Aug.; free

VANDERBILT UNIVERSITY FINE ARTS GALLERY

In 2009 this university gallery moved into the historical 1928 McKim, Mead and White building on Vanderbilt's pretty Peabody campus. The move prompted a shift of the gallery's mission as well. Today the gallery is home to a permanent collection of more than 6,000 objects of art. Exhibitions can be up for several months at a time and are often tied in with special lectures and other events on campus.

MAP 3: Vanderbilt University, 1220 21st Ave. S., 615/343-1702, http://as.vanderbilt.edu/gallery; 11am-4pm Mon.-Fri., 1pm-5pm Sat.-Sun. Sept.-early May; noon-4pm Tues.-Fri., 1pm-5pm Sat. early May-Aug.; free

CINEMA

BELCOURT THEATRE

Once the home of the Grand Ole Opry (as is true of so many buildings in Nashville), the Belcourt Theatre is the city's best venue for independent films. Built in 1925 as a silent movie house, the Belcourt now screens a refreshing variety of independent and unusual films, plus hosts live music concerts and other quirky performances and film fests. In the summer the Belcourt screens some films outdoors. Parking in the theater's Hillsboro Village lot is free for moviegoers. Ask for a code when you buy your ticket.

MAP 3: 2102 Belcourt Ave., 615/383-9140, www.belcourt.org; showtimes vary; $10 adults, $8 seniors, $8.50 students and military, $8 children under 12

Midtown and 12 South   Map 4

GALLERIES

AARON DOUGLAS GALLERY

Unassumingly nestled on the Fisk University campus is the Aaron Douglas Gallery, which houses the school's collection of African, African American, and folk art works. It also hosts visiting exhibits and works by Fisk students and faculty. The gallery is named after painter and illustrator Aaron Douglas, who also established Fisk's first formal art department, and located on the 3rd floor of the Fisk Library. Nearby Cravath Hall is home to several Aaron Douglas murals that are worth seeing.

MAP 4: Fisk University, 1000 17th Ave. N., 615/329-8685, http://fisk.edu; 10am-4pm Mon.-Wed. and Sat.; 10am-7pm Thurs.-Fri.; free

★ CARL VAN VECHTEN GALLERY

The Carl Van Vechten Gallery is named for the art collector who convinced artist Georgia O'Keeffe to donate to Fisk University a large portion of the work and personal collection of her late husband, Alfred Stieglitz. The college retains 50 percent interest in the collection, having sold the other half to Crystal Bridges Museum of American Art, in Arkansas, to raise funds for the cash-strapped private school. The collection rotates between Crystal Bridges and the Van Vechten every two years. Other exhibits are on display when the Stieglitz collection is in Arkansas. The collection includes works by Stieglitz and O'Keeffe, as well as acclaimed European and American artists including Pablo Picasso, Paul Cézanne, Pierre-Auguste Renoir, Diego Rivera, Arthur Dove, Gino Severini, and Charles Demuth. It is truly a remarkable collection and one worth seeing, but call ahead to confirm hours, particularly when school is not in session. Ring the bell to the right of the door to be let in.

MAP 4: Fisk University, 1000 17th Ave. N., 615/329-8720, http://fisk.edu; 10am-4pm Mon.-Wed. and Sat., 10am-7pm Thurs.-Fri.; $10 adults, $6 seniors, $5 students, free for children

Fisk's Stieglitz Collection

When photographer **Alfred Stieglitz** died in 1946, his wife, **Georgia O'Keeffe,** herself one of the most important artists of her generation, was left with the responsibility of giving away his massive art collection. Stieglitz had collected more than 1,000 works by artists including Arthur Dove, Marsden Hartley, O'Keeffe, Charles Demuth, and John Marin. He also owned several African sculptures.

Stieglitz's instructions regarding this art collection were vague. In his will he asked O'Keeffe to select the recipients "under such arrangements as will assure to the public, under reasonable regulations, access thereto to promote the study of art."

O'Keeffe selected several obvious recipients for parts of the collection: the Library of Congress, the National Gallery of Art in Washington, the Metropolitan Museum of Art, the Art Institute of Chicago, and the Philadelphia Museum of Art. Nashville's Fisk University was a surprise, and Carl Van Vechten, a writer, photographer, and friend of Stieglitz and O'Keeffe, is credited with making the suggestion. Van Vechten was keenly interested in African American art and was close friends with Fisk president Charles Johnson.

O'Keeffe and Fisk did not find an easy partnership. According to an account by C. Michael Norton, when she first visited the university, a few days before the Carl Van Vechten Gallery would open on campus, O'Keeffe ordered major changes to the gallery space, eventually flying in a lighting designer from New York on the day before the opening. At the opening ceremony on November 4, 1949, held at the Memorial Chapel at Fisk, O'Keeffe declined President Johnson's invitation to the lectern and spoke from her chair, saying curtly: "Dr. Johnson wrote and asked me to speak and I did not answer. I had and have no intention of speaking. These paintings and sculptures are a gift from Stieglitz. They are for the students. I hope you go back and look at them more than once."

The Stieglitz Collection at Fisk consists of 101 remarkable works of art, including 2 by O'Keeffe, 19 Stieglitz photographs, prints by Cézanne and Renoir, and 5 pieces of African tribal art.

For years, cash-strapped Fisk had sought to sell parts of the collection to raise funds. In 2012, Walmart heiress Alice Walton's Crystal Bridges Museum in Bentonville, Arkansas, acquired a 50 percent share in the collection for $30 million. Now the collection rotates between Crystal Bridges and Fisk's Carl Van Vechten Gallery every two years. While some decry the deal as not following the stipulations in O'Keeffe's will, others see it as the only option to keep the collection in the public eye and Fisk solvent. The influx of cash should help maintain the collection and provide for new resources, such as a printed catalog of the impressive works.

GALLERIES

ART + INVENTION GALLERY

The Art + Invention Gallery is an East Nashville institution. Proprietors Meg and Bret MacFayden put on five to six shows each year, including the signature Tomato Art Show, part of the annual **Tomato Art Festival** (www.tomatoartfest.com) in August, and are well loved for their support of other Music City creative types. The shop stocks handmade decorative art, jewelry, pottery, knit goods, and more. Art + Invention was the go-to East Nashville creative boutique before the streets were lined with them.

MAP 5: 1106 Woodland St., 615/226-2070, www.artandinvention.com; 11am-6pm Fri.-Sat., noon-5pm Sun., or by appointment; free

RED ARROW GALLERY

Founded in Joshua Tree, California, Red Arrow opened in Inglewood's Riverside Village in 2014. With an emphasis on emerging artists, Red Arrow brought a traditional gallery environment to a neighborhood that hasn't had one. In 2015 Red Arrow moved to a larger space on Inglewood's main drag, allowing it to be a bigger part of East Side Art Stumble walks.

MAP 5: 919 Gallatin Ave., 615/236-6575, http://theredarrowgallery.com; by appointment Fri. and Sun., noon-6pm Sat.; free

Music Valley   Map 6

DINNER THEATER

MISS JEANNE'S MYSTERY DINNER THEATRE

If mystery is what you're into, have dinner at Miss Jeanne's Mystery Dinner Theatre, where you and your friends try to guess who done it while eating a Southern feast. This dinner-and-a-show theater offers discounts for seniors, members of the military, and groups larger than 10, making a night of mystery more affordable. It's BYOB.

MAP 6: 2416 Music Valley Dr., 615/902-9566, www.missjeannes.com; 7pm Fri.-Sat., other days sporadically; $42-45

GALLERIES

DAVID LUSK GALLERY NASHVILLE

David Lusk Gallery started in Memphis in 1995, but now, with a new location in the state capitol next to Zeitgeist, it is part of the growing Wedgewood/Houston art scene. It makes sense, given the fact that Lusk has gravitated to transitional neighborhoods throughout his career. The gallery focuses on the works of emerging artists, many but not exclusively, from the South. Expect to see paintings, photography, and sculpture.

MAP 7: 516 Hagan St., Ste. 102, 615/780-9990, http://davidluskgallery.com; 11am-5pm Tues.-Sat.; free

FORT HOUSTON

Fort Houston is a 10,000-square-foot creative hub in the Wedgewood/ Houston neighborhood. There's a wood shop, print shop, bike shop, and photo studio. Artists pay a monthly membership fee to have space to make cool stuff. You can stop by the gallery and buy what they've made.

MAP 7: 2020 Lindell Ave., 615/730-8865, http://forthouston.com; 10am-8pm Mon.-Thurs., 10am-5pm Fri.; free

GALLERY LUPERCA

A participant in the monthly Wedgewood/Houston Art Night on the first Saturday of the month, Gallery Luperca mounts monthly exhibitions by emerging artists from the mid-South. Once located in East Nashville this business is not just an art gallery; it also serves as home to an experimental theater group.

MAP 7: 507 Hagan St., 615/669-1384, www.galleryluperca.com; 2pm-8pm Thurs., 6pm-9pm every first Sat. of the month, 4pm-7pm Sun.; free

TRACK ONE

In what once was a feed and seed warehouse built by Nashville Decatur Railroad in 1924 to serve nearby farming communities, Track One is a retail/arts/hipster paradise in Wedgewood/Houston. There are a number of galleries in this renovated space, and many artists who call Track One their studio. Hours vary, but the monthly Wedgewood/Houston Art Night on the first Saturday of the month is a good time to see lots of open doors.

MAP 7: 1201 4th Ave S., no phone, http://trackonenashville.com; hours vary

ZEITGEIST ARTS

For years Zeitgeist was the cornerstone—literally and figuratively—of Hillsboro Village (and before that in Cummins Station closer to downtown). Its small, bright space attracted high-quality artists and well-heeled collectors. In 2013 the gallery moved to a bigger, reclaimed historical space with Manuel Zeitlin Architects and helped welcome an artistic community to the Wedgewood/Houston neighborhood. The exhibited art changes monthly, depending on which artists the gallery is featuring.

MAP 7: 516 Hagan St., 615/256-4805, http://zeitgeist-art.com; 11am-5pm Tues.-Sat.; free

Greater Nashville Map 8

PERFORMANCE VENUES
DYER OBSERVATORY

A working space observatory operated by Vanderbilt University, Dyer Observatory has emerged as a popular venue for music. **Bluebird on the Mountain** ($135 per carload, up to 8 guests) with The Bluebird Cafe brings live music to this dramatic and one-of-a-kind spot. Imagine a night of fine music enjoyed under the stars with the fresh air and the atmosphere of the forest all around you.

MAP 8: 1000 Oman Dr., Brentwood, 615/373-4897, http://dyer.vanderbilt.edu; 8am-5pm Tues.-Fri.; additional hours vary by event

OZ ARTS

Founded in 2013 by Nashvillians who wanted to give back to the city that welcomed them as immigrants, OZ is a multiuse performance space with an emphasis on contemporary arts. Spoken word, music, performance art, film, and contemporary dance are often on the schedule. Yes, the location is on the far west side of town. But OZ presents some of the most cutting-edge performances in the city and should be on your radar.

MAP 8: 6172 Cockrill Bend Cir., 615/350-7200, http://ozartsnashville.org; hours and cost varies by event

GALLERIES
LEQUIRE GALLERY

Sculptor Alan LeQuire is known for two iconic Nashville works: *Musica*, the Music Row sculpture controversial for its unclad figures, and *Athena*, the massive golden goddess at the Parthenon. His Sylvan Park gallery is more diverse, exhibiting both his own work and that of other sculptors. In addition to having works on display, LeQuire Gallery also teaches classes and workshops for those who want to get in touch with their artistic side.

MAP 8: 4304 Charlotte Ave., 615/298-4611, www.lequiregallery.com; 10am-3pm Tues.-Sat.; free

THEATER
ACTORS BRIDGE ENSEMBLE

New theatrical works are given the spotlight by the Actors Bridge Ensemble, a theater company for both new and seasoned actors. The ensemble brings provocative and new plays to theaters across Nashville and hosts performances at Belmont University's Troutt Theater Complex and the Darkhorse

Theater. The ensemble approach means everyone gets to try everything, from acting to lighting to manning the box office.

MAP 8: Darkhorse Theater, 4610 Charlotte Ave., 615/498-4077, http://actorsbridge.org; show and class times vary; general admission $10-20

ARTISTS' COOPERATIVE THEATRE

Artists' Cooperative Theatre, or ACT 1, is an organization dedicated to bringing theatrical gems, both classic and modern, to Nashville audiences. Founded in 1989, ACT 1 has presented productions of more than 90 of the world's greatest plays, using both classical and modern plays to describe and comment on the human condition. Each year the theater puts on four to seven productions. Past productions have included *Dr. Horrible's Sing-Along Blog, Arsenic and Old Lace, The Night of the Iguana, Noises Off,* and *Pirates of Penzance.*

MAP 8: Darkhorse Theater, 4610 Charlotte Ave., http://act1online.com; showtimes and ticket prices vary

CIRCLE PLAYERS

Circle Players is the oldest nonprofit, all-volunteer arts association in Nashville. As a community theater, all its actors, stagehands, directors, and other helpers are volunteers. The company stages four or five performances every year at a variety of theater locations around the city. Performances include classic theater, plus stage adaptations of popular cinema and literature.

MAP 8: Looby Theatre, 2301 Rosa Parks Blvd., 615/332-7529, www.circleplayers.net; showtimes vary; $20

DINNER THEATER

CHAFFIN'S BARN DINNER THEATRE

Chaffin's Barn Dinner Theatre was Nashville's first professional theater and continues to put on Broadway-style plays for dinner patrons. As the name suggests, these performances take place in a theater that looks like a barn from the outside. There's nothing cutting-edge about the shows or the meal, but new ownership has helped bring them into the 21st century. These shows are family-friendly fun—buffet dinner included.

MAP 8: 8204 Hwy. 100, 615/646-9977, http://chaffinsbarntheatre.com; box office noon-8pm Tues.-Sat.; performances noon and 6pm Thurs., 6pm Fri.-Sat., noon Sun.; adults $60, students and children $30, less without dinner

Mural City

Call it the Banksy effect: In recent years many of Nashville's blank spaces, such as the sides of buildings in alleys, have been transformed into canvases of color.

The **Nashville Walls Project** (www.nashvillewallsproject.com) started in 2013 to put high-quality works of art in places where people could appreciate them and interact with them without going to a museum. Perhaps the most striking is on the side of a silo—160 feet tall—a sepia-toned portrait of a man who has lived in the neighborhood for more than 90 years. Some of these works do change over time, so the best way to find one is to check the map online and wander to your heart's and eyes' content.

Other artists have used walls as their medium, too. Favorites among the selfie crowd include: the Wings (giant white angel wings) in The Gulch; Hillsboro Village's dragon; **DCXV's** red, white, and blue "I Believe in Nashville" signs which are in several places in the city, including 12 South and Marathon Village; and **Draper James's** striking blue and white stripes.

Various Locations

THEATER
★ NASHVILLE SHAKESPEARE

The city's Shakespeare troupe brings the Bard to Music City audiences all year long. The winter performances take place at Belmont University's **Troutt Theater** (2100 Belmont Blvd.) and **Tucker Theatre,** on the campus of Middle Tennessee State University in Murfreesboro. But it is the summer show, held outside at **Centennial Park** (2500 West End Ave.) that really grabs headlines. Nashville Shakespeare was founded in 1988. Since then it has worked to get the Bard's words to audiences who might not otherwise be exposed to these classics. Many of its performances are designed to be inexpensive or free and often mounted in parks and schools. Also fun are the monthly **Shakespeare Allowed!** readings at the main public library. Everyday folks, not actors, gather to read the works as they were meant to be heard—aloud.

Various locations: 615/255-2273, www.nashvilleshakes.org; show times vary by performance; free, donations accepted

Festivals and Events

WINTER
NEW YEAR'S EVE
Also known as the Bash on Broadway, New Year's Eve near downtown Nashville includes—what else?—a music note drop. This is a huge celebration was moved from the riverfront to Bicentennial Mall to accommodate big crowds. It still offers lots of free outdoor fun. It has been part of the national program *Dick Clark's New Year's Rockin' Eve*. Musicians like Kings of Leon and Keith Urban play free concerts while the Music City Bowl game attracts football fans.

Downtown: Broadway, www.visitmusiccity.com; Dec. 31

MUSIC CITY BOWL
The Music City Bowl pits a Southeastern Conference team against a Big Ten or ACC rival. This nationally televised football game is held at Nissan Stadium. The festivities typically include a free night-before or postgame concert downtown and a parade of the collegiate athletes. Hometown team the Vanderbilt Commodores have played in the bowl several times in recent years. When that happens there is a big black and gold cheering section.

East Nashville: 1 Titans Way, www.musiccitybowl.com, late Dec. or early Jan.; $22-117

BATTLE OF NEW ORLEANS COMMEMORATION
At the Battle of New Orleans Anniversary, The Hermitage, Andrew Jackson's home, is free to the public. The free day is typically on a weekend closest to January 8, which is when the event took place in 1815. The Battle of New Orleans was one of the final battles in the War of 1812 and is considered one of President Jackson's biggest legacies. The event includes a traditional wreath-laying ceremony on the general's grave.

Greater Nashville: The Hermitage, 4580 Rachel's Ln., 615/889-2941, www.thehermitage.com; Jan.; free

ANTIQUES AND GARDEN SHOW OF NASHVILLE
More than 150 dealers set up in the Nashville Convention Center for the upscale Antiques and Garden Show of Nashville in February. One of the largest such shows that combines both indoor furniture and outdoor, garden antiques, the event includes workshops, demonstrations, and vintage finds to meet most budgets and tastes. Proceeds from the show benefit the Cheekwood Botanical Garden and Museum of Art.

Downtown: Nashville Convention Center, 1200 Forrest Park Dr., 615/352-1282, http://antiquesandgardenshow.com; Feb.; $20-25

TIN PAN SOUTH SONGWRITERS FESTIVAL

Many Nashville music events celebrate the performers. But the Tin Pan South Songwriters Festival honors the people who come up with the lyrics for all those great tunes. So while you may not recognize most of the names on the lineup, you're sure to get a good introduction to the people behind the famous words. Typically held the last week of March or first week in April, Tin Pan South, organized by the Nashville Songwriters Association International, schedules performances at venues across the city.

Citywide: www.tinpansouth.com; late Mar. or early Apr.

NASHVILLE FASHION WEEK

Nashville's creative class isn't just musically inclined. There's a rich fashion design community. And the first week of April is the time to see it in all its runway glory during Nashville Fashion Week. Events take place across the city all week, ranging from runways to workshops to parties with the city's best-dressed folks.

Citywide: www.nashvillefashionweek.com; early Apr.

ST. JUDE ROCK 'N' ROLL MARATHON

Part of the Rock 'n' Roll Marathon circuit, the St. Jude Rock 'n' Roll Nashville Marathon is good fun for both participants and spectators. In addition to the course's hard-core 26.2 miles, there are a half marathon, wheelchair marathons and half marathons, and a kids' event. Plenty of live music (more than 28 stages) is performed along the course, which winds its way through the city. High school cheerleading squads root for the runners.

Citywide: www.runrocknroll.com; late Apr.

NASHVILLE FILM FESTIVAL

Film lovers throughout the country look forward to the Nashville Film Festival, held every April or May at the Regal Cinemas Green Hills. The film festival was founded in 1969 as the Sinking Creek Film Celebration. These days more than 20,000 people attend the weeklong event, which includes film screenings, industry panels, and lots of parties. Lots of locals volunteer to help put on the event, which screens many regional films not shown at other festivals.

Greater Nashville: Regal Cinemas Green Hills, 3815 Green Hills Village Dr., www.nashvillefilmfestival.org; Apr. or May

TENNESSEE CRAFT FAIR

At the Tennessee Craft Fair, more than 200 artists are juried and selected for their quality works. You'll find jewelry, painting, ceramics, and many other media on display here, as well as food and activities to keep the kids busy. Held in Centennial Park, this is not a place to expect a bargain, but you may find a work of art you'll keep for years. The fair repeats in September.

Music Row: Centennial Park, http://tennesseecraft.org; early May; free

IROQUOIS STEEPLECHASE

For something a little different, plan to attend the Iroquois Steeplechase at Percy Warner Park. On the second Saturday of May, the race is the nation's oldest continuously run weight-for-age steeplechase in the country. Fans in sundresses or suspenders and hats enjoy watching some of the top horses in the country navigate the racecourse. A general admission ticket gets you a seat on the hillside overlooking the stadium. Pack a blanket, food, and drinks (and mud boots if it has rained recently, which is not uncommon), and you'll have an excellent day. Various tailgating tickets ($550-600) are available and are priced according to how good the view is from the parking spot. If you want to tailgate, you'll need to buy tickets well in advance.

Greater Nashville: Percy Warner Park, 7311 Hwy. 100, 800/619-4802, www. iroquoissteeplechase.org; May; general admission $20, infield $85-100

SUMMER

CMT MUSIC AWARDS

Country music fans vote on their favorite performers' videos and TV performances through CMT's website. The first weekend in June, the winners of the CMT Music Awards are feted in award-show style at a Music City venue like Bridgestone Arena. There's a red carpet, but in true Nashville fashion, you might see some boots with those black-tie outfits. Attendees will enjoy the many performances that occur between award presentations.

Various locations: www.cmt.com; early June

HERITAGE FOUNDATION TOUR

During the first full weekend of June you can join the Heritage Foundation of Franklin and Williamson County on the Heritage Foundation Tour. Tours go to private and historical homes that are closed to the public during the rest of the year.

Various locations: www.historicfranklin.com; early June; $30-35

CMA MUSIC FESTIVAL

CMA Music Festival is a four-day mega-music show in downtown Nashville. The stage at Riverfront Park along the Cumberland River is occupied by day with some of the top names in country music, with as many as 400 performers. At night the hordes move to Nissan Stadium to hear a different show every night. Four-day passes, which cost between $220 and $400 per person, also give you access to the exhibit hall, where you can get autographs and meet up-and-coming country music artists. This is one of Nashville's biggest events of the year, and you are wise to buy your tickets and book your hotel early. Get a room downtown so that you don't need a car; parking and traffic can be a nightmare during the festival.

Various locations: www.cmaworld.com; June

CRAFT BEER FESTIVAL

Hosted by the Nashville Predators and benefiting the Nashville Predators Foundation, the 21-and-up Craft Beer Festival features food, entertainment, and of course, an abundance of craft beer. The festival takes place in late June at the Bridgestone Arena.

Downtown: Bridgestone Arena, www.nhl.com; late June; $69-79

NASHVILLE PRIDE FESTIVAL

Late June sees Nashville's gay, lesbian, bisexual, and transgender community show its rainbow colors at the Nashville Pride Festival, a two-day event at Public Square Park. This is not just an average Pride parade. There's an artists' village, where local artisans show off their wares, plus live music, a drag stage, and much more.

Various locations: www.nashvillepride.org; late June

INDEPENDENCE DAY

Independence Day is celebrated in a big way in Music City with fireworks and a riverfront concert that's broadcast live on television. The event attracts more than 100,000 people every year. Like any Nashville event, the stage (often on a barge in Riverfront Park) is filled with lots of live music, and the fireworks display offers some serious pyrotechnics. Arrive downtown early to enjoy these festivities because you'll need extra time to park, and you'll want to stroll and listen before the fireworks begin.

Downtown: www.visitmusiccity.com; July 4

MUSIC CITY HOT CHICKEN FESTIVAL

The temperature is almost always hot at the Music City Hot Chicken Festival on July 4, but so is the chicken. This East Nashville event is a feast of the city's signature spicy panfried dish. Because hot chicken is made individually, the lines are long. But music, cooking contests, and other activities help pass the time. This is a great way to sample one of the classic Music City culinary delights.

East Nashville: http://hot-chicken.com/festival; July 4

MUSIC CITY BREWER'S FESTIVAL

The Music City Brewer's Festival is a one-day 21-and-up event held in late July at the Music City Walk of Fame downtown. Come to taste local brews, learn about making your own beer, and enjoy good food and live music. It typically has about 50 different brewers and 100 different beers, plus live music and other entertainment. Tickets are required; the event benefits local charities and typically sells out.

Downtown: Music City Walk of Fame, 4th Ave. S., www.musiccitybrewersfest.com, late July; $39-69

EAST NASHVILLE TOMATO ART FESTIVAL

The East Nashville Tomato Art Festival started as a tongue-in-cheek celebration of tomatoes and the hip, artsy vibe of East Nashville. Events include a parade of tomatoes, the "Most Beautiful Tomato Pageant," biggest and smallest tomato contests, tomato toss, and Bloody Mary taste-off, and has become one of the city's biggest weekends. The two-day festival takes place the second weekend of August. Costumes are encouraged, so feel free to come dressed as a tomato, or at least all in red.

East Nashville: Woodland St. and 11th Ave., www.tomatoartfest.com; Aug.; free

FALL

CUMBERLAND RIVER DRAGON BOAT FESTIVAL

The Cumberland River Dragon Boat Festival is a one-day race in early September that takes place at East Bank Landing and is part of a 2,300-year-old tradition. More than 40 boats with big dragon heads and 20 costumed paddlers each race each other on the water. There are plenty of river-themed activities for spectators, too, including a DragonLand-themed area for kids. Proceeds from the event benefit watershed conservation projects.

East Nashville: East Bank Landing, http://cumberlandrivercompact.org; early Sept.

JOHN A. MERRITT CLASSIC

The John A. Merritt Classic, held over Labor Day, starts with a pep rally, happy hour, and high school band showcase and culminates with a football contest between the Tennessee State University Tigers and another historically black collegiate football team at Nissan Stadium. The annual showdown is named for legendary former TSU football coach John Ayers Merritt.

East Nashville: Nissan Stadium, www.merrittclassic.com; early Sept.; $25-35

NASHVILLE GREEK FESTIVAL

The annual three-day Nashville Greek Festival is hosted by the Holy Trinity Greek Orthodox Church and held in early September. For more than 25 years Nashville residents have flocked here for homemade Greek food and entertainment, which includes dancing and tours of the historical cathedral. Opa!

Greater Nashville: 4905 Franklin Pike, www.nashvillegreekfestival.com; early Sept.

AMERICANA MUSIC FESTIVAL

A multivenue conference/music showcase, the Americana Music Festival in September has become one of the city's most popular events. Professionals (musicians, songwriters, producers, and more) come for the connections and the workshops during the day. Locals join them at night for concerts—more than 230 at nearly 40 different venues—that show off the genre. There's an award show and an end-of-week big-budget concert at Ascend Amphitheater.

Various locations: http://americanamusic.org; Sept.

JUBILEE DAY

Every October 6, the day in 1871 that the Fisk Jubilee Singers departed Fisk University for a worldwide tour, the school remembers their efforts with a convocation, a concert, a walk to the cemetery to lay wreaths made from campus magnolia trees, and more, on Jubilee Day. It's a moving day with remarkable live music.

Midtown and 12 South: Fisk University, 1000 17th Ave. N., www.fisk.edu; Oct. 6

CELEBRATE NASHVILLE CULTURAL FESTIVAL

International organizations set up in Centennial Park and offer food, dance, music, crafts, and other pieces of different cultures from around the world during the Celebrate Nashville Cultural Festival each October. There are separate activity areas for teens and younger children.

Music Row: Centennial Park, www.celebratenashville.org; Oct.

NASHVILLE BEER FESTIVAL

Held in October, the one-day Nashville Beer Festival is an indoor-outdoor drinking extravaganza dedicated to all things hops and barley. Expect to sample more than 150 beers (plus some wines and spirits, too), shop beer-related merchandise, and even hit the dance floor if the moment strikes.

Greater Nashville: 500 Wedgewood Ave., www.nashvillebeerfestival.com; Oct.; $15-100

OKTOBERFEST

Oktoberfest is a Nashville tradition. Held in historical Germantown north of the Bicentennial Mall, this weekend festival is enhanced by its setting in what was once Nashville's German enclave. The events include a walk-run, church services, a Dachshund Derby, a bratwurst-eating contest, and a street fair with German music, food, and other entertainment. Oktoberfest usually takes place in early or mid-October.

Germantown: www.thenashvilleoktoberfest.com; Oct.

SOUTHERN FESTIVAL OF BOOKS

The Southern Festival of Books is held during the second full weekend of October on Legislative Plaza in downtown Nashville. Featuring book readings, autograph sessions with well-known and regional authors, and discussions, the three-day festival, organized by Humanities Tennessee, is a must for book lovers. It has activities for children, too.

Downtown: Legislative Park, www.humanitiestennessee.org; Oct.

Bonnaroo: Tennessee's Music Festival

Bonnaroo Music and Arts Festival (www.bonnaroo.com) started out in 2002 as a jam band music festival, but diversification has made this summertime mega-event *the* destination for all types of music fans. Bonnaroo takes place over four days in June on a rural farm in Manchester. More than 65,000 people come each year.

Bonnaroo has a hippie heart with a slightly hard edge. Place-names are Seussian: The music tents are called, from largest to smallest, What Stage, Which Stage, This Tent, That Tent, and The Other Tent. Activities run the gamut from yoga to a 5K Roo Run to comedy performances. Of course, it's the music that really draws the crowds: reggae, rock, Americana, jam bands, world, hip-hop, jazz, electronic, folk, gospel, and country. The event is truly a feast for the ears.

In 2007, the Police were reunited at Bonnaroo. Past fests have hosted Lorde, U2, The Weeknd, and the Red Hot Chili Peppers. But quality permeates every echelon of the stage. Unknowns and barely knowns routinely wow audiences, including names like The Civil Wars, Moon Taxi, and Feist.

A few things to know about Bonnaroo: First, it's huge. The event takes place on a 700-acre farm, and the list of offerings is seemingly endless: 10 stages, whole villages dedicated to the arts, food vendors, and a whole lot more.

Second, Bonnaroo has above-average logistics. Organizers seem to consider everything, including the basics: drinking water, medical care, parking, traffic control, and a general store where you can buy necessities. Food vendors sell Tennessee barbecue, veggie burgers, and just about everything in between. A shuttle service between the Nashville airport (available with certain ticket packages) and Bonnaroo helps minimize traffic. Rules about camping, RVs, reentry, and security are common sense and easy to follow.

All that said, you can't turn up with the clothes on your back and expect to have much fun. It's important to pack well: A good camping tent, folding chairs, and water bottles are important. It is June in the South. It will be unspeakably hot. If it rains, it will be muddy. If it doesn't, it will be dusty. Even if you plan to buy most of your food at the festival, at least pack some snacks. There are ATMs at Bonnaroo, but lines can be very long, so bringing plenty of cash is also a good idea (but not so much that you attract trouble). Also bring garbage bags, sunscreen, and comfortable clothes for hot weather.

Beer—including good microbrews—is sold and consumed generously. Plenty of Bonnaroo fans take the opportunity to do a lot of drinking and drugs, partly because they're somewhere they don't have to drive for four days.

Most people buy a four-day pass to the festival, but day-pass tickets are available too. Four-day general admission passes cost $275 and up; a limited number of reduced-price early-bird tickets go on sale in January each year. Car and RV parking passes are extra. Regular tickets go on sale in the spring, after the lineup has been announced, typically in February. VIP packages are pricier (starting at $1,600 for a pair of two), but offer amenities that are priceless, as the meme would say, such as VIP restroom and shower facilities.

Sports and Activities

Look for ★ to find
recommended sports and activities.

Highlights

★ **Most TV-Worthy Green Space:**
The proximity to the river downtown and
the Tennessee Titans' stadium means
Cumberland Park is in many, many pan-
oramas of Music City on the small screen
(page 156).

★ **Only Sport in Town that Shows
the Score on a Guitar:** First Tennessee
Park is home to the minor league **Nashville
Sounds** and a guitar-shaped scoreboard
(page 156).

★ **Best for Golfers: Topgolf Nashville**
is more than a driving range: It's a grown-up
amusement park dedicated to all things golf
(page 157).

★ **Easiest Way to Rent a Bike:** Just
walk up to one of more than 36 **Nashville
B-Cycle** stations across the city, don your
helmet, and start pedaling (page 170).

★ **Most Fulfilling Way to Tour the
City:** Taste the work of some of the city's
best chefs while learning about one of its
neighborhoods on a guided **Walk Eat
Nashville** tour (page 170).

Nashvillians work hard, as evidenced by the number of businesses headquartered here, the number of venture capitalists who fund those companies, and the number of new music careers launched. But Nashvillians play hard, too.

Nashville's natural resources are notable and worth experiencing. In fact, folks who come to Music City from other parts of the country remark on how green and lush Nashville is. Nashville has good parks, numerous sports teams, accessible waterways, and nice weather to enjoy them all.

The Cumberland River is a great place for recreational opportunities. It winds its way through the city, offering up pretty vistas, ample paddling and boating access, and more. Walking, hiking, and even horseback riding are available on well-tended trails in the city's 108 parks. The Greenways connect large portions of the city with outdoor space. Bike and paddleboard rentals, kayak tours, and other options are available. An interactive map on the Metro website (www.nashville.gov) allows you to search for parks by geographic location or activity.

Hockey, football, and baseball are the trifecta of professional sports in Nashville. In 2017, Major League Soccer named Nashville as its 24th franchise location.

There are tours here for every interest: Music, celebrities, *Nashville* the TV show, food, drinks, and sports are just a few of the themes. Tours fill up in advance, particularly during months that are popular with bachelorette parties (a booming business in Music City), so plan ahead. If you want someone else to do the planning for you, try **BachWeekend Nashville** (www.bachweekend.com).

Previous: take a ride on the *General Jackson* showboat; kayak the Cumberland River with River Queen Voyages.

Rock Your Run

Every marathon is part spectacle. But the **Country Music Marathon** (www.runrocknroll.com) is as known for the performances as it is for the racing. (Officially, it is now called the St. Jude Rock 'n' Roll Marathon, but no one in town calls it that.) Spectators and runners alike cite the event's music vibe for keeping them motivated. In 2017, 28 stages were set up along the route to keep arms pumping and legs moving for the course of the race. After the 26.2 miles, all the runners and their families are invited to a postrace concert.

While some folks enter this event to win, it's not unusual to see runners hula-hooping or dancing to the music as they go by. It's all part of the Nashville beat.

Downtown

Map 1

SPECTATOR SPORTS

Ice Hockey
NASHVILLE PREDATORS

The NHL's Predators play in the 17,000-seat **Bridgestone Arena,** located on Broadway in the heart of downtown. In 2017, the whole country saw what a hockey town Nashville has become, when the Predators went to the Stanley Cup playoffs, the city closed off major streets for viewing parties, and game tickets were in extremely high demand. Home games include live country music performances between quarters and other activities for the fans. The regular season begins in October and ends in early April. Tickets for games against the archrival Chicago Blackhawks are particularly sought after.

MAP 1: 501 Broadway, 615/770-2355, www.nhl.com/predators; game times vary Oct.-Apr.; tickets $20-350

TOURS

EXPERIENCE NASHVILLE

What makes Music City Music City? Songwriter Kaysie Young will take you on her Famous Footsteps tour of downtown, which hits some of the area's music hot spots and historic sites. The two-hour tour only covers about six blocks, so you won't burn a lot of calories, but you will learn a lot about Patsy Cline, Dolly Parton, Keith Urban, and others who made the city what it is. Tours depart from the Ernest Tubb Record Shop on Lower Broad.

MAP 1: 417 Broadway, 615/788-6384, www.experiencenashvilletours.com; 10:30am and 12:30pm daily; $20 adults; $10 children, free for members of the military

EXPLORE CRAWLS

This tour company specializes in themed two-hour walking tours of Nashville, popular for bachelor and bachelorette parties and other groups.

Themes include a distillery crawl, a beer and barbecue tour, a downtown Nashville pub crawl, and the surprisingly fun and informative Instagram Scavenger Hunt Crawl for the social media-savvy. A six-person minimum typically applies. Times and dates are flexible, pending availability.

MAP 1: 800 3rd Ave. S., 615/640-0658, www.explorecrawls.com; $20-40 or two crawls for $45

IRIDE NASHVILLE
Explore Music City atop a different two-wheeled vehicle on a 2.5-hour sanctioned Segway tour. You'll cover about 10 miles, navigating past pedestrians and tourists stuck in car traffic and passing by many of the big tourist sites, including the Country Music Hall of Fame and Museum and the Bridgestone Arena. Riders must be older than 14. Helmets and other gear are provided, as is Segway training, which is included in the 2.5-hour tour time.

MAP 1: 330 Commerce St., 615/244-0555, http://iridenashville.com; 10:30am and 1:30pm daily; $75 pp

OFF THE WAGON TOURS
If you think Tennessee means tractors riding down the middle of city streets, well, Off the Wagon will sort of prove you right. These "party wagons" offer 105-minute tours of Nashville via a souped-up John Deere tractor that you and your tour mates pedal with your own feet, complete with a DJ on board. Tours can accommodate groups of up to 20 and are BYOB—you bring the alcohol (not in glass containers) and they'll provide coolers, ice, and cups.

MAP 1: 114 12th Ave. N., 800/979-3370, 11am-7pm daily, www.nashvillepartywagon.com; $35 pp or $480-500 groups up to 20

PONTOON SALOON
The Pontoon Saloon is billed as Nashville's only honky-tonk on the water. Cruise down the Cumberland sipping your own alcohol (cups and ice provided). This party barge holds up to 49 people, but you can book it for a private group with as few as 20 people. Cruises depart from near Nissan Stadium in East Nashville and last two hours.

MAP 1: 2 Victory Ave., 615/601-1464, http://pontoonsaloontn.com; tour times vary; $59, plus tips for crew

SPROCKET ROCKET
Party bikes have become the must-do activity of bachelor and bachelorette parties (and Nashville is now a prime location for pre-wedding merriment). On its party bike tour, Sprocket Rocket makes the drinking and cycling possible simultaneously thanks to a personal bartender (you bring the booze), an electric assist motor, and a DJ. Tours of downtown, which can accommodate teams of 8 to 16 people, include a souvenir photo album

so you can remember your outing. Other tour options include the Big Red Bus for larger groups or a Golf Cart Tour for smaller groups.

MAP 1: 516 5th Ave. S., 615/707-1368, http://sprockettours.com; tour times vary; $35

Germantown and Capitol Hill

Map 2

PARKS
★ CUMBERLAND PARK

Technically in East Nashville, this 6.5-acre park is one of the city's gems and, if you count the number of times it has been featured on the TV show *Nashville*, the most popular. TV drama aside, this is a remarkable space, nestled on the eastern bank of the Cumberland River, next to Nissan Stadium. It encompasses a kid-friendly rock climbing wall, trails with native plants, misting stations, and educational information about how the Cumberland River is essential to the area's ecosystem. There are nice public restrooms and a concession stand here. Right next to the park is the Riverfront Landing, an East Bank launch for canoes, kayaks, and paddleboards. The regular free parking (typically in Lot R) for both is not available when there is an event at Nissan Stadium.

MAP 2: 592 S. 1st St., 615/862-8508, http://nashville.gov/parks-and-recreation/parks.aspx; dawn-11pm daily; free

SPECTATOR SPORTS
Baseball
★ NASHVILLE SOUNDS

What an appropriate name for a minor league baseball team in Music City! The Sounds are a AAA affiliate of the Oakland A's, and they play about 40 home games a year April-September. In 2015 the Sounds got a spanking new stadium, **First Tennessee Park,** on the site of Sulphur Dell, which in the 1800s was the home of baseball in Nashville. The park, with its fancy stadium food from The Band Box and setting between Germantown and downtown, reinvigorated baseball fandom in the city. There's also a full miniature golf course called The Country Club designed by local artists inside the stadium. You can't miss the guitar-shaped scoreboard, just like in the team's old Greer Stadium, now with a view of the skyline behind it. Note: Junior Gillam Way was once called Jackson Street, so some GPS maps may still list the stadium at 401 Jackson Street.

MAP 2: 19 Junior Gillam Way, 615/690-4487, http://nashvillesounds.com; box office 9am-5pm or end of game on game days Mon.-Fri., 10am-end of game on game days Sat.-Sun. Apr.-Sept.; tickets $10-40; minigolf additional $5

TENNESSEE TITANS

You simply cannot miss the 68,000-seat Nissan Stadium, home of the NFL's Tennessee Titans. The stadium, which was finished in 1999 and renovated after the 2010 flood, towers on the east bank of the Cumberland River, directly opposite downtown. After the Titans moved to the stadium in 1999, they sold out almost every home game. But a spotty win-lose record in recent years has made tickets slightly easier to come by. If you want to see a game on short notice, your best bet is the online NFL ticket exchange, where season ticket holders can sell their seats to games they don't want to attend. Nissan Stadium is a venue for many other music and sporting events and frequently featured in photos of the skyline.

MAP 2: Nissan Stadium, 1 Titans Way, 615/565-4000, www.titansonline.com; Sept.-Dec.; tickets generally $130

GOLF

★ TOPGOLF NASHVILLE

In 2017 the eastern bank of the Cumberland River, near Germantown, became home to Topgolf, an outpost of a chain that has taken driving ranges to the next level. This 3,000-square-foot, three-level complex merges golf and entertainment, with 102 climate-controlled hitting bays that can accommodate up to six players each. Practice your swing, learn a new technique, listen to live music, and have a drink.

MAP 2: 500 Cowan St., 615/777-3007, http://topgolf.com; 9am-midnight Mon.-Thurs., 9am-2am Fri.-Sat.; $25/hour 9am-noon, $35/hour noon-5pm, $45/hour 5pm-close

TOURS

NASH TRASH TOURS

Nashville's most notorious tour guides are Sheri Lynn and Brenda Kay Jugg, sisters who ferry good-humored tourists around town in a big pink school bus. A Nash Trash Tour is a raunchy, rollicking, rib-tickling tour of city attractions, some of which you won't even find in this guidebook. Be prepared to be the butt of some of the jokes yourself—their "I Got Trashed" T-shirts have a double meaning. You'll snack on canned cheese, and there's even a pit stop to buy beer. These tours are not appropriate for children or adults who aren't comfortable laughing at themselves and others. As Sheri Lynn says: "If we haven't offended you, just give us some time." Nash Trash Tours sell out early and often. If you think you want this perspective on the city, make your reservation now. Tours depart from the Nashville Farmers' Market (900 Rosa Parks Blvd.).

MAP 2: Meeting point: 900 Rosa Parks Blvd., 615/226-7300 or 800/342-2123, www. nashtrash.com; generally 11am and 2pm daily; $33-36

PARKS

CENTENNIAL PARK

Nashville's best city park, Centennial is most known as home of the Parthenon, and that edifice is the center of activity in this 132-acre gem. In addition to housing the museum and historical site, the park is also a pleasant place to relax. A small lake provides a habitat for ducks and other water creatures; paved trails are popular for walking during nice weather. The park hosts many events during the year, including Shakespeare in the Park each August and September. Something is almost always going on here, particularly in the summer when live music frequently fills the trees. Centennial Park is home to one of Nashville's three official dog parks, as well as marked running trails, bicycle rental stations, children's play areas, and almost anything else you expect from a park.

MAP 3: 2500 West End Ave., 615/862-8424, http://nashville.gov; sunrise-11pm daily; free

BIKE SHOPS AND RENTALS

CUMBERLAND TRANSIT

One of the city's most beloved independent outdoors shops, Cumberland Transit stocks and services bikes. Brands carried include Trek, Gary Fisher, and Yakima. The store also hosts a number of how-to workshops, pint nights, and other outdoor-focused activities.

MAP 3: 2807 West End Ave., 615/321-4069, http://cumberlandtransit.com; 10am-6pm Mon.-Sat., noon-5pm Sun.

TOURS

NASHVILLE PEDAL TAVERN

Have 8 to 15 friends and a taste for beer? Then the Nashville Pedal Tavern is for you. You board a giant group bicycle and pedal together to move through downtown and Midtown, stopping at various pubs on the route. Members of your party pass out food and drink (BYOB; no glass containers) while you pedal. Each tour includes two or three pub stops; at each spot there's a special for Pedal Tavern customers. These tours are exceedingly popular with the booming bachelorette party crowd.

MAP 3: 1516 Demonbreun St., 615/390-5038, http://nashvillepedaltavern.com; times vary; $38 for individual seats, private group tours $380 Mon.-Wed., $325 Thurs., $440 Fri.-Sat., $400 Sun.

BIKE SHOPS AND RENTALS

EASTSIDE CYCLES

This neighborhood bike shop has everything anyone with two wheels could want. It offers high-end bikes for sale, rentals for just getting around town, and repair and service if you don't know what to do to get your own bicycle back on the road. There are bike seats and other gear to make biking with your kids easy (and even toys to keep them occupied while you shop). The store has bike tools around back for DIY repair during off-hours.

MAP 5: 103 S. 11th St., 615/469-1079, www.eastside-cycles.com; 11am-7pm Mon.-Fri., 10am-6pm Sat.; bike rentals $20-60/day, $5-15/day for racks, helmets, and locks

GOLF

SHELBY GOLF COURSE

The first public golf course in Music City is still one of Nashville's favorites. Located in the popular East Nashville Shelby Park, the 18-hole course (with a 9-hole option) is particularly friendly to new golfers. It also hosts a respected junior golf program. Tee times are recommended, but not required, and can be reserved up to seven days in advance.

MAP 5: 2021 Fatherland St., 615/862-8474, http://nashville.gov; hours vary based on season; $16/18 holes Mon.-Fri., $18/18 holes Sat.-Sun.

Music Valley Map 6

GOLF

GAYLORD SPRINGS GOLF LINKS

Golfers like this 6,842-yard Larry Nelson-designed 18-hole, par 72 course, saying it delivers one of the state's best golf experiences. Don't miss the comforts of the 43,000-square-foot clubhouse or the scenery of a links-like layout bordered by limestone cliffs and the Cumberland River. The location near the Gaylord Opryland Resort in Music Valley makes it easy to access from the airport and Briley Parkway.

MAP 6: 18 Springhouse Ln., 615/458-1730, www.gaylordsprings.com; 7am-sunset Mon.-Fri., 6:30am-sunset Sat.-Sun.; $67/18 holes Mon.-Thurs., $77/18 holes Fri.-Sun. Apr.-mid-Nov., $57/18 holes Mon.-Thurs., $67/18 holes Fri.-Sun. mid-Nov.-Mar.

TWO RIVERS GOLF COURSE

Near both the airport and the Music Valley Opryland complex is this public 18-hole course run by the Metro Parks department. It has great views of

SPORTS AND ACTIVITIES
MUSIC VALLEY

the downtown skyline and a design that is challenging for even the most experienced golfer.

MAP 6: 2235 Two Rivers Pkwy., 615/889-2675, www.nashville.gov; 8am-sunset Mon.-Fri., 7am-sunset Sat.-Sun. Feb.-Apr. and early Dec.-Jan., 7am-sunset Mon.-Fri., 6am-sunset Sat.-Sun. May-Labor Day, 7:30am-sunset Mon.-Fri., 6:30am-sunset Sat.-Sun. Labor Day-Sept. 30, 7:30am-sunset Mon.-Fri., 7am-sunset Sat.-Sun. Oct.-early Dec.; $26/18 holes Mon.-Fri., $28/18 holes Sat.-Sun.

AMUSEMENT PARKS

WAVE COUNTRY

When the summer gets hot, as it does in Tennessee, locals line up to take their kids to Wave Country. Located near Music Valley, this water park has exciting slides, a wave pool, and sand volleyball courts, as well as a play area for smaller kids. Wave Country is managed by Metro Parks.

MAP 6: 2320 Two Rivers Pkwy., 615/885-1052, www.nashville.gov/parks; 11am-5pm Mon.-Thurs., 10am-6pm Fri.-Sat., 11am-6pm Sun., May-Aug.; $12 adults, $10 children ages 3-12

TOURS

GENERAL JACKSON SHOWBOAT

Gaylord Opryland's *General Jackson* showboat offers campy, big-budget-style musical shows on the stage of a giant riverboat as it lumbers down the Cumberland River. Show dates and times vary by season but typically include midday lunch and evening dinner cruises. A smaller boat, the *Music City Queen,* offers tailgating cruises before Titans football games. Because of the meal and the live entertainment, these cruises aren't necessarily the best way to see the river, as you're focused on the stage, rather than the scenery.

MAP 6: 2812 Opryland Dr., 615/458-3900, http://generaljackson.com; showtimes generally noon and 7pm daily; $30-135

GRAY LINE TOURS

Nashville's largest tour company, Gray Line, offers more than 20 different sightseeing tours of the city. The three-hour Discover Nashville tour includes entrance to the Ryman Auditorium and the Country Music Hall of Fame and stops at other city landmarks. The three-hour Homes of the Stars tour takes you past the current and former homes of stars including Garth Brooks and Trisha Yearwood, Taylor Swift, Reese Witherspoon, and Dolly Parton. A one-hour downtown trolley tour and a downtown walking tour are also available, plus an option to see sights featured on the TV show *Nashville.*

MAP 6: 2416 Music Valley Dr., 615/883-5555 or 800/251-1864, http://graylinetn.com; tour times vary; $25-79 adults, $15-68 children

Clockwise from top left: First Tennessee Park, home to the Nashville Sounds; Topgolf Nashville; a Nashville Predators game.

PARKS

COLEMAN PARK COMMUNITY CENTER

A South Nashville jewel, Coleman Park is where neighborhood kids (and adults) congregate. Nice urban walking trails allow folks to run or walk before or after work. Inside is an indoor pool, dance studio, and more. There's a decent playground and full schedule of fitness classes.

MAP 7: 384 Thompson Ln., 615/862-8445, http://nashville.gov; dawn-11pm daily; indoor center 6am-8:30pm Mon.-Thurs., 6am-7:30pm Fri., 8am-noon Sat.; free

TOURS

TENNESSEE CENTRAL RAILWAY

The Tennessee Central Railway Museum offers an annual calendar of sightseeing and themed railway rides in central Tennessee, including kids' trips, Old West shoot-outs, and murder mysteries. Excursions include fall foliage tours, Christmas shopping expeditions, and trips to scenic small towns. All trips run on the Nashville and Eastern Railroad, which runs east, stopping in Lebanon, Watertown, Cookeville, or Monterrey. These tours are not just train rides, but well-organized volunteer-led events. You might get "robbed" by a Wild West bandit (the cash goes to charity) or taken to a scenic winery. The volunteers know their railroad trivia, so feel free to ask questions. The cars vary depending on what is available, but one car doubles as a gift shop and another as a concession stand, though you are welcome to bring your own food on the train. Trips sell out early, so book your tickets well in advance.

MAP 7: 220 Willow St., 615/244-9001, http://tcry.org; tour times and prices vary; museum 9am-4pm Tues.-Thurs., 9am-3pm Sat.

Greater Nashville Map 8

PARKS

EDWIN AND PERCY WARNER PARKS

The largest city parks in Tennessee, Edwin and Percy Warner Parks, also known as **The Warner Parks,** are a 2,600-acre oasis of forest, fields, and quiet pathways just nine miles southwest from downtown Nashville. Nashvillians come here to walk, jog, ride bikes and horses, and much more. The parks offer scenic drives, picnic facilities, playgrounds, cross-country running trails, an equestrian center, bridle trails, a model-airplane field, and athletic fields. Percy Warner Park is also home to the Harpeth Hills Golf Course, and Edwin Warner Park has a nature center that provides

Green in the City

Nashville has a remarkable network of connected green spaces thanks to its **Greenways** (615/862-8400, http://nashville.gov/greenways). The master plan is for this system to eventually connect the entire city. Today there are more than 190 miles of paved pathways and primitive trails used by bicyclists, runners, and dog walkers, all of which connect different parts of the city to each other. The Greenways run through the city's prettiest natural areas and, in places, along the Cumberland River. Some Greenways include nature centers and other educational facilities. For the most part, the routes are clean and safe. The long-term plan is for every Nashville resident to live within one mile of a greenway. Good maps are available for download from **Greenways for Nashville** (http://greenwaysfornashville.org) as well as from the official website.

year-round environmental education. The nature center also hands out maps and other information about the park.

MAP 8: 7311 Hwy. 100, 615/352-6299, http://nashville.gov; dawn-11pm daily; free

HAMILTON CREEK RECREATION AREA

Most of the access areas on J. Percy Priest Lake are managed by the U.S. Army Corps of Engineers, but Metro Nashville operates Hamilton Creek Recreation Area, on the lake's western shore. There's a sailboat marina here, where locals dock their boats, and this is a pretty spot from which to watch regattas and other sailing events. Storage for boats and paddleboards is available at a nominal fee for locals. This is also the site of Nashville Paddle Company, Music City BMX, and a challenging community-maintained mountain bike trail. A playground and traditional park offerings (room for Frisbee and picnic tables) round out the offerings.

MAP 8: 2901 Bell Rd., 615/862-8472, http://nashville.gov; sunrise-sunset daily (security gate open 6:30am-9:30pm); free

HORSEBACK RIDING
EQUESTRIAN CENTER

Those who love horses are fans of the Equestrian Center in The Warner Parks, best known for the annual Iroquois Steeplechase Horse Race it hosts each May. But a 10-mile bridle path is open to horseback riding year-round. Because these trails are the only public horse trails in the county, they are crowded, and your horses need to share the trails with dogs, runners, and walkers.

MAP 8: 2500 Old Hickory Blvd., 615/370-8051; dawn-11pm daily; free for 1-9 horses, $44 permit for 10-25 horses

TWIN FORKS HORSE TRAIL

Hikers and horseback riders alike appreciate this 18-mile trail located in the East Fork Recreation Area on the southwestern shore of J. Percy Priest

Lake and which dips into the Stones River. The trail is wooded and well maintained and perfect for horseback riding, but the emphasis here is on the trail, not the vistas. If what you really want is views of the water, select a different vantage point. Come prepared: This trail can be muddy after a rainstorm.

MAP 8: J. Percy Priest Lake, 3737 Bell Rd., 615/889-1975, www.percypriestlake.org; 24 hours daily; free

HIKING AND BIKING
ANDERSON ROAD FITNESS TRAIL

The 14,200-acre **J. Percy Priest Lake** is big and, as a result, is the heart of Nashvillians' water-based recreation. The big lake and its banks are divided into smaller pieces, and this trail is a good one to consider if you want to get out and stretch your muscles. It is called a "fitness trail," but all the fitness is on your own accord: There are no hurdles or obstacles or any equipment. It does have great views of the water and plenty of shade, which is welcome during Nashville's hot summers.

MAP 8: Anderson Rd. and Couchville Pike, 615/889-1975, www.percypriestlake.org; sunrise-sunset daily; free

LONG HUNTER STATE PARK

The state of Tennessee operates this park on the eastern shore of J. Percy Priest Lake. It offers mountain biking trails, both a two-mile loop and a four-mile loop. In addition there are several hiking trails around the lake, with a number of good vantage points and views of the water. Boats are available for rent during the summer season. Both group and backcountry camping is available.

MAP 8: 2910 Hobson Pike, Hermitage, 615/885-2422, http://tnstateparks.com; 7am-sunset daily; free

NATCHEZ TRACE PARKWAY

The primary destination for cyclists around Nashville is the Natchez Trace Parkway, a historic two-lane, 444-mile blacktop scenic drive that runs from Nashville and journeys south through the Tennessee and Mississippi countryside, eventually terminating in Natchez, Mississippi. The parkway, which is a designated bike route, is closed to commercial traffic, and the speed limit is strictly enforced, making it popular for biking. Cycling the Trace can be an afternoon outing or a weeklong adventure.

The National Park Service maintains three campgrounds along the Trace, plus five bicyclist-only campsites with more modest amenities. The northernmost bike campsite is located at the intersection of the Trace and Highway 50, about 36 miles south of Nashville. When biking on the Trace, ride in a single-file line (cars are encouraged to move to the opposite lane when safe to give cyclists plenty of room) and always wear reflective clothing and a helmet.

Each mile of the Trace is well-marked, and periodically there are

Exploring the Natchez Trace Parkway

Just to the west of Nashville is one of the National Park Service's little-known gems. The Natchez Trace Parkway is a 444-mile ribbon of green connecting three states and 10,000 years of military, Native American, musical, and U.S. history. As you walk in the footsteps of the Native Americans, Kaintuck boatmen, Confederate soldiers, Daughters of the American Revolution, and others, it's impossible not to feel connected to their journeys.

The first people to travel what is now considered the Natchez Trace were probably Choctaw and Chickasaw people, who made the first footpaths through the region. Early European settlers quickly identified the importance of a land route from Natchez to Nashville. In 1801, the Natchez Trace opened as an official post road between the two cities. One historian characterized the diverse array of people who used the Trace as "robbers, rugged pioneers, fashionable ladies, shysters, politicians, soldiers, scientists, and men of destiny, such as Aaron Burr, Andrew Jackson, and Meriwether Lewis." By 1820, more than 20 inns, referred to as "stands," were open. Many were modest—providing food and shelter only.

Then came the years of disuse and neglect. Steamboats, railways, and new roads rendered the Trace obsolete. Although it faded from use, the Natchez Trace was remembered. In 1909, the Daughters of the American Revolution in Mississippi started a project to mark the route of the Trace. The marker project continued for the next 24 years and eventually caught the attention of Mississippi Rep. Thomas J. Busby, who introduced the first bills in Congress to survey and construct a paved road along the route of the old Natchez Trace.

It took nearly another century for the project to be completed. In 1996 the final leg of the parkway was completed, and in 2005, sections near Jackson and Natchez, Mississippi (now some of the most traveled) were paved.

Today the 444-mile parkway follows the general path of the old, sunken, unpaved Natchez Trace; in a few places, they fall in step with each other. These spots are great for hikes and photographing the landscape. More than 100 miles of the parkway lie within Tennessee, and one of the beauties of the Trace is that you can feel like you are fully immersing yourself in it, whether you drive a few miles or the whole thing.

The Trace runs along the Western Highland Rim through Davidson, Williamson, Hickman, Maury, Lewis, and Wayne Counties. The **National Park Service** (800/305-7417, http://nps.gov/natr) publishes a foldout map and guide to the parkway. For more detailed information on the breadth and depth of opportunities on the Trace, see *Moon Nashville to New Orleans Road Trip*, a guide to all 444 miles and more.

turnouts from the road with signage about the spot and its history. Most stops have picnic tables and shade. A few have restrooms and other amenities. Highlights on the Trace near Nashville include the striking **Double Arch Bridge** (milepost 438) and the historic **Gordon House and Ferry site** (milepost 407.7).

MAP 8: Southwest of Nashville, 800/305-7417, http://nps.gov/natr; 24 hours daily; free

Just seven miles southwest of downtown Nashville, Radnor Lake State Natural Area provides a natural escape for visitors and residents of the city. Spanning 85 acres, Radnor Lake was created in 1914 by the Louisville and Nashville Railroad Company, which impounded Otter Creek to do so. The lake was built to provide water for the railroad's steam engines. By the 1940s, the railroad's use of the lake ended, and 20 years later the area was threatened by development. Local residents, including the Tennessee Ornithological Society, successfully rallied against development, and Radnor Lake State Natural Area was established in 1973.

Around the lake are six miles of hiking trails, and Otter Creek Road is closed to vehicular traffic and open to bicycles and walkers. The lake is not open to paddling or other recreation, and because this is a wildlife area, dogs are not allowed on the trails. A nature museum at the visitors center (8:30am-noon, 1pm-4pm daily) describes some of the 240 species of birds and hundreds of species of plants and animals that live at Radnor. The **Barbara J. Mapp Aviary Education Center** (http://radnorlake.org) houses non-releasable birds of prey.

MAP 8: 1160 Otter Creek Rd., 615/373-3467, http://tnstateparks.com; 6am-sunset daily; free

THREE HICKORIES NATURE TRAIL

The Three Hickories Nature Trail is an easy, 1.6-mile trail found in the Cook Recreational Area. It is the kind of walk you can do with a stroller, small children, and/or groups of varying fitness levels. Enjoy pretty views of the lake, and feel like you are miles away from the city, even though it takes fewer than 30 minutes to get here from downtown.

MAP 8: 2910 Hobson Pike, Hermitage, 615/885-2422, http://www.lrn.usace.army.mil; sunrise-sunset daily; $5

BIKE SHOPS AND RENTALS
TRACE BIKES

Trace Bikes is located in The Shoppes on the Harpeth. This is a picture-perfect spot for getting out and riding a bike on the lovely Natchez Trace or anywhere on the west side of town. Bikes and gear are also available for sale, and the shop leads biking events.

MAP 8: 8080 Hwy. 100, 615/646-2485, http://tracebikes.com; 10am-6pm Mon.-Fri., 10am-5pm Sat.; bike rentals $55/day

GOLF
HARPETH HILLS GOLF COURSE

Nestled in Percy Warner Park, Harpeth Hills is a public course with a solid reputation. It was designed in 1965 and renovated in 1991. Golfers can appreciate the natural beauty of the surrounding parks while they hit the

Biking Music City

Nashville is no Portland; you won't see a bicycle rack at every storefront. But the city has a growing bike culture, and it is easy to pedal your way across the city to see its highlights.

The first step is to bring your own bike, rent one, or borrow one. City residents (with a local ID) can check out a bike from **Nashville GreenBikes** (www.nashville.gov). Once you have your two wheels, it is easy to connect to more than 90 miles of greenways and 133 miles of on-road bike lanes and shared-use bike routes. **B-Cycle** (http://nashville.bcycle.com) offers 24-hour usage for just $5 plus hourly rental or membership for more frequent peddlers with more than 36 stations across town.

The Music City Bikeway (www.nashville.gov/bikeways) offers a 26-mile route that covers the city from east to west and includes city streets, Greenway paths, and more. It goes by the Nashville Farmers' Market, which has the most creative bike racks in the city, in the shape of bright vegetables. Eight miles of the bikeway include streets with designated bike lanes. The bikeway website offers a downloadable route map. Another good set of downloadable maps is available from **Walk/Bike Nashville** (www.walk-bikenashville.org).

links. Affordable lessons are available at many of Metro Nashville's public courses, including this one.

MAP 8: 2424 Old Hickory Rd., 615/862-8493, http://nashville.gov; hours vary based on season; $26/18 holes Mon.-Fri., $28/18 holes Sat.-Sun.

MCCABE GOLF COURSE

The city's Sylvan Park area is home to the public McCabe Golf Course, a large 27-hole course. Built in 1942 and renovated in 2007, the course is challenging enough for regular golfers but accessible for those who are new to the sport. There's also a driving range with target greens. Tee times can be reserved up to seven days in advance.

MAP 8: 100 46th Ave. N., 615/862-8491, http://nashville.gov; hours vary based on season; $24/18 holes Mon.-Fri., $26/18 holes Sat.-Sun.

NASHBORO GOLF CLUB

Larger bunkers and water hazards dot the 6,887 yards in this private golf course, which is open to the public. The course was designed by Benjamin J. Wihry. There's a clubhouse and pro shop for all your associated golfing needs.

MAP 8: 1101 Nashboro Blvd., 615/367-2311, www.nashborogolf.com; hours vary based on season; $39/18 holes Mon.-Thurs., $45/18 holes Fri., $49/18 holes Sat.-Sun.

TED RHODES GOLF COURSE

In 1992 this North Nashville golf course was renovated, thanks to a design by Gary Roger Baird. The greens run along the banks of the Cumberland River, which means pretty views and lots of wildlife alongside the putting greens and fairways. The 18-hole course is an easy one to walk, making it a good choice for a little extra exercise. Tee times can be reserved up to seven days in advance.

MAP 8: 1901 Ed Temple Blvd., 615/862-8463, http://nashville.gov; hours vary based on season; $26/18 holes Mon.-Fri., $28/18 holes Sat.-Sun.

WATER SPORTS
Marinas and Lakes
ELM HILL MARINA

Boating, fishing, and water sports are among the most popular activities on J. Percy Priest Lake. Elm Hill Marina is the marina closest to downtown Nashville and, as such, one of the busiest. Lots of locals rent slips and have their boats docked here. But even if you don't have a boat of your own, you can rent one. The pontoon boats ($265-425/half day) are popular with the bachelorette party crowd. Renting a 14-foot trolling motor fishing boat for two hours costs $25. Elm Hill also has an outdoors store, with essentials like sunscreen and key rings that float, and a restaurant with typical seaside fare.

MAP 8: 3361 Bell Rd., 615/889-5363 office, 615/739-9100 rentals, http://elmhillmarina.com; office and boathouse 8am-7pm daily, boat rentals until 6pm daily

J. PERCY PRIEST LAKE

J. Percy Priest Lake was created in the mid-1960s when the U.S. Army Corps of Engineers dammed the Stones River east of Nashville. The lake is a favorite destination for fishing, boating, swimming, paddling, and picnicking. Access to this lake sprawling over 14,200 acres is provided through more than a dozen different parks and entry points on all sides of the lake. Many of these areas bear the names of communities that were inundated when the lake was created.

The lake's visitors center, operated by the U.S. Army Corps of Engineers, is located at the dam site on Bell Road (at exit 219 off I-40 heading east from downtown Nashville). There you will find a lake overlook and one of four marinas on the lake. To rent a boat, head to Elm Hill Marina, about one mile south on Bell Road.

MAP 8: 3737 Bell Rd., 615/889-1975, www.lrn.usace.army.mil; 24 hours daily; free

OLD HICKORY LAKE

One of two lakes formed by the damming of the Cumberland River (the other is J. Percy Priest), Old Hickory is named after Andrew Jackson, whose plantation was nearby. The lakeshore is home to eight marinas, an arboretum, and more than 40 places to launch a boat (or paddleboard) and get out on the water or just sit on the banks and fish. There are beaches, picnic areas, and sailboat marinas, as well as two campgrounds.

MAP 8: 876 Burnett Rd., Old Hickory, 615/822-4846, http://www.lrn.usace.army.mil; 24 hours daily; free

FOGGY BOTTOM CANOE

Foggy Bottom generally offers floats down the Harpeth River between April and November in either canoes or kayaks. There are no set departure times; they aim to shuttle you as soon as you arrive and are ready to go. The Harpeth is typically a Class I river and generally very crowded on summer weekends. Because it can sometimes step up to a Class II, it's always a good idea to call ahead for river conditions.

MAP 8: 1270 Hwy. 70, Kingston Springs, 615/952-4062, www.foggybottomcanoe.com; hours and prices vary by season; trips up to 5 hours $34-39

NASHVILLE PADDLE CO.

Middle Tennessee's flatwater lakes and rivers are perfect for paddling. Nashville Paddle Company offers stand-up paddleboard (SUP) instruction and lessons for both adults and kids. Lessons take place at the company's boathouse at Hamilton Creek Recreation Area on J. Percy Priest Lake. Rentals are also available for those who want to take boards or kayak and go for a weekend. With more than a dozen yoga teachers, Nashville Paddle Co. offers SUP yoga as well as SUP Fitness classes, which are workouts that use both land and water to get your core in tip-top shape. (Full disclosure: The author of this book is one of the owners of Nashville Paddle Co.). Dogs are welcome for an additional $5 fee.

MAP 8: Hamilton Creek Recreation Area, 2901 Bell Rd., 615/682-1787, http:// nashvillepaddle.com; daily May-Sept.; $20-40 for paddleboard yoga, SUP lessons, or 1.5-hour rental

TIP-A-CANOE

Tip-a-Canoe has been offering canoe and kayak rentals on the Harpeth River on the west side of town since before the Narrows of the Harpeth was a state park. All that experience has paid off. Boat rentals include shuttle service from where you get off the river back to the beginning, where your car is parked. Shuttles are also available (for a fee) for those who have their own boats. The Harpeth is typically a Class I river, but at some times of the year bumps up to Class II. If you have concerns about your paddling ability, call ahead for river conditions.

MAP 8: 1279 Hwy. 70, Kingston Springs, 800/550-5810, www.tip-a-canoe.com; hours and prices vary by season; $50 (approx.) for two hours for two people

MUSIC CITY CANOE

This outfitter offers a variety of floats down the Harpeth, with trips and shuttles allowing you to opt for 2- to 9.5-mile routes on the Harpeth River on the west side of town. The Harpeth is typically a Class I river and generally so crowded on a summer weekend that it hardly seems like a nature experience. Other times of the year it's a Class II. It's always wise to call ahead for river conditions.

MAP 8: 1203 Hwy. 70, Kingston Springs, 615/952-4211, www.canoemusiccity.com; hours and prices vary by season; $40-43 per canoe

AMUSEMENT PARKS
NASHVILLE SHORES

Nashville Shores is a great destination for a hot summer day. This water and amusement park features miles of sandy beaches along the shore of J. Percy Priest Lake, pools, waterslides, and water sports. Admission to the park includes the opportunity to take a 15-minute lake cruise on *The Shoreliner,* which looks like an old steamboat and has a paddle wheel in the back.

MAP 8: 4001 Bell Rd., 615/889-7050, www.nashvilleshores.com; hours vary May-Sept.; $37 adults, $29 seniors and children under 52 inches tall

Various Locations

BIKE SHOPS AND RENTALS
★ NASHVILLE B-CYCLE

More than 310 bikes are available for rental at 36 different stations across Music City, with new locations being added regularly. A 24-hour pass is $5, plus hourly rental. The first hour is free, and each additional half hour is $1.50; the price is capped at $45/day. You can take an unlimited number of trips during your membership period. The idea is to bike from one attraction to another, return the bike, and then grab another bike when you need it, so you're not paying for a bike when you're not using it. You must sign up for a membership in advance and bring your own helmet.

Various locations: 615/625-2153, http://nashville.bcycle.com; 24 hours daily; up to $45 for 24 hours

TOURS
★ WALK EAT NASHVILLE

Formerly an editor at *The Tennessean,* Karen-Lee Ryan started her walking culinary tours as a way to show off her neighborhood of East Nashville. They were so popular she soon expanded to Midtown and downtown. The tours include about 1.5 miles of walking and food tastings at 5-6 restaurants and artisan food shops. Ryan and her expert guides narrate as you walk (and taste), and you get the benefit of their considerable knowledge of the city. You'll leave satisfied, but not full. One downtown tour, led by author Jennifer Justus, includes a signed copy of her cookbook, *Nashville Eats.*

Various locations: Meeting point disclosed when tour booked, 615/587-6138, www. walkeatnashville.com; 1:30pm-4:30pm Thurs., 11am-2pm Fri., 1:30pm-4:30pm Sat.; $58-88

Choose between several different canoe or kayak tours down the Cumberland River with River Queen Voyages. The one-hour, three-mile tour starts in Shelby Bottoms Greenway, winding under railway bridges and ending downtown with the skyline in sight. The two-hour, five-mile tour is self-guided and starts near Opryland, ending near Shelby Park with a view of the downtown skyline in the distance. Both are self-guided. When booking, you'll be provided with a meeting location to board a shuttle upstream to the tour start.

Various locations: 615/933-9778, http://rqvoyages.com; May-Oct.; $29-59 for 1-hour tours, $39-79 for 2-hour tours

Shops

Nashville's continued reputation as Music City means its shopping has gotten short shrift.

However, progress has been made in the Nashville retail scene, thanks in particular to the maker movement and the Nashville Fashion Alliance, a crowdsourcing effort devoted to highlighting and building Nashville's fashion chops. Hometown girl-made-good Reese Witherspoon opened the first outpost of her brand Draper James, in the 12 South neighborhood, and country/pop crooner Taylor Swift still loves to shop here, even if she sleeps in New York more often than Music City. Stylists to the stars—including Trish Townsend—have opened boutiques to share their secrets, too.

If you like the thrill of the hunt, you'll find more than enough stuff to fill extra space in your suitcase. Venture out beyond the malls, where there are endless opportunities for one-of-a-kind merchandise, from antiques and vintage goods to handmade treasures.

The area malls run the gamut from discount (the city's outlet mall is one of the state's most popular tourist destinations) to high end, and most of the big-name chain stores can be found in or near them (think Nordstrom, Lululemon, Urban Outfitters, Warby Parker, Kate Spade, Gap, Forever 21, and many, many others).

One of the best all-around shopping districts is Hillsboro Village, the commercial district that borders Vanderbilt University in Midtown. Critics have bemoaned that historical buildings have been demolished for new construction, and this is true. But designer clothing stores, affordable art, and trendy housewares are just a few of the things you'll find in this neighborhood, best explored on foot. Fine boutiques cater to the well-heeled in tony West End and 12 South, and East Nashville has become a maker paradise.

It may sound cliché, but don't pass up the opportunity to buy Western wear in Music City. Seriously, don't go home without a pair of boots.

Previous: leather handbags and shoes at Ceri Hoover; Jack White's Third Man Records.

Look for ★ to find recommended shops.

Highlights

★ **Most Iconic Nashville Images:** Since 1879 **Hatch Show Print** has been churning out letterpress signage for concerts, shows, and businesses. Take home a piece of the Music City aesthetic (page 175).

★ **Best Place to Buy Something Other than Country Music:** Jack White's **Third Man Records** is rock heaven, with music selected to fit the icon's favorite styles (page 177).

★ **Where to Buy Iconic Western Wear:** The appetite for boots, hats, and other cowboy goods is real. If cash is burning a hole in your pocket, stop at designer-to-the-stars **Manuel Exclusive Clothier** (page 179).

★ **Where to Find a Piece of Italy in Nashville:** Named for the Italian grandfather the owner never met, **Peter Nappi** offers high-end boots custom made in Italy (page 179).

★ **Best Place to Browse for Tunes:** **Grimey's New and Preloved Music** goes above and beyond the typical music shop with live music, helpful staff, and enthusiastic customers who love to hang out and browse (page 186).

★ **Best Indie Retail Strips:** East Nashville's **1108 Shops at Woodland** and **Shoppes on Fatherland** are chock-full of always-changing collections of one-of-a-kind purses, neckties, jewelry, and all other things made by local artists (page 192).

CLOTHING AND ACCESSORIES
TWO OLD HIPPIES

The owners of Two Old Hippies lived the era of "Peace, Love, and Rock 'n' Roll" with gusto, and they do their best to bring those ideals to the present day, particularly the rock 'n' roll part. There's an actual '69 VW Microbus right in the middle of the store to set the mood. Shop here for vintage-looking band shirts and other Nashville-style gifts. Non-shoppers can noodle away on premium guitars or listen to live music in a shop that is also a music venue (as seen on the TV show *Nashville*).

MAP 1: 401 12th Ave. S., 615/254-7999, http://twooldhippies.com/nashville; 10am-7pm Mon.-Thurs., 10am-8pm Fri.-Sat., 11am-6pm Sun.

GIFTS
FIRE FINCH BOUTIQUE

Country music sweetheart Taylor Swift has been known to shop here when in town, but it is a favorite of mere mortal locals, too. Fire Finch is the go-to shop for trendy jewelry, handbags, and accessories. Look here for candles, books, scarves, and more. There are a few sweet home decor items, too.

MAP 1: 305 Church St., 615/385-5090, www.welovefirefinch.com; 10am-6pm Mon.-Sat., noon-5pm Sun.

GOURMET AND SPECIALTY FOODS
PEANUT SHOP

Walking into the Peanut Shop is a trip back in time. The floorboards creak; nuts are roasting, boiling, or getting candied; and everything is still measured on the original over/under scale. This was the first home of Planters Peanuts and the original destination of generations of Nashvillians on coffee break (as it still is today). Though they specialize in nuts, there's also a generous assortment of candies and, in the summer, ice cream.

MAP 1: 19 Arcade Alley, 615/256-3394, http://nashvillenut.com; 9am-5pm Mon.-Fri. and during Art Crawls on Sat.

HOME DECOR
★ HATCH SHOW PRINT

Part gallery/part storefront, Hatch Show Print is one of the country's best-known places to buy and see art. Hatch has been making colorful posters for more than a century, and their iconic letterpress style is now one of the trendiest looks in modern design. They continue to design and print handouts, posters, and T-shirts for local and national customers. Visitors to the shop can gaze at the cavernous warehouse operation and buy small or large samples of their work, including reproductions of classic country music concert posters. This is a great place to find a special souvenir of your trip to Nashville or just to see another part of Music City's history.

Nashville Vintage

Folks rummaged their way through yard sales and flea markets long before there was a History Channel show that told them how. But even more people love the hunt for that long-forgotten gem thanks to *American Pickers*. The show's host, Mike Wolfe, has two **Antique Archaeology** stores in the country, and one of them is in Nashville (1300 Clinton St., 615/810-9906, http://antiquearchaeology.com), in the early-1900s Marathon Village car factory. See some of the shows favorite "picks," plus new logoed merchandise and the occasional real find.

Other favorite retailers who know how to salvage goods include East Nashville's **Old Made Good** (3701B Gallatin Pike, 615/432-2882, http://old-madegoodnashville.com) and **Hip Zipper** (1008 Forrest Ave., 615/228-1942, http://hipzipper.com). **High Class Hillbilly** (4604 Gallatin Pike, 615/840-7328, www.highclasshillbilly.com) stocks well-merchandised jewelry, clothing, and boots, some of which have been modernized or updated.

Gaslamp Antique and Decorating Mall (100 Powell Pl., Ste. 200, 615/297-2224, http://gaslampantiques.com) and East Nashville's **Wonders on Woodland** (1110 Woodland St., 615/226-5300) are known for their furniture and home decor.

If you'd rather sift through the parts and pieces yourself, Nashville has no shortage of flea markets and thrift stores. The best bet for furniture, art, and other funky finds is the **Nashville Flea Market** (500 Wedgewood Ave., 615/862-5016, www.thefairgrounds.com) held on the fourth weekend of every month at The Fairgrounds Nashville.

Hatch posters are up all over town, including in the airport. If you catch a show at the Ryman, you may have the chance to buy a Hatch poster from the evening there. Call ahead if you're interested in a tour or class; you may luck out in terms of timing.

MAP 1: 224 5th Ave. S., 615/256-2805, http://hatchshowprint.com; 9:30am-6pm Sun.-Wed., 9:30am-8pm Thurs.-Sat.

MUSIC
ERNEST TUBB RECORD SHOP

The Texas Troubadour, aka Ernest Tubb, founded his famous record store on Broadway in 1947. It remains a small but solid source of classic and modern country music recordings, as well as DVDs, books, clothing, and souvenirs. At the back of the shop you can see the stage where Ernest Tubb's Midnite Jamboree was recorded and aired after the Grand Ole Opry on Saturday nights. (The Jamboree still airs, but it's recorded at the Texas Troubadour Theatre in Music Valley.) It's great for late-night browsing after honky-tonking and eating on Lower Broad and remains one of the vestiges of old country in an area of town that's gone full-on pop-country.

MAP 1: 417 Broadway, 615/255-7503, http://etrecordshop.com; 10am-10pm daily

Third Man is a record label, recording studio, and record store all in one fairly small building. The idea behind the label is simple: All the music in the building has owner (and musician/producer) Jack White's stamp on it in some way. That's not a bad thing! Blue Series records are recorded by bands traveling through town, recording one or two songs, and available on seven-inch vinyl. Green Series are records of nonmusical ideas: spoken word, poetry, or instructional discussions. There are the bands on the label too, full-length LPs, and reissues of unusual and beautiful things. Even those who are not a fan of White's own music appreciate the noncountry street cred he gave the city before it was popular. The modern painted exterior makes the shop easy to find. Inside, there's a recording booth where you can opt to make a Music City souvenir of your own stylings.

MAP 1: 623 7th Ave. S., 615/891-4393, http://thirdmanrecords.com; 10am-6pm Mon.-Sat., 1pm-4pm Sun.

WESTERN WEAR
BOOT COUNTRY

It's all about the boots. Boot Country stocks a huge variety and organizes them by size. If you want boots, this is the place to go. If, in fact, you want three pairs of boots, this is the place to go, as they are always "buy one get two free." If you can't fit three pairs of boots in your luggage, organize a couple of friends and you can each get a pair. Buying a single pair is somewhat pricey.

MAP 1: 304 Broadway, 615/259-1691; 10am-10:30pm Mon.-Thurs., 10am-11pm Fri.-Sat., 11am-7:30pm Sun.

THE FRYE CO.

This U.S. boot- and shoemaker is a relative newcomer to Music City, but not to the leather game. The company has been around since 1863, and its 3,000-square-foot store in The Gulch shows off its timeless designs well. There's also space in the shop for live music events.

MAP 1: 401 11th Ave. S., 615/238-6170, http://thefryecompany.com; 10am-9pm Mon.-Sat., 11am-7pm Sun.

LUCCHESE BOOT CO.

A boot is not just a boot—at least not in Nashville, where boots are a status symbol as much as footwear. And in a town that loves boots, people really love Lucchese (pronounced "Lu-K-C"). This luxury brand has been around since 1883, but only since 2012 has it had its own retail shop in The Gulch. The boots (and belts and clothes) are made in the United States, and custom orders are taken.

MAP 1: 503 12th Ave. S., 615/242-1161, http://lucchese.com; 10am-7pm Mon.-Sat., noon-6pm Sun.

Top: Two Old Hippies offers both live music and great shopping. Bottom: Peter Nappi sells clothing and accessories in a jaw-dropping space.

★ **MANUEL EXCLUSIVE CLOTHIER**

The name says it all: Manuel Exclusive Clothier. Manuel Cuevas goes by just his first name, and he's the man who outfits all the stars with their stage-worthy clothing. The cowboy shirts start at $750 and jackets at more than $2,000, so this isn't the place for an impulse buy. This is the place to go when you've made it. You can stop by to admire the work even if you can't order your own Manuel suit … yet.

MAP 1: 800 Broadway, 615/321-5444, http://manuelcouture.com; 9am-6pm Mon.-Fri., or by appointment

Germantown and Capitol Hill

Map 2

CLOTHING AND ACCESSORIES

ABEDNEGO

One of a number of sleek Germantown boutiques, ABEDNEGO carries local- and American-made clothes and accessories. Owned by a local musician, ABEDNEGO stocks goods for men and women in a minimalist loftlike environment. The emphasis is on fashion-forward, yet affordable, togs you can't find elsewhere. The shop is named after a biblical character.

MAP 2: 1210 4th Ave. N., 615/712-6028, www.abednegoboutique.com; 11am-6pm Tues.-Sat., noon-5pm Sun.

EMIL ERWIN

The Buchanan Street shopping district is anchored by several high-end stores that make their own goods, including this one. The well-edited shop features luxury leather goods—handbags, belts, and items for the home such as coasters, baskets, and even chairs—in an art gallery-like setting.

MAP 2: 904 Buchanan St., 615/750-2735, www.emilerwin.com; 11am-5pm Thurs.-Sat. and by appointment

NISOLO

Feel guilty about shopping for shoes? Enter Nisolo. The company offers classic men's and women's leather shoes and accessories—all made without extra bells or whistles—by Peruvian craftspeople. The people who make the goods are paid more than a fair wage and have access to job training.

MAP 2: 1803 9th Ave. N., 615/953-1087, http://nisolo.com; 9am-5:30pm Mon.-Fri., 11am-5pm Sat., Sun. 1pm-5pm

★ PETER NAPPI

Phillip Nappi, grandson of the shop's namesake, has made boot- and shoe-making an art (based on research—he never met his grandfather, but had the craft in his bones). The shop's studio is in Italy, where artisans create footwear in the old-world style in limited runs with the highest-quality vegetable-tanned leathers. But the retail location in Germantown is totally Music City. The reclaimed space is a workshop, store, and live music venue where customers may purchase tempting shoes, handbags, hats, and jewelry or place custom orders. There's also a smaller second location in **12 South** (2308 12th Ave. S.). It carries the same goods, but the space isn't the jaw-dropper of the Germantown store.

MAP 2: 1308 Adams St., 615/248-3310, http://peternappi.com/studio; 11am-6pm Mon.-Sat. and by appointment

FLEA MARKETS
NASHVILLE FARMERS' MARKET FLEA MARKET
This flea market, located at the Nashville Farmers' Market, is chock-full of crafts and merchandise from local artisans as well as a few repurposed and vintage finds. This is a market in the making and likely not worth a separate trip. Instead, stop here on your way to the farmers market or Bicentennial Mall, and you may be pleasantly surprised.

MAP 2: 900 Rosa Parks Blvd., 615/880-2001, http://nashvillefarmersmarket.org; 8am-6pm Fri.-Sun.

GIFTS
SALEMTOWN BOARD CO.
Perhaps Nashville's best-loved social enterprise, Salemtown teaches inner city youth to make high-end, wood skateboards by hand. The craftsmanship is clear in every piece. Come check out their workshop, complete with a skate park and peruse the handmade goods, T-shirts, hats, and other apparel.

MAP 2: 1003 Buchanan St., no phone, http://salemtownboardco.com; 1:30pm-5:30pm Mon.-Fri.

HOME DECOR
WILDER
New York transplants Ivy and Josh (she was a Rockette and he was a member of Blue Man Group) brought their interior design eyes to the South. The duo opened a Germantown atelier to show off the kinds of wares with which they can transform a home. Come browse the furnishings, textiles, lighting, mirrors, and more, all with a modern sensibility and many not found elsewhere in the area. They also operate a spin-off store, **Wilder Etudes** (1200 Villa Pl., #301, 615/457-2529), near Music Row.

MAP 2: 1212 4th Ave. N., 615/679-0008, www.wilderlife.com, 11am-6pm Mon.-Sat., noon-5pm Sun.

CLOTHING AND ACCESSORIES

BOUTIQUE BELLA

Boutique Bella specializes in jeans. With a tremendous range of designers including J Brand, 7 for All Mankind, AG Adriano Goldschmeid, and Rock & Republic, and an equal selection of sizes, those looking for jeans that actually fit are bound to find their Holy Grail. The boutique is cute, but not twee, particularly the perfectly adorable dressing rooms. Sale racks are fantastic.

MAP 3: 2817 West End Ave., 615/467-1471; 10am-6pm Mon.-Sat.

NATIVE + NOMAD

This local favorite specializes in men's and women's clothing, including denim and workout wear, with a boho chic emphasis. The bright boutique is well-edited, with a focus on local labels. Barn wood accents show off denim, jewelry, and other accessories. The store has a second location in Franklin, in the **CoolSprings Galleria** (1800 Galleria Blvd., Franklin).

MAP 3: 1813 21st Ave. S., 615/840-7409, http://shopnativeandnomad.com; 10am-6pm Mon.-Fri., 10am-7pm Sat., 1pm-5pm Sun.

SCARLETT BEGONIA

For decades, Vanderbilt students have shopped in this boutique, which specializes in fair-trade goods. Walk by the window and inhale, and you might think it's all sweaters that smell like patchouli. There is some of that, but the merchandise is much more varied and sophisticated. Come here for pretty dresses, fun skirts, and jewelry in a variety of price ranges. Women's clothing is stocked in a wide cross section of sizes. Puppets, toys, and other gifts are also on the shelves.

MAP 3: 2805 West End Ave., 615/329-1272, www.scarlettbegonia.com; 10am-6pm Mon.-Sat., 1pm-5pm Sun.

UAL

Bargain-hunting fashionistas cannot skip UAL (which stands for United Apparel Liquidators). Designer samples of clothes, handbags, shoes, and jewelry are shoved onto crowded racks in this shop near the Vanderbilt campus. UAL stocks both men's and women's attire, but the women's selection is significantly larger. Label-loving shoppers can find great prices on goods, but a little digging is involved. A second location in Hillsboro Village (1814 21st Ave. S., 615/540-0211) is smaller, with more accessories and less clothing. If you are headed to the suburbs, there's also a Brentwood location (125 Franklin Rd., Brentwood, 615/922-4987).

MAP 3: 2918 West End Ave., 615/340-9999, http://shopual.com; 10am-8pm daily

SHOPS
MUSIC ROW

GIFTS

PANGAEA

Pangaea carries clothing, silver jewelry, mirrors, lanterns, frames, and trinkets that are funky, kitschy, eclectic, and boho-chic. The wares come from the Southwest, Mexico, Asia, India, Nashville, and everywhere in between—and in almost every price range. The shop is chock-full of goods. If you're the kind of browser who likes to look at every little thing, plan to be here a while.

MAP 3: 1721 21st Ave. S., 615/269-9665, www.pangaeanashville.com; 10am-6pm Mon.-Thurs., 10am-9pm Fri.-Sat., 1pm-5pm Sun.

HOME DECOR

CASTILLEJA

Owned by Grammy award-winning songwriter Liz Rose and her daughter, Castilleja brings a little taste of Texas to Tennessee. Expect to find home decor with a Lone Star twist, including blankets, leather goods, pillows, and lots of goods made with turquoise and silver. The shop is nestled in the Edgehill Village complex.

MAP 3: 1200 Villa Pl., Ste. 403, 615/730-5367, http://castillejanashville.com; 10am-7pm Mon.-Sat., noon-4pm Sun.

DAVIS COOKWARE

Davis Cookware has been in business in this location so long that they still have a painted sign on the side of the building that advertises their business. Like that sign, it's a little old-fashioned. The shop stocks all the essentials of cooking and crams them into every nook and cranny. The layout isn't entirely organized, but that's probably because the owners do like to show customers around and love a conversation. This is the only store in town that stocks Lodge Cast Iron cookware, and they sharpen knives on-site with skill. They also specialize in fine coffees and teas and have encyclopedic knowledge on the subject.

MAP 3: 1717 21st Ave. S., 615/298-4728; 8:30am-5:30pm Mon.-Sat.

HEY ROOSTER GENERAL STORE

Hey Rooster is a modern-day interpretation of an old-fashioned general store, located in Hillsboro Village. Proprietor Courtney Webb stocks the place with lovely handmade gifts, from art to jewelry to home decor, plus prepared foods and ingredients that are hard to find elsewhere.

MAP 3: 1711 21st Ave. S., http://heyrooster.com; 10am-6pm Mon.-Sat., 10am-4pm Sun.

SHOPPING DISTRICTS AND CENTERS

EDGEHILL VILLAGE

A former industrial laundry has become one of the city's lower-profile, but more engaging retail destinations. Come here to browse small boutiques ranging from home decor to baby clothes to jewelry to wedding dresses, along with chains such as Warby Parker and J. Crew. Stop and eat tacos, enjoy ice cream, or lounge in the coffee shop. Stores are on both sides of the street and also hidden from street view in the bigger building to the east. Street parking is mostly permit, but there are several affordable pay lots.

MAP 3: 1200 Villa Pl., http://edgehillvillage.com; hours vary by store

HILLSBORO VILLAGE

Some complain that Hillsboro Village, which runs several blocks along 21st Avenue South, has lost its indie cred, now that many historical buildings have been replaced with new construction. True, there are more chains here than there used to be, but this is still perhaps the city's best collection of boutiques, locally owned shops, and walkable options for a shopping outing. Hillsboro Village is located right next to the Vanderbilt campus and near Belmont's, so there is a student vibe. But the shops carry clothes, jewelry, gifts, cookware, and plenty of other stuff that wouldn't be at home in a dorm room. Hillsboro Village also has restaurants, bars, dessert spots, and the renovated Belcourt Theatre.

MAP 3: 1808 21st Ave. S.; hours vary by store

Midtown and 12 South   Map 4

ANTIQUES AND VINTAGE GOODS
ANTIQUE ARCHAEOLOGY

The second retail location for "American Picker" Mike Wolfe, this tiny store is almost a museum for American "things." All the pieces aren't necessarily for sale, but there are stories behind all of them. There are stories, too, about the building itself, which was the Marathon Motor Works car factory. Fans of the History Channel's *American Pickers* can find fun show T-shirts as well as rub elbows with some of the show's chief "pickers." There's almost always a line here, thanks to its TV reputation, but true thrifters and pickers have other favorite shops. There's also a small outpost inside the Omni Nashville Hotel.

MAP 4: 1300 Clinton St., 615/810-9906, www.antiquearchaeology.com; 10am-6pm Mon.-Sat., noon-5pm Sun.

EIGHTH AVENUE ANTIQUES MALL

Antiquers, pickers, and other lovers of vintage goods like to browse in this multidealer mecca of all things old. The folks with booths here specialize in dolls, jewelry, furniture, and other treasures of times gone by. There's ample parking, and individual dealers sometimes advertise sales on Facebook.

MAP 4: 2015 8th Ave. S., 615/279-9922; 10am-6pm Mon.-Sat., noon-5pm Sun.

BOOKS

HOWLIN' BOOKS

Howlin' is a literary offshoot of the wildly popular music store Grimey's. This small shop, which consists of several connected rooms, sells new and used books covering a variety of topics and genres, like music, art, poetry, and pop culture. They also sell magazines and children's books and host many public events. The shop adjoins with Grimey's Too, which sells used music.

MAP 4: 1702 8th Ave. S., 615/942-9648, http://howlinbooks.com; 11am-8pm Mon.-Fri., 10am-8pm Sat., 1pm-6pm Sun.

CLOTHING AND ACCESSORIES

CERI HOOVER

Local Ceri Hoover designs luscious high-end leather handbags, shoes, and wallets. These accessories are head-turners, and appear on the arms of most of the city's most fashionable people. The 12 South shop is tiny and minimally merchandised, but there are gems here to find. The strapless fold-over clutch has become a staple in the hands of Nashville women.

MAP 4: 2905 12th Ave. S., 615/200-0091, www.cerihoover.com, 11am-6pm Tues.-Fri., 10am-6pm Sat., 11am-5pm Sun.

DRAPER JAMES

Nashville native Reese Witherspoon launched the flagship location of her shop/lifestyle brand in her hometown. Find pillows, cocktail napkins, and more—with a Southern twist. Think J. Crew meets Kate Spade meets Southern hospitality. You'll be offered a glass of sweet tea as soon as you enter. The bright white and blue striped mural on the building's exterior is popular with Instagrammers. Being next door to a cupcake ATM is an extra perk.

MAP 4: 2608 12th Ave. S., 615/997-3601, www.draperjames.com; 10am-6pm Mon.-Wed., 10am-7pm Thurs.-Sat., 11am-5pm Sun.

FLIP

This pair of neighboring consignment stores stocks high-end clothing for men (at 1100 8th Ave.) and women (at 1016 8th Ave.). The selection is well curated, and the staff are good at finding something in your size, as well as helping you think about your style. The store stocks newer trends but is focused on classic suits and other items that have stood the test of time. Flip refers clients to a tailor for the perfect fit.

MAP 4: 1100 & 1016 8th Ave. S., 615/256-3547 (men's) or 615/732-3547 (women's), http://hip2flip.com; 10am-7pm Mon.-Sat.

HATWRKS

Owner/milliner Gigi Haskins creates fine custom hats for men and women, made on location with devices and machines that are as enchanting as the products themselves. Besides her own label of cloche, fascinators, boaters,

porkpies, bowlers, and fedoras, she carries an impressive array of some of
the most trusted brands available, including the ubiquitous Stetson, historical Dobbs, and gorgeous Louise Green. She can also rehab your grandfather's favorite hat to make it new again.

MAP 4: 1027 8th Ave. S., 615/491-9009, www.hatwrks.com; 10am-6pm Mon.-Sat.

IMOGENE + WILLIE

When this denim shop opened in an old gas station in 2009, it seemed like it was catering to a very niche market: a place to buy $200 jeans. But in the years since, the brand has thrived, getting into national retailers like Anthropologie, expanding into other product lines, and building a loyal local following, all by having products that are highly customizable and basically custom sewn to fit. If you have the splurge in your budget, come here to get your pair made; they're designed to last forever. The overall vibe is accessible and welcoming.

MAP 4: 2601 12th Ave. S., 615/292-5005, http://imogeneandwillie.com; 10am-6pm Mon.-Fri., 11am-6pm Sat., 1pm-5pm Sun.

MODA

MODA's elegantly eclectic boutique features women's designer clothing, accessories, jewelry, gifts, and even a bit of locally made baby clothes. The atmosphere is bright yet minimalist, adding to the spacious feel, and the style includes casual and the dressier side of casual. The staff are friendly and attentive without being intrusive.

MAP 4: 2511 12th Ave. S., 615/298-2271, http://modanashville.com; noon-5pm Mon., 10:30am-6pm Tues.-Sat.

GOURMET AND SPECIALTY FOODS
BANG CANDY COMPANY

Once a food cart hawking gourmet marshmallows around town, Bang Candy Company is now a candy store/coffee shop hybrid. It is the place to go for a sweet treat. The shop attracts a diverse clientele with Antique Archaeology shoppers and local hipsters all lingering among the sweets. The marshmallows and caramels are handmade in-house and include offbeat flavors such as absinthe and rose cardamom. Take home a flavored simple syrup for mixing your own cocktails.

MAP 4: 1300 Clinton St., 615/953-1065, www.bangcandycompany.com; 10am-3pm Tues., 10am-4pm Wed.-Thurs., 10am-6pm Fri.-Sat., 11am-4pm Sun.

HOME DECOR
WHITE'S MERCANTILE

White's Mercantile is owned by singer-songwriter Holly Williams. Yes, she's one of those Williams: Country legend Hank Williams Jr. is her father and Hank Sr. her grandfather. But she's not all about rhinestones and cowboy hats. Instead, this modern general store is a curated shop stocked with stuff she loves, some of which she found while on the road touring. Look for

Shop Like a Star

By now you know that Music City's name is well earned. Many bona fide stars call this fair city home. Not only that, they buy clothes (and boots, don't forget the boots) for their stage and screen appearances in Nashville.

You can emulate their style without looking like you're dressing for a Halloween party by starting at these favorite shops:

If you have serious cash to spend, head to **Manuel Exclusive Clothier** (800 Broadway, 615/321-5444, http://manuelamericandesigns.com), where you can have a bedazzled rhinestone suit made just for you.

Owned by a celeb herself (Hank Jr.'s daughter Holly), **H. Audrey** (4027 Hillsboro Pike, 615/760-5701, http://haudrey.com) is the choice for stars who want a more refined look, maybe for that talk show appearance.

How can you consider yourself a star until you have a custom-made signature hat? You can get that done at **Hatwrks** (1027 8th Ave. S., 615/491-9009, http://hatwrks.com).

jewelry, tasteful home decor, gifts for children, and holiday decor. Williams also owns clothing shop **H. Audrey** (4027 Hillsboro Pike, 615/760-5701, http://haudrey.com).

MAP 4: 2908 12th Ave. S., 615/750-5379; 10am-6pm Mon.-Sat., noon-5pm Sun.

MUSIC

★ GRIMEY'S NEW AND PRELOVED MUSIC

Grimey's is one of the best places in the city to go for new and used CDs, DVDs, and vinyl. You'll find a wide selection of not just country, but also rock, folk, blues, R&B, and other genres. But Grimey's is more than a store: It's an institution. The staff are knowledgeable and friendly, and the clientele passionate and loyal. In-store live performances literally make the sound come alive. Music fans could spend hours here. Plan accordingly. **Grimey's Too** (1702 8th Ave. S., 615/942-9683), down the block, is just as good as the original.

MAP 4: 1604 8th Ave. S., 615/254-4801, http://grimeys.com; 11am-8pm Mon.-Fri., 10am-8pm Sat., 1pm-6pm Sun.

GRUHN GUITARS

If you want to make your own music, head to Gruhn Guitars, a guitar shop with one of the best reputations in the music world. Founded by guitar expert George Gruhn, the shop is considered by some the best vintage guitar shop in the world. For 50 years shiny guitars, banjos, mandolins, and fiddles hung on the walls of the Broadway storefront. In 2013 the shop moved, but the sign—and the quality—remains the same.

MAP 4: 2120 8th Ave. S., 615/256-2033, http://gruhn.com; 10am-6pm Mon.-Sat.

OUTDOOR GEAR

HALCYON BIKE SHOP

This worker-owned bike shop sells both new and used bikes, including restored options that you can buy at a significantly lower price versus new. The shop offers bike repairs and also a workbench stocked with tools for do-it-yourself fixes.

MAP 4: 2802 12th Ave. S., 615/730-9344, http://halcyonbike.com; 10am-6pm Tues.-Sat., noon-5pm Sun.

East Nashville

Map 5

ANTIQUES AND VINTAGE GOODS

HIP ZIPPER

This East Nashville vintage stalwart is so packed with gems from days gone by that it can be hard to work your way around the racks. Working through the inventory is part of the fun, though. Hip Zipper was hip and here before the rest of the neighborhood was. Come here to find men's and women's vintage clothing, handbags, and accessories. Goods are also available for rent, if you're in town for a music video, film, or other production.

MAP 5: 1008 Forrest Ave., 615/228-1942, http://hipzipper.com; 11am-7pm daily

OLD MADE GOOD

Locals call this indie craft shop OMG. It's filled with everything vintage, reclaimed, repurposed, and locally made, ranging from housewares to clothing and jewelry. The proprietors have an eye for the quirky and a decidedly politically incorrect sense of humor. Beware: You may see a four-letter word embroidered on throw pillows. Over the years this shop has become a community center of sorts for local makers. Stop by for no other reason than to see the gold glitter floors and experience the good vibes.

MAP 5: 3701B Gallatin Pike, 615/432-2882, http://oldmadegoodnashville.com; noon-5pm Sun.-Mon., 11am-5pm Tues.-Sat.

BOOKS

HER BOOKSHOP

Don't let the name fool you—this isn't a feminist bookstore like you might experience on an episode of *Portlandia*. A play on the owner's last name, Herr, Her Bookshop offers a curated selection of unique, highly designed books on a wide range of topics. The stylish store has been so popular with locals it moved into a bigger location within two years of opening.

MAP 5: 1043 W. Eastland Ave., 615/485-5420, www.herbookshop.com; 11am-6pm Mon.-Fri., 10am-6pm Sat., 11am-4pm Sun.

CLOTHING AND ACCESSORIES

DCXV

All around town you'll see "I Believe in Nashville" murals painted on exterior building walls and garage doors with the elements of the state flag. This shop is owned by the minds behind those murals. In a small space in the hip strip mall along Porter Road (a repurposed housing complex), you'll find creative clothing and accessories, lots of great energy, and the best T-shirts to show off your Nashville love.

MAP 5: 727 Porter Rd., 615/295-8905, http://dcxvclothing.com; noon-6pm Tues.-Sat., noon-4pm Sun.-Mon.

TWO SON

Imagine the most minimalist shop you can conjure. Now, dial it back even more. The merchandise in this women's and men's clothing shop is the very picture of sleek and refined. You'll also find some accessories, small housewares, and personal care and beauty goodies. Brands stocked include Industry of All Nations and Norse Projects. The store was founded by two couples who each have two sons, hence the name.

MAP 5: 918 Main St., 615/678-4953, http://twoson.co; 10am-7pm Tues.-Sat., 1pm-5pm Sun.

WONDERS ON WOODLAND

Wonders on Woodland inhabits the front room of this East Nashville house. It is stocked with a well-curated selection of jewelry and other collectibles in a mix of midcentury and Victorian styles (yes, they can go together well). The jewelry comes in a range of costs and styles. It is a great place to find a quirky gift for quirky people.

MAP 5: 1110 Woodland St., 615/226-5300; 11am-5pm Sat.-Sun.

CRAFTS

BLACK DOG BEADS

Black Dog Beads in the Idea Hatchery is a small space jam-packed with beads, jewelry-making supplies, and finished pieces. There are also class offerings such as stringing parties for all ages and wire wrapping.

MAP 5: 1108 Woodland St., 615/530-1074, http://reddogbeads.com; 11am-6pm daily

GIFTS

GIFT HORSE

Located in the Shoppes on Fatherland, this sweet, hip shop stocks plenty of cards and art prints from local makers, contemporary jewelry, T-shirts, and other small gifts such as mugs, pins, and notebooks. Everything is well-designed and well-merchandised, making for fun browsing as well as shopping.

MAP 5: 1006 Fatherland St., #301, no phone, http://gifthorsenashville.com; 11am-6pm Tues.-Sat., 10am-6pm Sat., noon-4pm Sun.

Opry Mills

The Opry Mills discount mall in Music Valley remains the city's most maligned favorite destination.

Locals love to hate it, in part because it replaced the old Opryland amusement park on this same site and, in part, because it is so popular. As one of the area's leading tourist attractions, the lines for the parking lot back up along Briley Parkway around Christmas and during back-to-school shopping in summer.

If upscale shopping is your thing, or you live near other national-brand outlet malls, you don't need to come here. But if good deals on name-brand merchandise appeal to you, or you are looking to kill time before a show at the Opry, Opry Mills is the mall for you. Brands include Old Navy, Disney, LEGO, Coach, Kate Spade New York, Ann Taylor, H&M, and Torrid. It also has a 20-screen movie theater, IMAX, the Madame Tussauds Nashville wax museum, and a mammoth Bass Pro Shops with all sorts of outdoor equipment.

The mall is the destination in the area, and the only real shopping on this side of town, outside of a few interesting, albeit expensive, stores inside the **Gaylord Opryland Resort** (433 Opry Mills Dr., 615/514-1000, http://simon.com/mall/oprymills).

HARLAN RUBY GIFT SHOP

It's a family affair at Harlan Ruby, an umbrella for several creative businesses run by a mother and her daughters. You'll be delighted by the surprises in this modern party supply and gift shop, stocking locally made artwork, housewares, and hipster greeting cards, plus a "balloon bar" with unusual options like unicorns, cacti, margarita glasses, and oh-so-trendy rose gold letters and numbers. The youngest daughter (who is school-age) runs Hankabee Button Co., which is a part of the shop.

MAP 5: 805 Woodland St., #301, 615/955-0565, www.harlanruby.com; 10am-6pm Mon.-Sat., noon-5pm Sun.

KIDS

FAIRYTALES BOOKSTORE

This is kid heaven. Housed in one-half of a cute little house in East Nashville, this bookstore has what children—and adults—need to express themselves in most every art form. The books are wonderful, but there are toys, games, and crafting supplies, too. Everything is touchable, and there's a secure play area for trying things out. There's a quiet room with a couch and a cup of tea for parents needing a break. They also host events: story time and art classes for kids and adults. Be forewarned: The other side of the house is home to the **Pied Piper Creamery** (114 S. 11th St., 615/227-4114, www.thepiedpipercreamery.com), an excellent ice cream shop.

MAP 5: 114B S. 11th St., 615/915-1960, http://fairytalesbookstore.com; noon-5pm Wed.-Fri., 10am-6pm Sat.-Sun.

Top: White's Mercantile is a celeb-owned shopping hotspot. **Bottom:** Browse a curated book selection at Her Bookshop.

MUSIC

FANNY'S HOUSE OF MUSIC

In another city, Fanny's might be considered an unusual place. It's a woman-owned, guitar-centered music store with a vintage clothing shop mixed in. But in Nashville, it's par for the course. The staff can help you find a guitar that's comfortable for you to play, regardless of gender or size. There are new, used, and vintage guitars and gear, and the guitar techs do a superb job of getting the road dings out of your axe. There are almost always folks sitting around jamming while you shop.

MAP 5: 1101 Holly St., 615/750-5746, http://fannyshouseofmusic.com; 11am-6:30pm daily

FOND OBJECT

Inglewood's Fond Object is the ultimate Nashville hangout: part record store, part live music venue, part boutique, part art gallery, and part community center. Come here to browse for your favorite tunes, learn about new music you didn't know existed, and meet locals who can point you toward other cool under-the-radar places to hear music. Unlike many Nashville music shops, the focus here is rock 'n' roll, not country. There's also a **second location downtown** (535 4th Ave. S., 615/499-4526).

MAP 5: 1313 McGavock Pike, 615/499-4498, www.fondobjectrecords.com; 11am-7pm Mon.-Thurs., 11am-8pm Fri.-Sat., noon-5pm Sun.

THE GROOVE

The Groove stocks some CDs, but mainly it's all about the vinyl, new and used. The folks behind the counter know what they're doing, so the records are in the right genre. In contrast with many stores for record diggers, this is a bright and airy place in a sunny house. Instead of smelling like dust and basement, it smells faintly of incense. They have a turntable listening station and host live bands.

MAP 5: 1103 Calvin Ave., 615/227-5760, http://thegroovenashville.com; 11am-8pm Mon.-Sat., noon-6pm Sun.

PETS

WAGS & WHISKERS

Wags & Whiskers carries holistic dog and cat food and offers self-serve dog washing stations. The washing stations are big metal tubs set at a height that won't break your back. They also stock a cornucopia of treats, including dog-safe bones in the freezer. Wags & Whiskers is a little tricky to find, on the back side of vintage purveyor Hip Zipper, in the basement, but it's worth the trip. Look for other locations in **12 South** (2222 12th Ave. S., 615/292-9662, no dog wash at this location) and **West Nashville** (3731 Charlotte Ave., 615/454-2665) with the same hours.

MAP 5: 1008 Forrest Ave. (back of building), 615/228-9249, www. wagsandwhiskersnashville.com; 10am-8pm Mon.-Fri., 10am-6pm Sat., noon-5pm Sun.

SHOPPING DISTRICTS AND CENTERS

★ 1108 SHOPS AT WOODLAND

A collection of quirky shops nestled near East Nashville's 5 Points intersection, 1108 Shops at Woodland is a good destination for one-of-a-kind goods you won't find at home. Expect locally made crafts, a bookstore with a local bent, home goods, vintage clothes for men and women, letterpress stationery, and more.

MAP 5: 1108 Woodland St., 615/226-6670; hours vary by store and season

★ SHOPPES ON FATHERLAND

The tiny stores that comprise the Shoppes on Fatherland strip are hip to the point of humor. It can be somewhat surreal, like an episode of *Portlandia*. But beyond silliness is a nice community of more than 20 local businesses primarily selling handmade goods and repurposed vintage items. There's a fun energy in these East Nashville businesses. Hours vary by store, but weekends are when you'll see locals strolling by and hanging out. Some businesses pop up just for the holiday season, so you'll always be able to find something new. A number of local shops have started here to test the retail waters before moving to bigger (more expensive) spaces.

MAP 5: Fatherland St. between 10th and 11th Sts., 615/227-8646, www.fatherlanddistrict. com; vary by store

South Nashville
Map 7

ANTIQUES AND VINTAGE GOODS

GASLAMP ANTIQUE AND DECORATING MALL

Near the old 100 Oaks Mall in South Nashville, you'll find one of the city's largest and most popular antiques malls. It may be squeezed behind a Staples store and next to a Home Depot, but its wares are anything but big-box style. It has more than 150 vendors, many of them local interior designers, and a great selection of all types of antiques.

MAP 7: 100 Powell Pl., Ste. 200, 615/297-2224, http://gaslampantiques.com; 10am-6pm Mon.-Sat., noon-6pm Sun.

FLEA MARKETS

NASHVILLE FLEA MARKET

Nashville's largest flea market takes place on the fourth weekend of every month at the Fairgrounds Nashville. It's a bargain lover's dream, with thousands of sellers peddling clothes, crafts, and all sorts of vintage and used housewares, often at lower prices than you'd find in bigger cities. The free; parking is $5.

GIFTS
HESTER & COOK

It might look like a simple place for high-end party supplies, but this off-the-beaten-track shop is a gem. Browse through a sophisticated selection of tabletop wares, home decor (including some cool lighting fixtures), paper goods, and greeting cards. The framed art is particularly interesting. There's a second location (84 White Bridge Rd., 615/457-2799) in West Nashville.

MAP 7: 2728 Eugenia Ave., 615/736-2692, http://hesterandcook.com; 10am-6pm Mon.-Sat.

HOME DECOR
GILCHRIST GILCHRIST

Country/pop singer and Nashville favorite Taylor Swift shops here. Whether or not you're a fan of her music, if you love vintage finds with a shabby chic patina, you'll enjoy this stop on her Music City list. When it comes to furniture, expect to find real antiques, not items made to look old, most of which are in the beige and white color family. There are also new lampshades, picture frames, and other goods that would be easier to pack in a suitcase.

MAP 7: 2823 Bransford Ave., 615/385-2122, http://gilchristgilchrist.com; 10am-4pm Mon.-Sat.

MUSIC
PHONOLUXE RECORDS

Phonoluxe Records owner Mike Smyth has always marched to the beat of his own drum. He never lost faith in vinyl, so in the 1990s, when everyone started buying CDs, he stocked up on LPs. Now that people remember why they loved vinyl in the first place, he has the stock to attract collectors and music lovers. The location is a bit out of the way, and the hours are eccentric, but this only increases the romance. Smyth pulls gems from his own vault every week, so it's worth checking back regularly. All genres are represented.

MAP 7: 2609 Nolensville Pike, 615/259-3500; 10am-7pm Fri.-Sat., noon-6pm Sun.

PETS
CAT SHOPPE/DOG STORE

This store is an animal lover's dream, worth the trip just to soothe the nerves and relax. The atmosphere is peaceful, and kittens and cats, available for adoption, roam everywhere. The staff are knowledgeable about pet issues and extremely helpful. The dog half of the store features discounted high-end dog food, Thundershirts, and a seemingly endless array of dog paraphernalia sorted by breed.

MAP 7: 2824 Bransford Ave., 615/297-7877, http://thecatshoppedogstore.com; 10am-6pm Mon.-Sat.

Greater Nashville Map 8

BOOKS

MCKAY

A Knoxville institution with locations across the state, McKay encourages readers to return books, CDs, and DVDs for store credit after they've read or listened to or watched them. That means the mammoth Nashville location is always buzzing with sellers as well as buyers. McKay has a fun energy and is cleaner and better organized than most used bookstores. The space is large—and also includes some electronics—so allot plenty of time to browse.

MAP 8: 636 Old Hickory Blvd., 615/353-2595, http://mckaybooks.com; 9am-9pm Mon.-Thurs., 9am-10pm Fri.-Sat., 11am-7pm Sun.

PARNASSUS BOOKS

A famous co-owner (novelist Ann Patchett) and the willingness to open an independent bookstore in the "books-are-dead" year of 2011 allowed Parnassus Books to make national headlines. Located in a strip mall across from the Mall at Green Hills, Parnassus specializes in a well-edited selection, personal service, and literary events for both kids and adults. The shop isn't huge, but it's chock-full of new and local books. The shop hosts many literary events.

MAP 8: 3900 Hillsboro Pike, Ste. 14, 615/953-2243, http://parnassusbooks.net; 10am-8pm Mon.-Sat., noon-5pm Sun.

CLOTHING AND ACCESSORIES

H. AUDREY

This women's clothing boutique, owned by renowned singer-songwriter Holly Williams (Hank Jr.'s daughter), aims to fill a niche in Nashville for the well-heeled. The store is aimed at clients who shop at Barney's, Saks, and Bergdorf's—or would, if they had Nashville locations. The clothing here could take you from work to a red-carpet event. The shop is exquisitely edited with an eye for detail. Upstairs, a small loft space showcases portraits of renowned musicians by equally renowned photographers.

MAP 8: 4027 Hillsboro Pike, 615/760-5701, http://haudrey.com; 10am-6pm Mon.-Sat., noon-5pm Sun.

HABIT

This little white cottage, with whitewashed floors and a bright country loft feel, satisfies casually sophisticated tastes. Habit's owners find the best of new and known clothing designers, including Joie, Rebecca Taylor, and Ella Moss, to offer lovely selections to their discriminating customers.

MAP 8: 2209 Bandywood Dr., 615/292-9399; 10am-5:30pm Mon.-Sat.

JAMIE

Jamie has long been the height of couture for Nashville women who want something without rhinestones. Brands stocked include Prada, Missoni, Vera Wang, and Jason Wu, so come here for attentive service and killer shoes, but be prepared to pay for it. There's also an on-site salon for makeup and hair services.

MAP 8: 4317 Harding Pike, 615/292-4188, http://jamie-nashville.com; 10am-5pm Mon.-Fri., 10am-4pm Sat.

THE PERFECT PAIR

For women who love the pursuit of the perfect shoe, there's no better place than this well-edited shop. High-fashion pumps and flats meet the quintessential Music City boots on these shelves. The inventory is limited, so you leave feeling like what you've purchased won't be worn by every woman in town. The shop also stocks jewelry and handbags, but shoes are what makes The Perfect Pair a regular stop for those who are well-heeled.

MAP 8: 4103 Hillsboro Cir., 615/385-7247, www.theperfectpairnashville.com; 10am-5:30pm Mon.-Sat.

POSH

One of the city's hippest clothing shops, Posh stocks a large selection of clothing for both men and women, as well as a drool-worthy shoe department, handbags, and other accessories. The back room's sales area is a bargain hunter's dream. Regular prices can be on the higher end. Fashions are stylish and run the gamut from casual to a night on the town. There's also another location in **Hillsboro Village** (1801 21st Ave. S., 615/383-9840) with the same hours.

MAP 8: 4027 Hillsboro Pike, 615/269-6250, www.poshonline.com; 10am-7pm Mon.-Sat., noon-5pm Sun.

CRAFTS

HAUS OF YARN

Both local knitters and those from out of town flock here. Haus of Yarn's large, well-stocked shop offers things stores in bigger cities don't. The shelves here are filled with some of the country's best selection of yarns. The staff and owner are avid knitters, so there are hundreds of shop models that help you visualize what the yarns will look like in a finished garment. If you're lucky you'll meet Stanley, a sweet rat terrier rescued

Get Outdoor Gear

If you're continuing onward from Nashville on an outdoor adventure, such as the 444-mile trip down the Natchez Trace, you'll need to stock up. These are the best places in the area to find quality camping and hiking gear, waterproof supplies, water bottles, and everything else you might need. The salespeople at these spots know the area well.

- **Bass Pro Shops at Opry Mills** (323 Opry Mills Dr., 615/514-5200, http://basspro.com)

- **Binks Outfitters** (4017 Hillsboro Pike, 615/298-1700, www.binksoutfitters.com)

- **Cumberland Transit** (2807 West End Ave., 615/321-4069, http://cumberlandtransit.com)

- **Friedman's Army/Navy Surplus & Outdoors** (2101 21st Ave. S., 615/297-3343)

- **LifeView Outdoors** (2190 Nolensville Pike, 800/395-5433, http://lifeviewoutdoors.com)

- **Mountain High Outfitters** (1608 21st Ave. S., 615/465-6447, http://mountainhighoutfitters.com)

by one of the staff from in front of the store. He models many knit goods from the shop's stock. Keep your eyes peeled around town for The Yarn Bus, a mobile outpost of the Haus of Yarn, serving surrounding communities without their own independent textile shops.

MAP 8: 265 White Bridge Rd., 615/354-1007, http://hausofyarn.com; 10am-5:30pm Mon.-Fri., 10am-4pm Sat., noon-5:30pm Sun.

GIFTS
FABU

Fabu is located in a cute little converted house, and the owners have done a sweet job making that location work. Each room has its own theme or style: pop culture, masculine, kids, kitchen, and of course, a room devoted to the holiday that's just around the corner. It is the kind of place to go to find something for the person that has everything, the folks holding down the fort at home, or a gift for yourself.

MAP 8: 4606 Charlotte Pike, 615/383-0505, http://shopfabu.com; 10am-6pm Mon.-Sat., 1pm-5pm Sun.

HOME DECOR
ASHBLUE

Imagine a shop that carries everything from fine jewelry to funky furniture to garden accessories—that's AshBlue. People come here for everything from bridal registries to hostess gifts. If you're visiting Music City via airplane, you'll likely have to ship your finds home, because you're not going to want to limit yourself to what will fit in a carry-on.

MAP 8: 2170 Bandywood Dr., 615/383-4882, http://ashblue.com; 10am-6pm Mon.-Sat.

KIDS

PHILLIPS TOY MART

Phillips Toy Mart is the sort of toy store both children and adults dream about. They not only have the nostalgia factor on their side with Lincoln Logs and Tinker Toys, but they also have the modern crazes like Webkinz. Not to be missed is the model train setup in the back, which most likely will enchant grandpa and grandson into starting a train set together. Phillips is also old-school enough to carry a full selection of kites, from beginner to stunt, and model-making supplies.

MAP 8: 5207 Harding Pike, 615/352-5363, http://phillipstoymart.com; 9am-5:30pm Mon.-Sat.

SHOPPING DISTRICTS AND CENTERS

MALL AT GREEN HILLS

The signature shopping mall in Nashville is the Mall at Green Hills, an indoor mall about a 15-minute drive south from downtown Nashville along Hillsboro Road. Stores include Macy's, Brooks Brothers, Tiffany & Co., and Nordstrom. The mall has spawned additional shopping opportunities nearby, including the upscale Hill Center, so this is a good place to head if you're in need of just about anything. Call the concierge (615/298-5478, ext. 0) to find out if your favorite store is here. The parking lot can get packed on weekends, but the mall offers free valet service, which makes it tolerable.

MAP 8: 2126 Abbott Martin Rd., 615/298-5478, www.shopgreenhills.com; 10am-9pm Mon.-Sat., noon-6pm Sun.

Hotels

PRICE KEY

$ Less than $100 per night

$$ $100–200 per night

$$$ More than $200 per night

M usic City's status as a tourist mecca may be most noticeable in the hotel room rates.

In recent years Nashville went from a city with no shortage of places to stay to one with a premium on accommodations.

The good news is Nashville has more than 39,900 (and growing) hotel rooms, with options for places to sleep ranging from historical downtown hotels to standard chain motels to nontraditional options (home and apartment short-term rentals). Many seemingly standard hotels have unique Music City touches, such as recorded wake-up calls from country stars or guitar-shaped swimming pools.

The sight of cranes across the skyline confirms the construction of more hotels (with as many as 11,000 more rooms), including Richard Branson's third Virgin Hotel in the United States. As they open their doors, prices may come down some, but expect to pay a premium in a traditional hotel if visiting in high season.

CHOOSING A HOTEL

Because one of Nashville's drawbacks is a lack of a robust public transportation system, that old saw of location, location, location applies to selecting the right place to stay. If you're in town to see the Commodores play, you'll want to be near the Vanderbilt University campus. If you're attending a conference at the Gaylord Opryland, staying somewhere in Music Valley or near the airport will reduce your commute time by at least 30 minutes, but then you'll have a drive to see most of the city's attractions.

The bulk of hotels are concentrated in three areas: downtown, Midtown (near Vanderbilt), and Music Valley (near Opryland), but options are everywhere, from East Nashville to the airport. This chapter highlights a selection of top places across the city, but there are many more (particularly decent, moderately priced chains, near the airport and in Music Valley).

Previous: the sleek Omni Nashville Hotel; the Hermitage Hotel.

Look for ★ to find recommended hotels.

Highlights

★ **Best Place to Experience a Sense of History:** Almost everyone who's anyone in Nashville has stayed at the **Hermitage Hotel** at some point, even Gene Autry's horse! You get a feel for the significance of this place just by walking into the lobby (page 201).

★ **Most Artistic:** In addition to housing a wonderful art collection on-site, the **21c Museum Hotel Nashville** also stocks every guest room with original art (page 203).

★ **Best Home Away from Home:** With kitchens that can be stocked for your arrival and living areas with board games and record players, **SoBro Guest House** feels more like a house than a hotel (page 206).

★ **Best Place to Listen to Music Without Leaving the Hotel:** The **Aloft West End** has a listening room in the lobby where talented singer-songwriters play on weekday evenings. Lots of locals come to hear their friends play (page 208).

★ **Best Resort:** Other hotels in town, even the nicest ones, are just that: hotels. **Gaylord Opryland Resort** is a full-on resort, with enough attractions to allow you to fill a weekend without leaving the property (page 212).

For more options, plus a guide to nearby campgrounds, see http://visit-musiccity.com.

As is the case anywhere, prices fluctuate based on the time of year. Summer and winter holidays are in-demand times for Nashville hotel rooms. If you intend to come to town for the music extravaganzas CMA Music Fest or Bonnaroo in June, book your rooms at least a year in advance. Other music festivals can also put a strain on hotel availability, as can football (NFL and college) and college basketball games. The rates in this chapter are based on double occupancy in such high seasons.

Downtown

Map 1

COURTYARD BY MARRIOTT $$$

This 181-room renovated hotel occupies a century-old downtown highrise. It is located right next to Printers Alley and is set midway between the downtown business district and Broadway's entertainment attractions. Guest rooms are tastefully decorated, with amenities including web and cable TV, wired and wireless internet access, coffeemakers, ironing boards, voice mail, and supercomfortable beds. There is a restaurant on-site, and guests can take advantage of valet parking for $34 per day.

MAP 1: 170 4th Ave. N., 615/256-0900, www.marriott.com

404 HOTEL $$$

With just five rooms and an on-site manager who provides "invisible service," the 404 is a luxury hotel for people who don't want to stay in a hotel. Expect to pay for the high-end service. Rooms have sumptuous linens, works by local artists, fruit and pastries, free Wi-Fi, keyless entry, and other amenities as needed. Centrally located in The Gulch, this is not a place for kids under the age of 15 or pets.

MAP 1: 404 12th Ave. S., 615/242-7404, http://the404nashville.com

★ HERMITAGE HOTEL $$$

The last of a dying breed of hotels, the Hermitage Hotel has been the first choice for travelers to downtown Nashville for more than a century. The 122-room hotel was commissioned by prominent Nashville citizens and opened for business in 1910, quickly becoming the favorite gathering place for the city's elite. Prominent figures including Al Capone, Gene Autry, and seven U.S. presidents have stayed at the Hermitage, not to mention some of country music's biggest names. Guests enjoy top-of-the-line amenities, including 24-hour room service, pet walking, valet parking, and laundry services. Rooms are furnished in an opulent style befitting a luxury urban hotel. Many rooms have lovely views of the capitol and city. With a nod to

Historic Sleeps

Nashville is a city rich in heritage, with Civil War tales and musical history lore woven through its narrative. Fortunately, those stories aren't just reserved for tours and attractions. You can choose to stay somewhere that has a past.

Among the most famous historical picks for a hotel is downtown's **Hermitage Hotel.** Opened in 1910, the hotel has been at the center of historic events from the very beginning. In 1914 it hosted the National American Woman Suffrage Association's national convention, playing a role in women's right to vote. Presidents, senators, and movie and music stars have stayed there, and for eight years pool legend Minnesota Fats lived (and played) there. You don't have to be famous to stay at the Hermitage, but having plenty of cash will help your cause. Rooms start at $300 a night, but check on its website for last-minute specials, when rates may dip to $250.

A restored 19th-century railroad station, **Union Station** is an example of Richardsonian-Romanesque elegance. Train schedules still adorn the lobby as decor, and the guest rooms have cathedral ceilings, stylish furnishings, and a subtle art deco touch, not to mention expansive marble vanities in the bathrooms. The track level of the hotel once held two alligator ponds, but today the luxury hotel is alligator-free.

The small **Germantown Inn** is one of the neighborhood's oldest buildings, but the interior is updated, so you get the feeling of both 19th-century and 21st-century life.

state pride, you can choose to have $2 from your room rate contributed to the Land Trust for Tennessee.

MAP 1: 231 6th Ave., 615/244-3121, www.thehermitagehotel.com

HILTON NASHVILLE DOWNTOWN ⑤⑤⑤

The all-suite Hilton Nashville is next door to the Country Music Hall of Fame, just south of Broadway's honky-tonks, and near the home of the Nashville Symphony. All of the hotel's 330 suites have two distinct rooms— a living room with sofa, cable television, microwave oven, refrigerator, and coffeemaker, and a bedroom with one or two beds. The rooms are appointed with modern, stylish furniture and amenities. An indoor pool, workout room, valet parking, and two restaurants round out the hotel's offerings. Valet parking is $38 per day.

MAP 1: 121 4th Ave. S., 615/620-1000, http://nashvillehilton.com

NOELLE ⑤⑤⑤

Nashville's über-creative class has come together in this 220-room luxury hotel in the former Noel Place hotel building. The artwork in the rooms and public spaces is from Bryce McCloud of Isle Printing, who also runs a print shop/art gallery on the hotel's ground floor. Two of the places to eat and drink—**Makeready Libations & Liberation** and **The Trade Room** lobby bar—are open to the public. The rooftop deck is for hotel guests only. Back on the ground floor, check out **Drug Store Coffee**, operated by

Andy Mumma of Barista Parlor, and fashionable **Keep Shop,** run by local creative consultant Libby Callaway.

MAP 1: 200 4th Ave. N., 615/649-5000, http://noelle-nashville.com

OMNI NASHVILLE HOTEL ⑤⑤⑤

Opened in late 2013, the Omni is adjacent to the 1.2-million-square-foot Music City Convention Center. It has more than 80,000 square feet of meeting and event space, more than 800 guest rooms, plus easy access to the convention center, the Hall of Fame, restaurants, and other attractions south of Broadway. Don't miss the cool displays of musicians' costumes in the hallway that connects Hatch Show Print to the hotel. There are also several on-site restaurants, a fitness center, a rooftop pool deck, and a seriously indulgent spa.

MAP 1: 250 5th Ave. S., 615/782-5300, www.omnihotels.com

RENAISSANCE HOTEL ⑤⑤⑤

Located north of Broadway, this hotel stands 25 stories, making views of the city below one of its charms. The Renaissance's 673 rooms offer web TV, hair dryers, ironing boards, crisp linens, coffeemakers, and business services. High-speed wired internet access is available for a fee. The fitness center is next door to an indoor heated swimming pool, whirlpool, and sauna. Daily valet parking is $40; self-parking is $13.

MAP 1: 611 Commerce St., 615/255-8400, http://marriott.com

THOMPSON ⑤⑤⑤

The Thompson offers Nashville a lot of things that seem at odds with one another: It is in the heart of The Gulch, but still quiet enough to sleep. It's in a modern high-rise, but feels like a small, boutique hotel. Enjoy pet-friendly rooms with hardwood floors, midcentury modern-style furnishings, honor bars with local spirits, Bluetooth speakers, and rain showers. There's also a hipster coffee shop on the first floor and great retail options (including a Frye boot shop) adjacent.

MAP 1: 401 11th Ave. S., 615/262-6000, www.thompsonhotels.com

★ 21C MUSEUM HOTEL NASHVILLE ⑤⑤⑤

In 2017 Nashville became the newest city to welcome a 21c Museum Hotel, a 124-room hotel with a contemporary art museum inside. The public is welcome to tour the museum for free (and everyone should: This collection is above and beyond what others would charge museum patrons to peruse). Perks for guests include free Wi-Fi, free bottled water, smartphone docking stations, bathrobes, and more original art in every room. Some suites have lovely balconies with city views. The hotel also features a bar and restaurant with a menu by Levon Wallace, seven suites with terraces and a spa, and a vibrant downtown atmosphere.

MAP 1: 221 2nd Ave. N., 615/610-6400, www.21cnashville.com

UNION STATION ⑤⑤⑤

One of Nashville's most notable downtown hotels is the Union Station, a 125-room hotel located in what was once the city's main train station. Distinctions include magnificent ironwork and molding and an impressive marble-floored great hall that greets guests, contributing to what makes this one of the National Trust's Historic Hotels of America. One of Nashville's great old buildings, the hotel has high ceilings and lofty interior balconies, and amenities include a fitness center, wireless internet, plasma televisions, complimentary morning newspapers, and room service. Packages include a recording session at the Ryman and other Nashville-centric perks. It's remarkable how cozy and quiet the spaces inside feel, just steps from the traffic and sounds of Broadway.

MAP 1: 1001 Broadway, 615/726-1001, www.unionstationhotelnashville.com

WESTIN NASHVILLE ⑤⑤⑤

Opened in late 2016, the 27-story Westin Nashville is a big-city type of hotel, with a full-service spa, a rooftop pool and bar (called L27), and valet-only parking. The on-site restaurant **Decker & Dyer** serves breakfast, lunch, dinner, and craft cocktails in a shared space in the lobby, so you can see-and-be-seen. **Oak Steakhouse,** an outpost of the Charleston original, serves a seasonal steak house menu downstairs. The 453-room hotel is pet-friendly.

MAP 1: 807 Clark Pl., 615/248-2800, http://westinnashville.com

HOLIDAY INN EXPRESS NASHVILLE-DOWNTOWN ⑤⑤

Across Broadway from the Frist Center for the Visual Arts, the Holiday Inn Express offers a comfortable compromise between value and location. There is an on-site fitness room, free wireless internet, a business center, and a guest laundry. Guest rooms have desks and coffeemakers. Suites have refrigerators and microwave ovens. All guests enjoy free continental breakfast, and on-site valet parking is available for $28. The Holiday Inn is located about five blocks away from the Lower Broadway honky-tonk action.

MAP 1: 920 Broadway, 615/244-0150, www.ihg.com

HOTEL INDIGO DOWNTOWN ⑤⑤

Housed in the restored historical American Trust and Nashville Trust building, the Hotel Indigo is one of downtown Nashville's oft-overlooked hotels. This boutique hotel is on the north side of downtown, making it convenient to the Tennessee Performing Arts Center, the courthouse, and other government buildings. Business travelers will have their needs met with high-speed internet access, an on-site restaurant (which often has live music), and a nearby FedEx business center. There's a small on-site fitness center, or pay extra to use a nearby full gym. Valet parking is $35 per day. The hotel's pet-friendliness is clearly conveyed by a doghouse in the lobby.

MAP 1: 301 Union St., 615/891-6000, www.ihg.com

Top: the rooftop at The Westin Nashville. Bottom: The historic Union Station is modern on the inside.

SHERATON NASHVILLE DOWNTOWN $$

The Sheraton Nashville Downtown is a city landmark. The 472-room hotel stands tall above neighboring buildings, providing most guest rooms with views of the city below. Located in the middle of Nashville's bustling downtown business district, it is another good option for business travelers. The hotel has a fitness room, business center, indoor pool, and laundry and concierge services. Club-level rooms have perks such as free breakfast and evening hors d'oeuvres. Internet access ($10 per day) and on-site parking ($31-35 per day) are available.

MAP 1: 623 Union St., 615/259-2000, www.sheratonnashvilledowntown.com

★ SOBRO GUEST HOUSE $$

An old apartment building converted into a modern hotel, SoBro is one of the area's best-kept secrets. Every room is a smartly decorated suite, with kitchens, record players with vinyl, games, free Wi-Fi, and a real downtown perk: free parking. It is walking distance to downtown, but still very quiet. You can ask for your grocery shopping to be done ahead of time for you: The fridge will be stocked when you arrive. There's no front desk; you check in with your mobile phone.

MAP 1: 310 Peabody St., 615/965-4545, www.sobroguest.com

Germantown and Capitol Hill

Map 2

THE GERMANTOWN INN $$$

One of the oldest buildings in historic Germantown, this two-story, Federal-style house constructed in 1865 has been transformed into an inspired six-bedroom luxury boutique inn, with a remarkable garden, rooftop decks and views, and an ambience that combines modern amenities with original charm. Once known in the neighborhood as the Wallman House (for the building's first owner, H. H. Wallman, a prominent shoemaker), today the inn is an oasis in an urban environment. Eat breakfast in the light-filled lobby, sleep in a luxurious, quiet bedroom, and walk to many Germantown and downtown attractions. The staff are attentive, but not overbearing.

MAP 2: 1218 6th Ave. N., 615/581-1218, www.germantowninn.com

DOUBLETREE HOTEL NASHVILLE $$

Located just steps from the Tennessee State Capitol and near dozens of downtown office buildings, the Doubletree is a popular choice for business travelers. Rooms are spacious and bright. The hotel boasts a beautiful indoor swimming pool, business center, above-average fitness center, and on-site restaurant and coffee shop. Valet is the only option for parking at the Doubletree and costs $35 per day.

MAP 2: 315 4th Ave. N., 615/244-8200, http://doubletree.hilton.com

QUALITY INN NASHVILLE 💲💲

The Quality Inn looks unassuming from the exterior, in an East Nashville location sandwiched between the interstate and a Nissan Stadium parking lot. The hotel's proximity to the stadium makes it a favorite of football fans, who can tailgate and walk to Titans or TSU games. The hotel also boasts a guitar-shaped pool, free continental breakfast, a fitness room, and free wireless internet.

MAP 2: 303 Interstate Dr., 615/244-6690, http://choicehotels.com

CLARION HOTEL AT THE STADIUM 💲

On the east bank of the Cumberland River, the hotel's name refers to neighboring Nissan Stadium, where the Tennessee Titans play. The hotel's 180 rooms have clock radios, cable TV, and wireless internet. Some have decent views of the Nashville skyline. Guests enjoy access to a fitness room, indoor pool, and laundry facilities, plus free breakfast. There is a bar and restaurant inside the hotel. While not in the heart of downtown Nashville, it is just across the river from the city's premier attractions. Free parking is a plus, particularly during events when downtown parking is at a premium.

MAP 2: 211 N. 1st St., 615/254-1551, http://choicehotels.com

Music Row

Map 3

HUTTON HOTEL 💲💲💲

When it opened in 2009, the Hutton became Nashville's ecofriendly darling. Even as many more luxury hotels have opened, the Hutton still holds its own. This swanky hotel near the Vanderbilt campus also offers an easy commute to Music Row and downtown, but regular visitors stay here less for the great location and more for the ambience. It's designed for creative types: There are recording studios and a writers room, a turntable in the lobby, and a 300-seat concert venue. The bathrooms include sleek showers, which have a modern aesthetic and oversize ceiling-mounted showerheads. Turn the water on, and you'll feel like you're in a serious rainstorm in the privacy of your well-appointed bathroom. The contemporary bathrooms also feature quality bath products and thick, fluffy towels.

MAP 3: 1808 West End Ave., 615/340-9333, www.huttonhotel.com

KIMPTON AERTSON HOTEL 💲💲💲

Opened in June 2017, this 180-room hotel rises next to the Vanderbilt campus. Perks include free bike rentals (also available to nonguests), an 8th-floor pool deck with cabanas, and a 17th-floor indoor/outdoor event space.

Enjoy free coffee and tea in the morning in the lobby, cutely referred to as the living room. **Henley,** the restaurant featuring James Beard Award-winning chef RJ Cooper, has quickly become a favorite of locals (don't skip the cocktail list) and adjacent **Caviar & Bananas** is an excellent place to grab better-than-average takeout for a picnic. Kimpton hotels are well-known for their pet-friendliness; there's no extra charge for pet beds, mats, or water bowls in your room.

MAP 3: 2021 Broadway, 615/340-2269, http://aertsonmidtown.com

LOEWS VANDERBILT HOTEL ⑤⑤⑤

This luxurious 340-room hotel on West End Avenue close to Centennial Park and Hillsboro Village boasts 24-hour room service; luxurious sheets, towels, and robes; natural soaps; and spacious bathrooms. Guests enjoy in-room Keurig coffeemakers and top-of-the-line coffee, iHome docking stations, evening turndown service, and free high-speed internet access. Many rooms have views of the Nashville skyline; premium rooms provide guests with access to the concierge lounge, continental breakfast, and evening hors d'oeuvres. All guests can enjoy a fine fitness room (or ask about in-room fitness sessions), spa, art gallery, and gift shop. The parking garage includes charging stations for electric vehicles. If you want to stay here during a Vanderbilt reunion or graduation weekend, reserve well in advance.

MAP 3: 2100 West End Ave., 615/320-1700, www.loewshotels.com

NASHVILLE MARRIOTT AT VANDERBILT UNIVERSITY ⑤⑤⑤

You can't get closer to Vanderbilt University than the Marriott Nashville Vanderbilt. Set on the northern end of the university campus, the Marriott has 301 guest rooms, 6 suites, and plenty of meeting space. It is located across West End Avenue from Centennial Park, home of the Parthenon, and a few steps from Vanderbilt's football stadium. There is an indoor pool, a full-service restaurant, a concierge lounge, an ATM, a fitness center, and a business center. Plan ahead if you want a room during a Vanderbilt game weekend or parents' weekend.

MAP 3: 2555 West End Ave., 615/321-1300, http://marriottvanderbilt.com

★ ALOFT WEST END ⑤⑤

This hotel has changed names and ownership over the years, but it has remained a favorite of visitors to the Vanderbilt area. The lobby's café is more of a Nashville-style listening room than a traditional hotel lobby coffee shop. It hosts regular singer-songwriter nights, attracting locals who come to support their favorite musicians. The hotel offers free Wi-Fi and amenities that travelers welcome, such as dry cleaning and both valet and self-parking ($30 per day).

MAP 3: 1719 West End Ave., 615/329-4200, www.aloftnashvillewestend.com

HAMPTON INN VANDERBILT $$

Free breakfast, free parking, and free wireless internet make this chain hotel a popular choice for folks who want to stay near the Vanderbilt campus. Rooms are clean with good amenities for business travelers, and there's an outdoor pool for Nashville's summer nights. Rooms available during Vanderbilt events—such as graduation or homecoming—tend to book a year in advance.

MAP 3: 1919 West End Ave., 615/329-1144, http://nashvillevanderbilt.hamptoninn.com

HOLIDAY INN NASHVILLE-VANDERBILT $$

The closest hotel to Vanderbilt football stadium and Centennial Park, this renovated hotel has clean, if small, guest rooms, as well as an excellent bar with live music seven days a week. Free Wi-Fi, shuttle service downtown, an outdoor pool, and a fitness center round out the offerings, but the location—walking distance to all the Vanderbilt campus must-sees—makes this hotel in demand for reunions and graduations. Parking is $22 per night if you do it yourself and $25 per night for valet (street parking near campus is hard to find during the school year).

MAP 3: 2613 West End Ave., 615/327-4707, www.ihg.com

BEST WESTERN PLUS MUSIC ROW $

This is a no-nonsense motel with an outdoor pool, fitness center, free continental breakfast, and free Wi-Fi. Rooms have cable TV, refrigerators, and coffeemakers. Pets are allowed for $10 a day, and parking is free (though it's typically easy to find in this neighborhood). The 102-room hotel is located a few steps away from the Music Row traffic circle, *Musica* sculpture, and nearby restaurants and bars.

MAP 3: 1407 Division St., 615/242-1631, www.nashvillebestwestern.com

MUSIC CITY HOSTEL $

The Music City Hostel is set amid doctors' offices, restaurants, and commercial buildings in between downtown and Vanderbilt. The low-slung, 1970s-style building looks like nothing much on the outside, but inside it is cheerful, welcoming, and a comfortable home base for budget travelers. The hostel offers the usual dorm-style bunk-bed accommodations (coed or female-only), as well as a handful of private apartments. You can also have a private bedroom with private bath plus shared kitchen and common room. Common areas include a large kitchen, dining room, reading room, cable TV room, computer with internet access, an outdoor grill, and a coin laundry. Parking is free, and the hostel is within walking distance of restaurants, a bus stop, car rental agency, post office, and hospitals, but a bus or car would be best for getting downtown. Note: You must have a residence at least 60 miles outside of Nashville to stay here.

MAP 3: 1809 Patterson St., 615/692-1277, http://musiccityhostel.com

DAISY HILL B&B $$

Stay in a 1925 Tudor home, which has a spot on the National Register of Historic Places. Tucked into a brick house near Hillsboro Village and the Vanderbilt and Belmont campuses are three guest rooms, each with its own European decor (Scottish, French, and Scandinavian). Amenities include fireplaces and a family-style breakfast with an emphasis on local produce. Cancellation policies differ during Titan game weekends and other big events, so check when making reservations during these times.

MAP 4: 2816 Blair Blvd., 615/297-9795, www.daisyhillbedandbreakfast.com

LINDEN MANOR BED AND BREAKFAST $$

Housed in a 19th-century Victorian house, this bed-and-breakfast has private baths in every room and other amenities that B&Bs sometimes lack, such as cable TV and Wi-Fi. The guest rooms at this cheerful yellow-brick home on a corner lot have stylish furniture and hardwood floors, while the separate carriage house offers even more privacy. One room has a private whirlpool, and another has a fireplace.

MAP 4: 1501 Linden Ave., 615/298-2701, http://nashville-bed-breakfast.com

12 SOUTH INN $$

This sweet B&B with contemporary decor has four suites, giving you lots of extra room with private porches, private entrances, and in the case of the King Suite, a separate living room. Unlike some B&Bs that lack hotel-style amenities, the 12 South Inn has free wireless internet, TV, refrigerators, and other perks, as well as the home-style digs that separate an inn from a traditional hotel. Instead of serving a traditional group breakfast, the inn has partnered with Frothy Monkey a few blocks away to provide breakfast. Discounted rates are available for extended stays.

MAP 4: 918 Knox Ave., 615/260-8015, http://bedandbreakfastnashville.com

East Nashville Map 5

URBAN COWBOY B&B $$$

The bones of the Urban Cowboy were built in the 1890s by a doctor who used the space both as a residence and as an office to see patients. He likely wouldn't be able to imagine how his historic Queen Anne mansion has been turned into an ultrahip, super-Instagrammable B&B. These eight rooms (including five suites) may be some of the most photographed in the city. Each room has a claw-foot tub. The property is pet-friendly. Locals flock to the **Public House** restaurant, which once served as the stables for the

Clockwise from top left: the Hutton Hotel; modern bathroom at the Kimpton Aertson Hotel; the Gaylord Opryland Resort.

doctor's home, for great cocktails, food, and campfires (what else would an Urban Cowboy do?).

MAP 5: 1603 Woodland St., 347/840-0525, http://urbancowboybnb.com

THE BIG BUNGALOW ⑤⑤

A Craftsman-style early-1900s town house, the Big Bungalow offers three guest rooms, each with its own private bath and television. Guests have shared access to a computer, microwave, and refrigerator. Common areas are comfortable and stylish, with tasteful decor and hardwood floors. Hostess Ellen Warshaw prepares breakfast for her guests and sometimes hosts in-the-round concerts in her living room. She is also a licensed masseuse and sometimes offers discounted massage rates with the room. This is a pet-free facility; children over 10 are welcome. It is located about seven blocks from the Shelby Street Pedestrian Bridge (seen often on the TV show *Nashville*), which takes you to the heart of downtown.

MAP 5: 618 Fatherland St., 615/256-8375, http://thebigbungalow.com

Music Valley

Map 6

★ GAYLORD OPRYLAND RESORT ⑤⑤⑤

Said to be the largest hotel without a casino in the United States, the Gaylord Opryland Resort is more than just a hotel. Completely renovated after the 2010 flood, the 2,882-room luxury resort and convention center is built around a nine-acre indoor garden. Glass atriums invite sunlight, and miles of footpaths invite you to explore the climate-controlled flora. Highlights include a 40-foot waterfall and flatboats that float along an artificial river. Service is impeccable. Press the "consider it done" button on the phone in your room, and any of your needs will be met. Guests can buy onetime or daily passes on the downtown shuttle for about $20 a day or $36 for three days, and the airport shuttle costs $30 round-trip. Self-parking is $29, and valet parking is $38 per day.

MAP 6: 2800 Opryland Dr., 615/889-1000, http://www.marriott.com

COURTYARD BY MARRIOTT OPRYLAND ⑤⑤

This 87-room hotel offers all the basic amenities, as well as a few pluses: It is close to the mammoth Opryland complex and offers shuttles to and from the resort as well as the airport. Convention-goers and others who are on a budget but attending an event at Opryland can save by staying here.

MAP 6: 125 Music City Cir., 615/882-9133, http://marriott.com

HYATT PLACE NASHVILLE-OPRYLAND ⑤⑤

After the Gaylord resort, this is perhaps Music Valley's nicest hotel property, and if you ask for a room that faces the resort, you may even be able to see Opryland's famous holiday lights in season. This hotel caters to folks who want to take in the Music Valley attractions, with free shuttles (and friendly shuttle drivers) to the Gaylord resort, Grand Ole Opry, the airport, and Opry Mills mall. For a small fee there's even a shuttle that will take you downtown. The hotel offers a 24-hour fitness center, free wireless internet, 24-hour room service, HDTVs, and other better-than-average amenities.

MAP 6: 220 Rudy's Cir., 615/872-0422, http://nashvilleopryland.place.hyatt.com

BEST WESTERN SUITES NEAR OPRYLAND $

The all-suite Best Western Suites near Opryland is a comfortable compromise between the luxury of the Gaylord Opryland Resort and the affordability of a motel. Each of the hotel's 100 suites has a couch, desk, high-speed internet access, coffee/tea maker, microwave, ironing board, and refrigerator. Rooms with whirlpool tubs are available. Guests enjoy an on-site fitness room, 24-hour business center, outdoor pool, free continental breakfast, and weekday newspaper. The Best Western is located along a strip of motels and restaurants about one mile from the Grand Ole Opry and other Opryland attractions.

MAP 6: 201 Music City Cir., 615/902-9940, http://bestwestern.com

FIDDLER'S INN $

If you're looking for a clean, comfortable room, and no more, look no further than the Fiddler's Inn. This 202-room hotel is seriously no frills, but it offers a solid Tennessee welcome to its guests, who come in droves to see the Opry and enjoy other Music Valley attractions. It's right next to a restaurant, and it has plenty of parking for cars and tour buses. Guests enjoy cable TV, free continental breakfast in the morning, an outdoor pool, and a gift shop stocked with perfectly kitschy Music City souvenirs. Pet-friendly rooms are available.

MAP 6: 2410 Music Valley Dr., 615/885-1440, http://fiddlers-inn.com

QUALITY INN OPRYLAND AREA $

About two miles from Opryland, Quality Inn Opryland Area offers 121 clean, comfortable guest rooms with cable TV, free HBO, wireless internet, ironing board, hair dryer, and free daily newspaper. It has free outdoor parking and an outdoor pool. Pets are permitted for an additional fee.

MAP 6: 2516 Music Valley Dr., 615/889-0086, http://choicehotels.com

Hotel Alternatives

Not every trip calls for a traditional hotel. Sometimes the best way to see Music City is by booking a guest room, a condo, or even a room at a farm. These options are often more economical than a hotel, particularly for groups, who may appreciate having a kitchen and not eating every meal out.

Websites **Airbnb** (www.airbnb.com) and **VRBO** (www.vrbo.com) list options across the city. Many of these locations have the advantage of being in neighborhoods where locals live, rather than in tourist-heavy areas. As the hotel inventory has gotten tighter, Airbnb offerings in Nashville have increased, so much so that the Metro government has limited the number of short-term lease licenses available. But there are plenty of houses and condos, often with free parking and Wi-Fi, available for those who want to stay awhile.

For more specialized non-hotel options, check out **Nashville Farm Stay** (615/425-3616, from $120/night, with a two-night minimum), just off the Natchez Trace Parkway. This is an option for cyclists and others who want to experience Nashville's great outdoors (and pet a goat or donkey while in town).

Scarritt-Bennett Center (1008 19th Ave. S., 615/340-7500, www.scarrittbennett.org, $50) is a religious conference center near both the Vanderbilt campus and Music Row. There are 125 spartan rooms in three former residence halls that can be rented like hotel rooms, and many standard hotel amenities, including wireless internet, are provided. However, bathrooms are shared with other guests. The real appeal of Scarritt-Bennett is the lovely grounds and the meditative vibe you get from just being there.

Greater Nashville

Map 8

INN AT FONTANEL $$$

With just six guest rooms, this ecofriendly inn (and related buildings) has become one of Nashville's most-sought-after places to stay. Nestled in the Fontanel complex, the former home of Barbara Mandrell, the inn was part of *Southern Living* magazine's Ideal House project. The house has beautiful views of Mandrell's former wooded acreage, plus close proximity to the complex's restaurants, distillery, outdoor music venue, and walking trails. There's an attendant on duty 24 hours per day and daily maid service. Some of the detached rooms are pet-friendly (with a $50 service fee).

MAP 8: 4225 Whites Creek Pike, 615/876-2357, http://fontanel.com

HOTEL PRESTON $$

Hotel Preston is a boutique hotel near the airport. Youthful energy, modern decor, and up-to-date rooms set this property apart from the crowd. Rooms are stocked with Tazo tea and Starbucks coffee, and there's a 24-hour fitness center and free airport shuttle. The "You-Want-It-You-Got-It" button in each room beckons the 24-hour room service, and whimsical extras, including a lava lamp, pet fish, and a pillow menu, are available by request when you check in. High-speed internet is an extra add-on. Whimsical packages—like the bachelorette package with late checkout, a bottle of prosecco, transportation to downtown, and a hangover kit—prove that this isn't your parents' hotel, though the property caters equally to business travelers, with meeting rooms and a business center. Two restaurants, including the **Pink Slip** bar and nightclub, which features a sculpture by local artist Herb Williams, provide food and entertainment.

MAP 8: 733 Briley Pkwy., 615/361-5900, www.hotelpreston.com

ALEXIS INN AND SUITES NASHVILLE AIRPORT $

The Alexis Inn and Suites Nashville Airport is a comfortable and convenient place to stay near the airport. Rooms have all the usual amenities, plus guests get free popcorn in the lobby, a free airport shuttle (7am-9pm daily), and free continental breakfast. All rooms have refrigerators, and most have microwaves. There is a business center on-site.

MAP 8: 600 Ermac Dr., 615/378-5168, www.alexisinn.com

MILLENNIUM MAXWELL HOUSE NASHVILLE $

Located in MetroCenter, just off the interstate and north of downtown, the Maxwell House is one of Nashville's overlooked, but reliable, hotels. The common areas are light, airy, and clean. Amenities for the 287-room hotel include a fitness center and outdoor pool, free Wi-Fi, and a business center. This isn't a neighborhood in which you'll likely want to stroll and explore, but there's a free shuttle to most of the city's main attractions. Free parking is ample, and the hotel often offers discounted government rates on rooms.

MAP 8: 2025 Rosa L. Parks Blvd., 615/259-4343, www.millenniumhotels.com

SHERATON MUSIC CITY $

The Sheraton Music City is another good option for business travelers who want to be in the Music Valley area but don't need (or want) the full-on resort amenities of the Gaylord. This is a very large convention hotel, with plenty of meeting room space, plus amenities for leisure travel, like both indoor and outdoor swimming pools. Spa services are available, and the free shuttle to the airport is a nice perk. There is a charge for wireless internet access. Self-parking is free. Security ensures no one other than guests drive onto the property at night.

MAP 8: 777 McGavock Pike, 615/885-2200, http://starwoodhotels.com

Excursions

Nashville's geographic location (within one day's drive for about half of the country's population) is one of the reasons it's such a good road-trip destination.

And the inverse is true, too. Nashville is a great place to set off on an awesome day trip, because so much is nearby. In almost every direction there's something worth seeing. Middle Tennessee doesn't have the high-profile reputation of, say, the Smoky Mountains. But the landscape is rural and pure relaxation. If you're planning to be in Nashville for a week or more, take the time to get in the car and explore some nearby attractions.

Chief among these must-sees are suburban Franklin and Leiper's Fork, upscale communities that are a mecca for both history buffs and shoppers (how many destinations can say that?), quaint Bell Buckle, and the recreation paradise of Land Between the Lakes. All of them are easily accessed from Nashville by car. Much of the drive is on interstates, but of course, taking the back roads is often more interesting.

PLANNING YOUR TIME

Tennessee is a long state. From tip to tip, the Volunteer State stretches 432 miles, so if you're planning to visit more than just Nashville's surrounding areas, you'll want to gas up the car and download an audiobook or two.

If you have limited time to explore, no worries. Just one day is ample (though you'll leave wanting more) to check out Franklin, Leiper's Fork, and Bell Buckle. A two- or three-day weekend is perfect for Land Between the Lakes, with time for paddling, fishing, hiking, and more.

Previous: the gardens and grounds at Carnton; downtown Franklin.

Look for ★ to find
recommended sights and activities.

Highlights

★ **Most Updated Blast from the Past:** The 1937-era **Franklin Theatre** has been renovated with modern amenities, but that old-world charm remains (page 221).

★ **Place to Honor the Fallen:** The cemetery for the Confederate dead at **Carnton** is a solemn reminder of the area's past (page 222).

★ **Best Place to Find a Treasure Worth Shipping Home:** Leiper's Fork's **Serenite Maison** is the pick of local celebs looking for drool-worthy antiques and decor (page 233).

★ **Most Iconic Distillery:** Small-batch whiskey is enjoying a renaissance, but **Jack Daniel's Distillery** is still the best-known liquor in the state (page 236).

★ **Best Chance for Seeing Wildlife:** Land Between the Lakes's **Elk and Bison Prairie** is a 700-acre plot of land where you are likely to see these magnificent beasts at close range (page 240).

Excursions

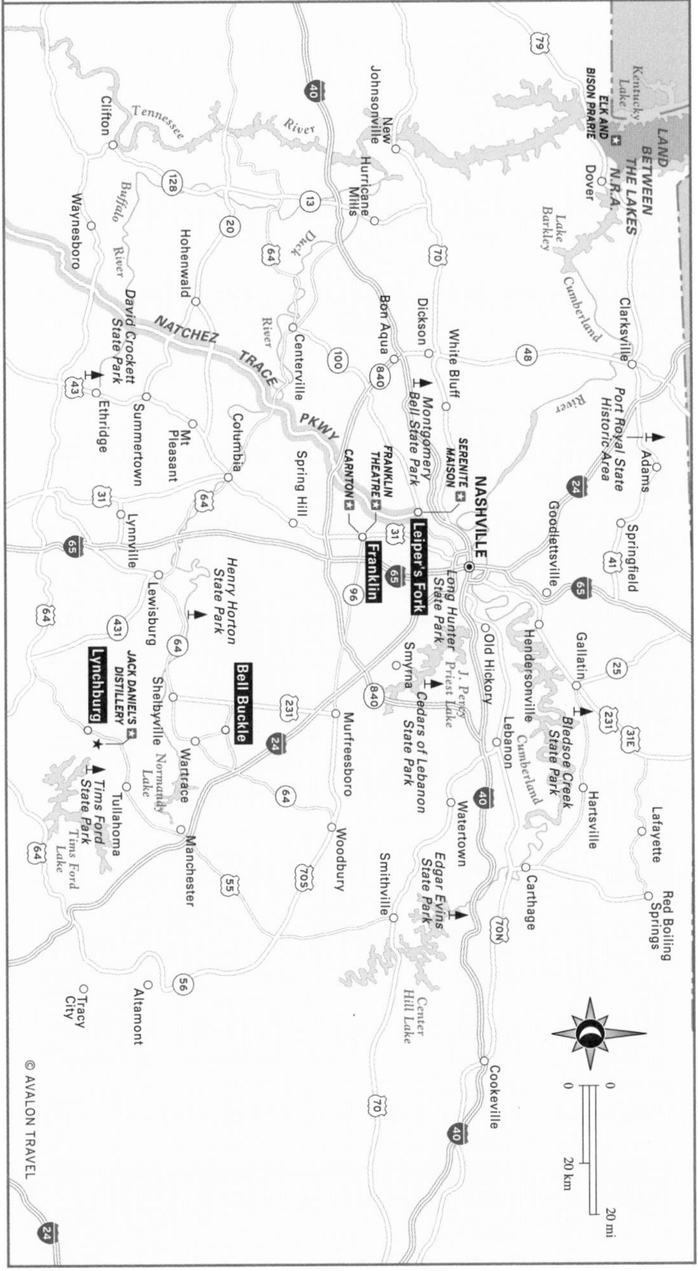

EXCURSIONS

The bloody Battle of Franklin that took place in the fields surrounding the town on November 30, 1864, was one of the single most important events to take place on this land. Like other towns in the region, it took many years for Franklin to fully recover from the impact of the Civil War, and even today its Civil War roots are a large part of what makes Franklin what it is.

Starting in the 1960s, Franklin underwent a metamorphosis. Construction of I-65 near the town spurred economic development. Today, Franklin is a well-heeled bedroom community for Nashville professionals and music industry bigwigs, with attractions that rival those in Nashville. The city, whose population runs around 68,800, is the 7th largest in Tennessee and one of the wealthiest in the state. What sets Franklin apart from other small towns in the state is the efforts it has made to preserve and protect the historical downtown. The area is quaint and pedestrian-friendly. Its location only 20 miles from Nashville is also a major plus.

Franklin's attractions are all within a few miles of the city center, except for Cool Springs Galleria, a megamall several miles out of town along I-65.

SIGHTS
Historical Downtown

Franklin is one of the most picturesque small towns in Tennessee. Contained within four square blocks, downtown Franklin consists of leafy residential streets with old and carefully restored homes. The center of town is a traffic circle crowned by a simple white Confederate monument. The circle is fronted by banks, more offices, and the 1859 Williamson County courthouse.

The best way to explore downtown Franklin is on foot. Free parking is available along the streets or in two public garages, one on 2nd Avenue and one on 4th Avenue. Pick up a printed walking-tour guide from the **visitors center** (400 Main St.) or download the free iPhone app.

The walking tour takes you past 39 different buildings, including the **Hiram Masonic Lodge** (115 2nd Ave. S.), the oldest Masonic lodge in Tennessee and also the building where in 1830 Andrew Jackson signed the treaty that led to the forced removal of thousands of Native Americans from Tennessee, Georgia, and other Southern states. You will also see the old city cemetery and the old **Franklin Post Office** (510 Columbia Ave.), as well as lots of beautiful old houses and churches, all of which remain in use today. The walking tour is a good way to become familiar with the town and to appreciate the different types of architecture. It takes 1-2 hours to complete.

Guided walking tours of Franklin are offered by **Franklin on Foot** (615/400-3808, http://franklinonfoot.com). The Classic Franklin tour provides an overview of the history of the town and its buildings. Other tours include a children's tour, a Southern food tour, and the Haunted Franklin tour. Tours cost $5-20 per person.

Franklin

Map labels:

To Nashville

HILLSBORO RD

Harlinsdale Farm Park

LANCASTER DR

FRANKLIN RD

★ THE FACTORY
▼ SAFFIRE

LIBERTY PIKE

OLD LIBERTY PIKE

To Cool Springs Galleria via Memorial Parkway

MOUNT HOPE CEMETERY

MARGIN ST

5TH AVE N

MT HOPE ST

GLASS ST

9TH AVE

GREEN ST

96

11TH AVE

3RD AVE

BRIDGE ST

2ND AVE

E MAIN ST

1ST AVE

PUBLIC SQUARE ★

■ VISITOR CENTER

FRANKLIN THEATRE ✚

MERRIDEE'S BREADBASKET ▼

PUCKETT'S GROCERY AND RESTAURANT ▼

CHURCH AVE

4TH AVE

S MARGIN ST

FORT GRANGER ★

FORT GRANGER RD

EDDY LN

Pinkerton Park

FAIR ST

W MAIN ST

NATCHEZ ST

COLUMBIA AVE

246

FOWLKES ST

LEWISBURG AVE

MUFREESBORO RD

96

Harpeth River

To Quality Inns and Suites, SOAR Adventure Tower, and Best Western

Strahl Street Park

● LOTZ HOUSE
★ THE CARTER HOUSE

▼ BUNGANUT PIG

GRANBURY ST

CLEBURNE ST

JENNINGS ST

● MAGNOLIA HOUSE B&B

ADAMS ST

GIST ST

EVERBRIGHT AVE

BATTLE AVE

FAIRGROUND ST

CAROLYN ST

DOWNS BLVD

CARNTON LN

To Leiper's Fork

COUNTRY CLUB OF FRANKLIN

★ ✚ CARNTON

0   0.25 mi

0   0.25 km

© AVALON TRAVEL

★ Franklin Theatre

One of the brightest gems of historical downtown Franklin is the **Franklin Theatre** (419 Main St., 615/538-2076, www.franklintheatre.com, box office noon-5pm Mon., 11am-6pm Tues.-Sat.), a 1937 movie theater that had seen better days until it finally closed in 2007. In 2011 it reopened after an $8 million restoration funded primarily by donations from locals through the efforts of the Heritage Foundation. The renovation is spot on, bringing the theater, including its striking outdoor marquee, back to its former glory. Lush carpeting, detailed wallpaper, comfortable seats—everything about the theater evokes moviegoing in a different era.

Civil War Sights

Fought on November 30, 1864, the Battle of Franklin was one of the biggest hits the Confederate army took during the U.S. Civil War. By the time the fighting ended, more than 10,000 soldiers had lost their lives, been wounded, or gotten captured, all in about a five-hour period.

For those who want to learn all they can about the War Between the States, suburban Franklin is one of the best places to immerse oneself in all things Civil War. The history of the South comes alive, not only through occasional reenactments, but through cemeteries, former war hospitals, and other landmarks that help you understand the rigors of war.

Five of Franklin's Civil War highlights include **Carnton** (1345 Carnton Ln., 615/794-0903, www.carnton.org, 9am-5pm Mon.-Sat., noon-5pm Sun., adults $15, seniors $12, children 6-12 $8, children under 5 free), **Fort Granger** (113 Fort Granger Dr., 615/794-2103, dawn-dusk daily, free), **The Carter House** (1140 Columbia Ave., 615/791-1861, http://battleoffranklin-trust.org, 9am-5pm Mon.-Sat., 11am-5pm Sun., $15), **Lotz House** (1111 Columbia Ave., 615/790-7190, http://lotzhouse.com, 9am-5pm Mon.-Sat., 1pm-4pm Sun., adults $10, seniors $9, children ages 7-13 $5, children under 6 free), and **McLemore House** (11th Ave. N. and Glass St., 615/794-2270, tours available). Carnton, in particular, has accomplished guides who know enough to keep historians interested, but also can draw in those who aren't as familiar with the era.

But the Franklin Theatre isn't stuck in the past. It has many modern amenities that make it a great place to have a night out, complete with a concession stand that serves beer, wine, and spirits. Its menu delineates Jack Daniel's from bourbon and whiskey, as a nod to the locally made, favorite spirit. The Franklin Theatre hosts live concerts (many by local residents of acclaim) as well as films.

McLemore House

Five generations of the McLemore family lived in the white clapboard home at the corner of Glass Street and 11th Avenue in downtown Franklin. **McLemore House** (11th Ave. N. and Glass St.) was built in 1880 by Harvey McLemore, a former slave and farmer. Inside, a small museum has been created that documents the story of African Americans in Williamson County.

McLemore House offers **tours** (on the hour, 10am-2pm Fri.-Sat., $10, cash only). Contact Mary Mills at 615/794-2270 for more information.

★ Carnton

When Robert Hicks's novel *The Widow of the South* became a best seller in 2005, the staff at **Carnton** (1345 Carnton Ln., 615/794-0903, www.carnton. org, 9am-5pm Mon.-Sat., noon-5pm Sun., adults $15, seniors $12, children 6-12 $8, children under 5 free) noticed an uptick in the number of visitors. The novel is a fictionalized account of Carrie McGavock and how her home, the Carnton Plantation, became a Confederate hospital during the

Battle of Franklin in the Civil War (how fictionalized is subject for discussion on the tours here).

The Carnton mansion was built in 1826 by Randal McGavock, a former Nashville mayor and prominent lawyer and businessman. Randal had died by the time of the Civil War, and it was his son, John, and John's wife, Carrie, who witnessed the bloody Battle of Franklin on November 30, 1864. Located behind the Confederate line, the Carnton Plantation became a hospital for hundreds of injured and dying Confederate soldiers. As late as six months after the battle, the McGavock home remained a refuge for recovering veterans.

In the years that followed the battle, the McGavocks raised money, donating much of it themselves, to construct a cemetery for the Confederate dead and donated two acres of land to the cause.

A new visitors center opened at Carnton in 2008, providing much-needed space for the museum and gift shop. Visitors to Carnton can pay full price for a guided tour of the mansion and self-guided tour of the grounds, including a smokehouse, slave house, and garden. You can also pay just $5 for the self-guided tour of the grounds. There is no admission charged to visit the cemetery.

Packages include discounts if you want admission to nearby **Lotz House** (http://lotzhouse.com), the Carter House, and Carnton. It's a good choice for hard-core history buffs but perhaps too much Civil War lore for one day for the average visitor.

Fort Granger

An unsung attraction, **Fort Granger** is a lovely and interesting place to spend an hour or so. Built between 1862 and 1863 by Union forces, the earthen fort is set on a bluff overlooking the Harpeth River just south of downtown Franklin. The fort was the largest fortification in the area built by Capt. W. E. Merrill during the Federal occupation of Franklin. It saw action twice in 1863 and also in 1864 during the Battle of Franklin.

Many features of the fort remain intact for today's visitors. You can walk around portions of the breastworks. The interior of the fort is now a grassy field, perfect for a summer picnic or game of catch. An overlook at one end of the fort provides an unmatched view of the surrounding countryside.

You can reach Fort Granger two ways. One is along a short but steep trail departing Pinkerton Park on Murfreesboro Road east of town. Or you can drive straight to the fort by heading out of town on East Main Street. Turn right onto Liberty Pike, right onto Eddy Lane, and finally, right again onto Fort Granger Drive.

The fort, which is maintained by the city of Franklin, is open during daylight hours only. Although there is no office or visitors center at the fort, you may contact Franklin's **parks department** (615/794-2103) for more information.

Carter House

Some of the fiercest fighting in the Battle of Franklin took place around the farm and house belonging to the Carter family, on the outskirts of town. The family took refuge in the basement while Union and Confederate soldiers fought right above them. Today **Carter House** (1140 Columbia Ave., 615/791-1861, www.boft.org/carter-house.htm, 9am-5pm Mon.-Sat., 11am-5pm Sun., $15) is the best place to come for a detailed examination of the battle and the profound human toll that it exacted on both sides.

You will see hundreds of bullet holes, which help to illustrate the ferocity of the fight. Guides describe some of the worst moments of the battle and bring to life a few of the people who fought it. The house also holds a museum of Civil War uniforms and memorabilia, including photographs and short biographies of many of the men who were killed in Franklin. A video about the battle shows scenes from a reenactment.

If you can't get enough Civil War history, consider one of the packages that offer discounts on joint admission to nearby **Lotz House** (http://lotzhouse.com), Carter House, and Carnton.

RESTAURANTS

The best choice for baked goods, coffee, and light fare, including soups, salads, and sandwiches, is **Merridee's Breadbasket** (110 4th Ave., 615/790-3755, www.merridees.com, 7am-5pm Mon.-Wed., 7am-9pm Thurs.-Sat., $3-11). Merridee grew up in Minnesota and learned baking from her Swedish mother. When Merridee married Tom McCray and moved to Middle Tennessee in 1973, she kept up the baking traditions she had learned as a child. In 1984, she opened Merridee's Breadbasket in Franklin. Merridee McCray died in 1994, but her restaurant remains one of Franklin's most popular. Come in for omelets, scrambled eggs, or sweet bread and fruit in the morning. At lunch choose from the daily soup, casserole, or quiche, or order a cold or grilled sandwich. Merridee's also bakes fresh bread daily; take home a loaf of the always-popular Viking bread. Merridee's attracts a variety of people—students, businesspeople, and families out on the town. The creaky wood floors and comfortable seating make it a pleasant and relaxing place to refuel.

Puckett's Grocery & Restaurant (120 4th Ave. S., 625/794-5527, http://puckettsgro.com, 7am-3pm Mon., 7am-9pm Tues.-Sat., 7am-7pm Sun., $7-10) offers traditional breakfasts with eggs, bacon, country ham, and biscuits, and plate lunches during the day. In the evening, order up a handmade burger (the locals swear that they're the best in town), a Southern dinner of fried catfish, or a traditional steak, chicken, or fish entrée. For vegetarians, they offer a veggie burger or a vegetable plate, as well as salads. Do not skip the fried green beans. The food is well prepared and the service friendly, and there's almost always a crowd, regardless of whether or not there's live music on tap. There are other locations in Leiper's Fork and downtown Nashville.

On Friday and Saturday nights, the **Cool Cafe** (1110 Hillsboro Rd.,

615/538-7456, 10:30am-2pm and 5pm-8pm Mon.-Thurs., 10:30am-2pm and 4pm-9pm Fri., 4pm-9pm Sat., 10:30am-2pm Sun., $6-11, Steak Night $14-30) hosts Steak Night. The menu features steaks, burgers, catfish dishes, and decadent steak house-style side dishes. At other times, the café serves meat-and-threes.

NIGHTLIFE

Venues that sometimes offer live music include restaurants like **Puckett's Grocery & Restaurant** (120 4th Ave. S., 625/794-5527, http://puckettsgro. com), **The Bunganut Pig Pub & Eatery** (1143 Columbia Ave., 615/794-4777, www.bunganutpigfranklin.com, 11am-10pm Mon.-Thurs., 11am-1am Fri.-Sat., 11am-9pm Sun.), and **Jack and Jameson's Smokehouse** (509 Hillsboro Rd., 615/465-6253), which is co-owned by singer/actor Jonathan Jackson. The **Franklin Theatre** (419 Main St., 615/538-2076, www.franklin-theatre.com) has an impressive concert schedule, typically with affordable ticket prices.

ARTS AND CULTURE

Franklin's community theater is the **Pull-Tight Players** (112 2nd Ave. S., 615/791-5007 or 615/790-6782, www.pull-tight.com, tickets $18 adults, $16 seniors, $12 students). Performing in an intimate theater in downtown Franklin, Pull-Tight Players puts on about six productions each season, which runs September-June. Productions include many classic stage favorites.

The restored **Franklin Theatre** (419 Main St., 615/538-2076, www. franklintheatre.com) shows classic black-and-white films as well as recent releases (but not first-run movies). Movie ticket prices are typically $5, and there are many kid-friendly flicks shown on the weekends.

In just a few years the **Pilgrimage Music & Cultural Festival** (The Park at Harlinsdale Farm, 239 Franklin Rd., 615/794-2103, http://pilgrimagefes-tival.com, Sept.) has become a major player on the concert festival circuit, which is really saying something in the land of Bonnaroo. The fest, which takes place in September, attracts acts including The Avett Brothers, Grace Potter, Hall & Oates, and Kacey Musgraves. Megastar and Tennessee native Justin Timberlake is one of the partners in the festival.

For more than 30 years people in Franklin have been donning period Christmas attire each December for **Dickens of a Christmas** (http://his-toricfranklin.com, downtown Franklin, Dec.). This free street festival recreates the time of Charles Dickens, thanks, in part, to historic downtown Franklin's Victorian architecture. Festivities include caroling, Victorian-style entertainment, and chestnuts roasting on an open fire.

SPORTS AND ACTIVITIES

Pinkerton Park (405 Murfreesboro Rd., 615/794-2103), just southeast of town off Murfreesboro Road, is a pleasant city park. Walking trails, playgrounds, and picnic tables draw dozens of town residents, who come to exercise or simply relax. A short hiking trail takes you to Fort Granger, overlooking the city. You can also take the Sue Douglas Berry Memorial pedestrian bridge over the Harpeth River and walk the six blocks to the town square.

Jim Warren Park (705 Boyd Mill Ave., 615/794-2103) is a large public park with baseball and softball fields, tennis courts, covered picnic areas, and 2.5 miles of walking trails.

To add a little height (and adrenaline) to your time in Franklin, head to **SOAR Adventure Tower** (3794 Carothers Pkwy., 615/721-5103, www. soaradventure.com, 10am-9pm Tues.-Thurs., 10am-10pm Fri.-Sat., 10am-8pm Sun. June-July, hours vary seasonally; adults $45, children 8-17 $40, children 3-7 $35), where you can climb obstacles in the sky. Or opt for the easy float of **Middle Tennessee Hot Air Adventures** (615/584-6236, www.tnballoon.com, shared flight $200/passenger, private two-passenger flight $750).

The Park at Harlinsdale Farm

One of the most famous Tennessee Walking Horse breeding farms became a public park in 2007. **The Park at Harlinsdale Farm** (239 Franklin Rd., 615/794-2103) was a famed Franklin landmark for many years, thanks to a very famous horse. Midnight Sun, a stallion, was a world champion walking horse in 1945 and 1946, and all subsequent champions can trace their ancestry to him. The Park hosts the popular **Pilgrimage Music Festival** (http://pilgrimagefestival.com) each September. In 2004, Franklin bought the 200-acre farm for $8 million, and three years later the first 60 acres opened as a public park. It is a pleasant place to walk or picnic, with a dog park, a pond for catch-and-release fishing, an equestrian trail, and a 5K turf track for running or walking.

Golf

A few miles southeast of Franklin, **Forrest Crossing Golf Course** (750 Riverview Dr., 615/794-9400, www.forrestcrossing.com, $34 Mon.-Fri., $50 Sat.-Sun., $28 seniors) is an 18-hole par 72 golf course designed by Gary Roger Baird. Just shy of 7,000 yards, the course rating is 77.8, and the slope is 135.

There are more golf courses in Cool Springs, a few miles north of Franklin. **Vanderbilt Legends Club** (1500 Legends Club Ln., 615/791-8100, www.legendsclub.com, $75-85) is a top-of-the-line golf club. It has two 18-hole courses, as well as a complete array of club services, including a putting green and chipping green. Greens fees include a cart. Lower rates are available after 3pm. No blue jeans, T-shirts, or athletic shorts are allowed.

The **Fairways on Spencer Creek** (285 Spencer Creek Rd., 615/794-8223, www.fairwaysonspencercreek.net, $16) is a nine-hole alternative. The course rating is 64.6, and the slope is 105.

SHOPS

In many respects, shopping is Franklin's greatest attraction. Trendy downtown boutiques, the unique environment of The Factory, and proximity to a major mall make this a destination for shoppers. It is also one of Tennessee's most popular antiques shopping destinations.

Antiques

Franklin declares itself "the new antiques capital of Tennessee." Indeed, antiquing is one of the most popular pursuits of Franklin's visitors, and at least two dozen antiques shops serve to quench the thirst for something old. The town's antiques district is huddled around the corner of Margin Street and 2nd Avenue. Here you'll find no fewer than six major antiques stores. Other shops are found along Main Street in the downtown shopping district.

The best place to start antiquing is the **Franklin Antique Mall** (251 2nd Ave. S., 615/790-8593, 10am-5pm Mon.-Sat., 1pm-5pm Sun.), inside the town's old icehouse. The mall is a maze of rooms, each with different goods on offer. Possibilities include books, dishware, quilts, furniture, knickknacks, and housewares. You can also follow 5th Avenue about two blocks south of downtown to find **Country Charm Antique Mall** (301 Lewisburg Ave., 615/790-8998, www.countrycharmmall.com, 10am-5pm Mon.-Sat., 1pm-5pm Sun. summer, 10am-5pm Tues.-Sat., 1pm-5pm Sun. winter), whose three buildings house a vast array of furniture, quilts, glassware, china, and home decor.

Just outside the Franklin Antique Mall are at least five other antiques shops to roam through, including **J. J. Ashley's** (125 S. Margin St., 615/791-0011, 10am-5pm Mon.-Sat.), which specializes in French and English country accessories, as well as European furniture. **Scarlett Scales Antiques** (212 S. Margin St., 615/791-4097, 10am-5pm Mon.-Sat., 1pm-5pm Sun.), located in a 1900s shotgun house, has American country furnishings, accessories, and architectural elements arriving daily.

Downtown

Independent retail is alive and well in Franklin's downtown. West Main Street is the epicenter of the shopping district, though you will find stores scattered around other parts of downtown as well. Home decor, classy antiques, trendy clothes, and specialty items like candles, tea, and gardening supplies are just a few of the things you'll find in downtown Franklin.

Most shops in downtown Franklin are open by 10am, and many stay open until the evening to catch late-afternoon visitors. You can easily navigate the downtown shopping district on foot, but you may need to stow your parcels in the car now and then.

Bink's Outfitters (421 Main St., 615/599-8777, http://binksoutfitters.com, 10am-9pm Mon.-Sat., 11am-7pm Sun.) sells outdoor clothing and equipment, perfect for stocking up for a trip down the nearby Natchez Trace.

The city's best bookstore is **Landmark Booksellers** (114 E. Main St.,

615/791-6400, 10am-5pm daily), found on the other side of the town square. They have a wide selection of used and new books, including many regional titles. It is friendly and welcoming, with fresh coffee for sale in the mornings.

For the best in paper, gift wrap, and stationery, go to **Rock Paper Scissors** (317 Main St., 615/791-0150, www.rockpaperscissor.com, 10am-6pm Mon.-Fri., 10am-5pm Sat.). **Heart and Hands** (418 Main St., 615/794-2537, www.heartandhandsonline.com, 10am-5pm Mon.-Sat., noon-5pm Sun.) is one of several area shops specializing in crafts and home decor.

THE FACTORY AT FRANKLIN

The most distinctive retail center is **The Factory at Franklin** (230 Franklin Rd., 615/791-1777, www.factoryatfranklin.com). A 250,000-square-foot complex of 11 different old industrial buildings, The Factory once housed stove factories and a textile mill. In the mid-1990s, Calvin Lehew bought the dilapidated eyesore and began the lengthy process of restoring the buildings and converting them into a space for galleries, retail shops, restaurants, and other businesses.

Today, The Factory is a vibrant commercial center for the city of Franklin. It houses a refreshing array of local independent retailers, including galleries, **Luna Record Shop** (615/806-9435, http://lunarecordshop.com, 10am-5pm Tues.-Sat.), a jewelry store, and a pet boutique. **The Little Cottage** (615/794-1405, www.thelittlecottagechildrensshop.com, 9:30am-5pm Mon.-Thurs., 9:30am-6pm Fri., 10am-6pm Sat., noon-5pm Sun.) sells children's fashions.

The **Franklin Farmer's Market** (230 Franklin Rd., http://franklinfarmersmarket.com, 8am-1pm Sat.), held at The Factory, is one of the finest small-town farmers markets in the state, featuring a wide variety of fruit and vegetable growers; cheese, milk, and meat sellers; and craftspeople and live music.

In addition to retail, The Factory has a handful of restaurants, a fish market, bakery, a coffee roaster, and an ice cream shop. It also offers free wireless internet.

COOL SPRINGS GALLERIA

Cool Springs Galleria (1800 Galleria Blvd., Cool Springs, 615/771-2128, http://coolspringsgalleria.com, 10am-9pm Mon.-Sat., noon-6pm Sun.) is a mall with more than 165 specialty stores, 4 major department stores, 15 restaurants, and a 500-seat food court. It is located a few miles north of Franklin, convenient to I-65. Shops include **Zales** (615/771-1886, http://zales.com), **Talbots** (615/771-1822, http://talbots.com), **Pier 1 Imports** (615/771-7884, http://pier1.com), **Pottery Barn** (615/771-0166, http://potterybarn.com), **Macy's** (615/771-2100, http://macys.com), and **JCPenney** (615/771-7743, http://jcpenney.com). The mall is found at exits 68B and 69 on I-65.

Near the mall in Cool Springs Market is **Marti & Liz Shoes** (2000

Mallory Ln., 615/435-8125, www.martiandliz.com, 9am-9pm Mon.-Sat.), a shoe-shopper's bargain dream. **Happy reTales** (101 Creekside Crossing #700, Brentwood, 615/309-1835, http://happyretalesonline.com, 10am-7pm Mon.-Sat., noon-4pm Sun.) is a dog and cat supply store that sends all profits to Happy Tales Rescue, a no-kill dog and cat rescue in Franklin. The store is staffed almost entirely with volunteers (the manager is employed). Besides all of the healthy food that one might expect at a boutique pet store, they also have a wide selection of pet and people clothing, a variety of dog treats for every purpose, and pet-inspired artwork.

HOTELS

Franklin has two types of accommodations: cozy bed-and-breakfasts and chain motels. The bed-and-breakfasts are located in downtown Franklin and the surrounding countryside. The chain motels are clustered around exit 65 off I-65, about two miles from the city center. The bed-and-breakfasts are far more congruous with Franklin's charm than the interstate motels. This is also a good area to search for alternative accommodations, like those offered on **Airbnb** (www.airbnb.com).

Several chain motels surround the interstate near Franklin. Closest to town are the 89-room **Quality Inn and Suites** (1307 Murfreesboro Rd., 615/794-7591, $68-110) and the 142-room **Best Western** (1308 Murfreesboro Rd., 615/790-0570, $55-70). Both offer wireless internet, free continental breakfast, and an outdoor pool. The Quality Inn is pet-friendly with a mere $10 fee.

The **Comfort Inn Franklin** (4202 Franklin Commons Ct., 800/916-4339, http://comfortinn.reservations.com, $95-110) offers free Wi-Fi and complimentary breakfast and allows pets.

The **Magnolia House Bed and Breakfast** (1317 Columbia Ave., 615/794-8178, http://bbonline.com/tn/magnolia, $160) is less than a mile from downtown Franklin, near the Carter House. A large magnolia tree shades the early 20th-century Craftsman home. There are four carpeted guest rooms, each with a private bath. Three have queen-size beds; the fourth has two twin beds. Common areas include a polished sitting room, cozy den, and sunroom, which looks out onto the quiet residential neighborhood. Hosts Jimmy and Robbie Smithson welcome guests and prepare homemade breakfasts according to your preferences.

A hip, urban-feeling hotel option is **Aloft/Cool Springs** (7109 South Springs Dr., 615/435-8700, http://aloftnashvillecoolsprings.com, $149-184). The hotel boasts a saltwater pool, a better than average bar, and a good location for business or recreation in Franklin.

The log cabin that is now **The Cabin at Cedar Run Farm** (5330 Old Harding Rd., 615/799-9391, http://cabinatcedarrunfarm.com, $175-250) may have been built in 1840, but staying here isn't roughing it by any stretch of the imagination. The two-story cabin has a full kitchen, internet access, and a cute front porch perfect for sipping your morning coffee.

Visit Franklin (615/791-7554 or 866/253-9207, http://visitfranklin.com) publishes guides and maintains a website about Franklin and the surrounding area. They also operate the **Visit Franklin Visitor Center** (209 E. Main St., 615/591-8514, 9am-6pm Mon.-Sat., noon-5pm Sun.).

The **Williamson Medical Center** (4321 Carothers Pkwy., 615/435-5000) is a 185-bed full-service medical facility with a 24-hour emergency room.

TRANSPORTATION

Traffic can be heavy in and around Franklin. As a thriving bedroom community for commuters working in Nashville, the morning and afternoon rush hours are to be avoided. The city of Franklin offers a **trolley bus service** around the town and to outlying areas, including Cool Springs Galleria, Williamson Medical Center, Watson Glen Shopping Center, and Independence Square. The trolleys run three different routes 6am-6pm. It can take anywhere from 30 minutes to an hour to get to downtown Franklin from downtown Nashville, depending on traffic. You can pick up a full schedule and route map from the visitors center or download it from http://tmagroup.org. Fares for the Cool Springs Galleria bus are $3 for a one-way trip and $5 for a round-trip.

If you need a taxi, call **Brentwood Taxi** (615/376-8294), or try a ride-hailing app such as **Lyft.**

Leiper's Fork

Part bucolic small town, part yuppified enclave, Leiper's Fork is a pleasant place to spend a few hours. It is located about a 15 minutes' drive from Franklin and near milepost 420 on the Natchez Trace Parkway. The town runs for several miles along Leiper's Fork, a tributary of the West Harpeth River. Beautiful old farmhouses line Old Hillsboro Road, which serves as the main thoroughfare through town.

Some of the earliest settlers of the area were the Benton family, including Thomas Hart Benton, who would go on to become a U.S. senator from Missouri. For many years, Leiper's Fork was called Hillsboro after Hillsborough, North Carolina, where many of its early settlers came from. There is another Hillsboro in Coffee County, Tennessee, however, so when this Hillsboro petitioned for a post office in 1818, the U.S. Postal Service insisted that it change its name. Leiper's Fork was born.

Acclaimed furniture maker Dick Poyner was from the Leiper's Fork area. Poyner, a former slave, was famous for his sturdy ladder-back wooden chairs, one of which is on display at the Tennessee State Museum in Nashville.

Leiper's Fork is a pleasant community, with a die-hard group of locals who are proud of their town. Art galleries and antiques shops line the short main drag. Unusually good food can be found at local restaurants, and a

Clockwise from top left: The Factory at Franklin; Puckett's Grocery & Restaurant, a must-eat and -visit in Franklin; Fort Granger.

laid-back let's-laugh-at-ourselves attitude prevails. Many music powerhouses live here; if you see a celebrity, don't make a fuss. That's why they choose to live in Leiper's Fork.

Bed-and-breakfasts in the area make it a viable destination or a pleasant pit stop during a tour of the region.

RESTAURANTS

Puckett's Grocery & Restaurant (4142 Old Hillsboro Rd., 615/794-1308, www.puckettsofleipersfork.com, 6am-7pm Mon.-Thurs., 6am-10:30pm Fri.-Sat., 6am-6pm Sun. summer, reduced hours Dec.-Feb., $6-25) is the heartbeat of Leiper's Fork. An old-time grocery with a small dining room attached, Puckett's serves breakfast, lunch, and dinner to the town faithful and visitors alike. The original country store opened about 1950. In 1998, Andy Marshall bought the store and expanded the restaurant offerings. Solid country breakfasts are the order of the day in the mornings, followed by plate lunches. The pulled pork is a favorite, as is the Puckett Burger. Dinner specials include catfish nights, family nights, and a Saturday-night seafood buffet. Friday night the grocery turns upscale with a supper club and live music. Puckett's hours vary by the season, so it's best to call ahead, especially for dinner. This is the location that started it all, but there's also a location in Franklin (120 4th Ave. S., 625/794-5527) with a more varied menu.

NIGHTLIFE

Friday night is songwriter night at **Puckett's Grocery & Restaurant** (4142 Old Hillsboro Rd., 615/794-1308, www.puckettsofleipersfork.com). For $30 you can enjoy a dressed-up dinner (fresh seafood, poultry, and steak are usually among the options) at 7pm and an in-the-round performance from Nashville singer-songwriters starting at 8:30pm. If you prefer, pay $15 for the concert only. Reservations are essential for either, so call ahead. Check the website to find out who is performing.

ARTS AND CULTURE

Jailhouse Industries operates the Leiper's Fork **Lawn Chair Theatre** (4144 Old Hillsboro Rd., May-Sept.), behind Leiper's Creek Gallery. Bring your lawn chair or blanket and enjoy classic movies and kids' favorites on Friday and Saturday nights, plus concerts. Call 615/477-6799 for more information, or just ask around.

SPORTS AND ACTIVITIES

The **Leiper's Fork District** of the **Natchez Trace National Scenic Trail** runs for 24 miles, starting near milepost 427 and ending at milepost 408, where State Highway 50 crosses the Natchez Trace Parkway. The trail follows the old Natchez Trace through rural countryside. The best access point is from Garrison Creek Road, where there are parking, restrooms, and picnic facilities. You can also access the trail from Davis Hollow Road.

Leiper's Fork's retailers are open 10am-5pm Wednesday-Saturday and 1pm-5pm Sunday. Park the car and set off on foot to explore.

Part record store, part pickin' corner, and part curio shop, **Finds in the Fork** (4165 Old Hillsboro Rd., 615/628-8716, www.findsinthefork.com) embodies much of what makes Leiper's Fork what it is. Owner Karen Whitford was once married to Brad Whitford of Aerosmith, and he donated some of the guitars available to pick up and play when you are in the shop. Lights made from cigar boxes are favorites of locals.

The **Leiper's Creek Gallery** (4144 Old Hillsboro Rd., 615/599-5102, www.leiperscreekgallery.com) is the finest gallery in town. It shows a wide selection of paintings by local and regional artists, and hosts a variety of arts events year-round.

★ Serenite Maison

The 3,000-square-foot **Serenite Maison** (4149 Old Hillsboro Pike, 615/599-2071, www.serenitemaison.com) houses a well-edited inventory thanks to the smart design sense of Alexandra Cirimelli. A California transplant, Cirimelli has appeared on an episode of *American Pickers* and is known for finding her well-heeled clients (including Holly Williams and several actors and actresses from the TV show *Nashville*) the perfect farm table or pie safe for their kitchen. Don't overlook the pickin' corner, where locals stop in to play the antique guitars, banjos, and mandolins that hang on the walls.

HOTELS

Innkeepers Eric and Samantha offer three different places to stay under the name **Pot N' Kettle Cottages** (5527 Joseph St., 615/864-3392, www.potnkettlecottages.com, $150-295). The cottages, all on the same street, are within walking distance of downtown Leiper's Fork and sleep 5-9 people. Amenities include bicycles to cruise around town and Wi-Fi. Discounts are available for groups that book more than one cottage at a time.

Bell Buckle

A tiny town nestled in the northern reaches of the Walking Horse region, Bell Buckle is a charming place to visit. Founded in 1852 and once a railroad town, Bell Buckle has successfully become a destination for antiques shopping, arts and crafts, small-town hospitality, and country cooking. The town's single commercial street faces the old railroad tracks; handsome old homes—some of them bed-and-breakfasts—spread out along quiet residential streets.

What makes Bell Buckle so appealing is the sense of humor that permeates just about everything that happens here. T-shirts for sale on the main street proclaim "Tokyo, Paris, New York, Bell Buckle," and the town's quirky residents feel free to be themselves. Tennessee's poet laureate,

Margaret "Maggi" Britton Vaughn, who operates the Bell Buckle Press shop and had an office on Main Street for many years, once told an interviewer that William Faulkner "would have killed" for a community with the ambience and characters of Bell Buckle.

Bell Buckle's name is derived from Bell Buckle Creek, named thus because a cow's bell was found hanging in a tree by the creek, attached by a buckle.

The town's annual RC and Moon Pie Festival in June attracts thousands to the tiny town, and the well-respected Webb School Arts and Crafts Festival in October is one of the finest regional arts shows in the state. This is also home to the annual Tennessee Shakespeare Festival each summer.

SIGHTS

Bell Buckle is noted as the home of the elite and well-regarded **Webb School** (319 Webb Rd. E., 931/389-9322, www.thewebbschool.com). Founded in 1870 and led by William Robert Webb until his death in 1926, Webb School has graduated 10 Rhodes scholars, several governors and attorneys general, and numerous successful academics. The school now has about 300 students in grades 8-12 from around the country and the world. It was all male for many years, but Webb School now admits both male and female students. Its athletic mascot is the "Webb Feet."

The Webb campus is about three blocks north of downtown Bell Buckle. You can visit the main administrative office during regular business hours, where there are photographs and school memorabilia on display. Pay attention as you drive by; the speed limit in this school zone is considerably lower than that on all the nearby country roads.

RESTAURANTS

There's no debate about where to eat in Bell Buckle. The **Bell Buckle Café** (16 Railroad Sq., 931/389-9693, www.bellbucklecafe.com, 10:30am-2pm Mon., 10:30am-8pm Tues.-Thurs., 10:30am-9pm Fri.-Sat., 11am-5pm Sun., $4-18) is not only a Bell Buckle institution, but it is also one of the only games in town. The menu is Southern, with a few refined touches (like ostrich burgers and spinach-strawberry salad) you won't find at most small-town cafés. The menu is also mighty diverse, with seafood, pasta, and sandwiches in addition to the usual plate lunches and dinner entrées. The large dining room fills up quick, especially for lunch, so there's no shame in coming a bit early. The Bell Buckle Café takes care of your entertainment needs, too. Live music every Thursday, Friday, and Saturday night is usually bluegrass or country. Local radio station WLIJ broadcasts a musical variety show from the café 1pm-3pm on Saturday, which is a great reason to come to the café for lunch.

If you managed to pass up homemade dessert at the Bell Buckle Café, then head to **Bluebird Antiques and Ice Cream Parlor** (15 Webb Rd., 931/389-6549, 10am-5pm Mon.-Sat., noon-5pm Sun.). Here you'll find a turn-of-the-20th-century soda fountain with hand-dipped ice cream and homemade waffle cones. Come in the morning to see (and smell) them making the cones.

SHOPS

The single most popular pursuit in Bell Buckle is shopping. Antiques are the main attraction, but arts and crafts are a close second. Several Nashville interior designers and antiques dealers have booths in shops in Bell Buckle because of the goods found here. You can spend an entire day rummaging through these shelves, though it is generally too crowded to do so on the day of the Moon Pie Festival.

Start with the **Bell Buckle Antique Mall** (112 Main St., 931/389-6174, http://bellbuckleantiquemall.com, 10am-4pm Mon.-Thurs., 10am-5pm Fri.-Sat., 1pm-5pm Sun.) and the nearby **Livery Antique Mall** (107 Main St., 931/389-6354, http://bellbuckleantiquemall.com, 10am-4pm Mon.-Sat., noon-5pm Sun.). The booths at these spots are run by different dealers, so there's a wide cross-section of vintage and antique goods; there's a heavy emphasis on ceramics and metal signs.

Farm Girlz Goodz (26 Railroad Sq., 931/389-0011, 11am-4pm Sun.-Mon., 11am-5pm Tues.-Thurs., 11am-5:30pm Fri.-Sat.) carries more than the name might indicate. Browse locally made and fair-trade goods ranging from jewelry and essential oils to quilts, metal sculpture, and hand-woven rugs.

Serendipity Mercantile (10 Railroad Sq., 931/813-3141, 10am-2pm Tues.-Thurs., 10am-4pm Fri.-Sat.) stocks a wide variety of giftable items and souvenirs, including handmade soap, mugs, kids' toys, clothing and sweet treats.

INFORMATION

The **Bell Buckle Chamber of Commerce** (4 Railroad Sq., 931/389-9663, http://bellbucklechamber.com) publishes brochures and operates as a clearinghouse for information.

Lynchburg

A 1.5-hour drive southeast of Nashville, Lynchburg was once a town with a population of 361. It has been transformed by the popularity of Jack Daniel's Tennessee Whiskey, which is made a few blocks from the town square. No other small town in Tennessee sees as many visitors from as many different places as this one.

Critics may object to the tour buses and crowds, but for now, the town has managed to survive its success with relative grace. It has maintained its small-town feel, and it offers its guests a hospitable and heartfelt welcome.

Lynchburg is centered on the Moore County courthouse, a modest red-brick building. Souvenir shops, restaurants, and a few local businesses line the square. Outside of this, Lynchburg is quiet and residential. The Jack

Daniel's Distillery is about three blocks away from the town square; a pleasant footpath connects the two.

★ JACK DANIEL'S DISTILLERY

As you drive into Lynchburg, or walk around the town, you might notice some odd-looking gray warehouses peeking out above the treetops. These are barrel houses, where Jack Daniel's Distillery ages its whiskey. Around Moore County there are 74 of these warehouses, and each one holds about one million barrels of whiskey.

Thousands of whiskey drinkers make the pilgrimage every year to **Jack Daniel's Distillery** (visitors center 133 Lynchburg Hwy./Hwy. 55, 931/759-6357, www.jackdaniels.com, 9am-4:30pm daily) to see how Jack Daniel's is made. And what they find is that, aside from the use of electricity, computers, and the sheer scale of the operation, things have not changed too much since 1866 when Jack Daniel registered his whiskey still at the mouth of Cave Spring near Lynchburg.

Jack Daniel was introduced to the whiskey business by a Lutheran lay preacher named Dan Call, who sold the distillery to Daniel shortly after the Civil War. In 1866, Daniel had the foresight to register his distillery with the federal government, making his the oldest registered distillery in the United States. He never married and had no known children. After Daniel died in 1911, the distillery passed to his nephew, Lem Motlow. The distillery remained in the Motlow family until it was sold in 1957 to the Brown-Forman Corporation of Louisville, Kentucky.

Tours offered include the all-ages **Dry County Tour** (9am-4:30pm daily, $14 adults, $7 ages 10-17, free 9 and under), a 70-minute whiskey-free tour that will teach you about the distillery and its history. For those who want a taste, the **Flight of Jack Daniel's Tour** (9am-4:30pm Mon.-Sat., 11am-4:30pm Sun., 21 and up, $17) lasts 90 minutes and includes tastings of five of the distillery's whiskeys. All tours are offered first-come, first-served, and they sell out, so get there early.

The tour of the distillery begins with a video about the master distillers—Jack Daniel's has had seven in its lifetime—who are the final authority on all facets of the product. You then board a bus that takes you up to the far side of the distillery, and from here you'll walk back to the visitors center, stopping frequently to be told about the key steps in the process. The highlight of the tour for some is seeing Cave Spring, where the distillery gets its iron-free springwater. Others enjoy taking a potent whiff of the sour mash and the mellowing whiskey.

Moore County, where Lynchburg is located, is a dry county, and for 86 years the irony was that Jack Daniel's could not sell any of its whiskey at the distillery. In 1995, however, the county approved a special exemption that allows the distillery to sell souvenir bottles of whiskey at its visitors center. That is all they sell, however; you have to buy other Jack Daniel's merchandise at one of the other gift shops in town.

OTHER SIGHTS

A stately two-story brick building on the southwest corner of the square is the **Moore County Old Jail Museum** (231 Main St., no phone, 8am-3pm Tues.-Sat., $1 adults, suggested donation), which served as the sheriff's residence and the county jail until 1990. The building is now a museum and operated by the local historical society. You can see law enforcement memorabilia, old newspaper clippings, and vintage clothes. Go upstairs to see the prisoners' cells.

RESTAURANTS

Be prepared: It can be tough to get an evening meal in Lynchburg; by 6pm the place clears out, as the attractions are geared to daytime visitors.

The most popular place to eat in Lynchburg is **Miss Mary Bobo's Boarding House** (295 Main St., 931/759-7394, seating 1pm Mon.-Fri., 11am, 1pm Sat. summer and fall; 1pm daily winter and spring, $25). Miss Mary's started life as the home of Thomas Roundtree, the founder of Lynchburg. In 1908, Lacy Jackson Bobo and his wife, Mary Evans Bobo, bought the house and operated it as a boardinghouse until the 1980s. Over the years, word of Mary Bobo's legendary home-cooked meals spread, and this boardinghouse became one of the region's best-known eating houses. Today, Miss Mary's is no longer a boardinghouse, and the restaurant is operated by Miss Lynne Tolley, who has worked hard to keep up the traditions established by Miss Mary. The restaurant is owned by the Jack Daniel's Distillery, and servers are hired from the local community college. A meal at Miss Mary's will easily be the most unique of your trip. Arrive at least 15 minutes early to check in, pay, and be assigned to a dining room. You will be taken to your dining room by a hostess, who stays with you throughout the meal. Everyone sits family-style around a big table. The meal is a traditional Southern dinner, with no less than six side dishes and two meats, plus iced tea (unsweetened), dessert, coffee, and bread. Almost every meal features fried chicken. Side dishes may include green beans, mashed potatoes, fried okra, carrot slaw, and corn bread. Your hostess will answer questions about the food and tell you some stories about the restaurant—if you ask. Call well ahead to make reservations. Meals are fully booked weeks and even months in advance, especially during the busy summer months and on Saturdays.

For a more low-key meal, go to the **Bar-B-Que Caboose Cafe** (217 Main St., 931/759-5180, http://bbqcaboose.com, 11am-4:30pm Mon.-Fri., 10am-5pm Sat., 11:30am-5pm Sun., $4-22). The menu offers pulled-pork or smoked chicken sandwiches, jambalaya, red beans and rice, and hot dogs. On Saturday mornings (10am-11am), a live country music radio show is broadcast from the café.

There are a handful of other restaurants in Lynchburg, all on the town square. **Southern Perks** (10 Short St., 931/759-5552, 7am-3pm daily, $10) serves breakfast sandwiches, hand-tossed pizza, salads, wraps, and panini.

The **Belle Fleur Cottage** (Mulberry Creek, 931/580-0671, www.cottage-bellefleur.com, $115-125) is a quick walk from the town square and Jack Daniel's Distillery. The three rooms in the B&B are set up for you to relax back to an earlier time, but still have some modern-day comforts. Families can enjoy board games or lounge on private patios and porches.

The **Tolley House** (1253 Main St., 931/759-7263, www.tolleyhouse.com, $145-165) is located about a mile from the town square and a pleasant country retreat. A handsome antebellum farmhouse once owned by Jack Daniel's master distiller Lem Motlow, the Tolley House provides touches of luxury. Rooms have private baths, television, and wireless internet access and are furnished tastefully with antiques. Hosts Frank and Karen Fletcher provide your choice of a full country or light continental breakfast. Discounts are available for stays of two or more nights.

The closest thing to a motel in Lynchburg is the **Lynchburg Country Inn** (423 Majors Blvd., 931/759-5995, www.lynchburgcountryinn.com, $79). Its 25 rooms are each furnished with a microwave, refrigerator, free Wi-Fi and cable TV. There's a pool out back and rocking chairs on the front and back porches. The motel-style building is modern, constructed in 2003, but the decor is pure country.

Land Between the Lakes

This narrow finger of land that lies between the Cumberland and Tennessee Rivers is a natural wonderland. Comprising 170,000 acres of land and wrapped by 300 miles of undeveloped river shoreline, the **Land Between the Lakes National Recreation Area** (100 Van Morgan Dr., Golden Pond, 270/924-2000, www.landbetweenthelakes.us) has become one of the most popular natural areas in this region of the country. Split between Tennessee and Kentucky, the area provides unrivaled opportunities to camp, hike, boat, play, or simply drive through quiet wilderness.

Land Between the Lakes is about a 1.5-hour drive northwest from Nashville. The area lies between what is now called Kentucky Lake (the Tennessee River) and Lake Barkley (the Cumberland River). At its narrowest point, the distance between these two bodies of water is only 1 mile. The drive from north to south is 43 miles. About one-third of the park is in Tennessee; the rest is in Kentucky. It is managed by the U.S. Forest Service, an agency of the U.S. Department of Agriculture.

History

Land Between the Lakes was not always a natural and recreational area. Native Americans settled here, drawn to the fertile soil, proximity to the rivers, and gentle terrain. European settlers followed, and between about 1800 and the 1960s the area, then called Between the Rivers, saw thriving small settlements. Residents farmed and traded along the rivers, which were served by steamboats.

In many respects, settlers in Between the Rivers were even more isolated than those in other parts of what was then the western frontier of the United States. They did not necessarily associate with one state or another, instead forming a distinct identity of their own. During the Civil War, it was necessary to finally determine the border between Tennessee and Kentucky, since this line also marked the border between the Union and the Confederacy.

It was during another period of upheaval in the United States that the future of the Between the Rivers region changed forever. In the midst of the Great Depression, Congress created the Tennessee Valley Authority; it improved soil conditions, eased flooding, brought electricity, and created jobs in Tennessee. One of TVA's projects was the Kentucky Dam, which was built between 1938 and 1944 and impounded the Tennessee River. In 1963, 25 years after work began on Barkley Dam, President John F. Kennedy announced that the U.S. government would buy out residents of the land between the Cumberland and Tennessee Rivers to create a new park to serve as an example of environmental management and recreational use. The project's goal was to bring much-needed development to the area by attracting visitors to the park.

The project was not without opponents, who objected to the government's use of eminent domain to take over lands that were privately owned. Residents lamented the loss of unique communities in the lake region. More than 2,300 people were removed to create Land Between the Lakes (LBL). In all, 96,000 of the 170,000 acres that make up LBL were purchased or taken from private hands.

Over time, however, the controversy of the creation of the park has faded, and the Land Between the Lakes has become well loved. It is the third most visited park in Tennessee, behind only the Smoky Mountains and Cherokee National Forest.

Planning Your Time

Some of the best attractions at Land Between the Lakes charge admission. If you are planning to visit all or most of them, consider one of the packages offered by the U.S. Forest Service. The discount package allows you to visit each attraction once over a seven-day period at a 25 percent discount. Another option is the $30 LBL Fun Card: 10 admissions to any of three attractions. It does not expire. You can buy packages at either the north (Kentucky) or south (Tennessee) welcome stations or the Golden Pond Visitor Center.

During certain summer weekends there are free two-hour tours of **Lake Barkley's Power Plant and Navigation Lock** (270/362-4236). You must call in advance to reserve a spot and complete a registration form.

There are no restaurants in Land Between the Lakes. Vending machines with snacks and sodas can be found at The Homeplace, Golden

Pond Visitor Center, and the Woodlands Nature Station. Picnic facilities abound. A McDonald's sits near the southern entrance to the park. Dover, five miles east, has a number of other fast-food and local eateries. Twenty miles to the southwest, Paris has dozens of restaurants.

SIGHTS
Great Western Iron Furnace

About 11 miles inside the park is the **Great Western Iron Furnace,** built by Brian, Newell, and Company in 1854. If you have traveled around this part of Tennessee much, you will have come to recognize the distinctive shape of the old iron furnaces that dot the landscape in the counties between Nashville and the Tennessee River. Like the Great Western Furnace, these plants were used to create high-quality iron from iron ore deposits in the earth.

The Great Western Furnace operated for less than two years. By 1856 panic over reported slave uprisings and the coming of the Civil War caused the plant to shut down. It would never make iron again.

The Homeplace

Just beyond the furnace is **The Homeplace** (4512 The Trace Rd., Dover, 931/232-6457, 9am-5pm Mon.-Sat., 10am-5pm Sun. Apr.-Oct., 9am-5pm Wed.-Sat., 10am-5pm Sun. Mar. and Nov., $5 ages 13 and up, $3 children 5-12, free for children 4 and under), a living-history museum that depicts life in Between the Rivers circa 1850. At the middle of the 19th century, Between the Rivers was home to an iron ore industry and hundreds of farmers. These farmers raised crops and livestock for their own use, as well as to sell where they could. In 1850, about 10,000 people lived in Between the Rivers, including 2,500 slaves and 125 free blacks.

The Homeplace recreates an 1850 farmstead. Staff dress in period clothes and perform the labors that settlers would have done: They sow seeds in the spring, harvest in the summer and fall, and prepare the fields for the next year in the winter. The farm includes a dogtrot cabin, where you can see how settlers would have lived, cooked, and slept. Out back there is a small garden, a plot of tobacco, pigs, sheep, oxen, and a barn. You may see farmers splitting shingles, working oxen, sewing quilts, making candles, or another of the dozens of tasks that settlers performed on a regular basis.

The Homeplace publishes a schedule that announces when certain activities will take place, such as canning, shearing of sheep, or harvesting tobacco. Even if you come when there is no special program, you will be able to see staff taking on everyday tasks, and you can ask them about any facet of life on the frontier.

★ Elk and Bison Prairie

Archaeological evidence shows that elk and bison once grazed in Tennessee and Kentucky, including the area between the rivers. Settlers quickly destroyed these herds, however. Both bison and elk were easy to hunt, and they were desirable for their meat and skins. By 1800, bison had been killed off, and about 50 years later elk were gone, too.

When Land Between the Lakes was created, elk and bison were reintroduced to the area. The South Bison Range across the road from The Homeplace is one of the places where bison now live. The bison herd that roams on about 160 acres here can sometimes be seen from the main road or from side roads bordering the range.

You can see both bison and elk at the **Elk and Bison Prairie** (dawn-dusk daily, $5 per vehicle), a 700-acre restoration project located near the midpoint of the Land Between the Lakes. In 1996, 39 bison were relocated here from the south prairie, and 29 elk were transported from Canada. Since then, the population of both animals has grown.

Visitors may drive through the range along a **one-mile loop** (The Trace Rd./TN-453), the entrance to which is directly across The Trace Road from the Jenny Ridge Picnic Area. Take your time, roll down your windows, and keep your eyes peeled for signs of the animals. The best times to view elk and bison are in the early morning or late afternoon. At other times of day, you may just enjoy the sights and sounds of the grassland. Pay attention to the road as well as the animals, as the car in front of you may slow to take photos of one of these magnificent creatures. You may also see some bison from the Natchez Trace en route. The loop drive is about one mile north of the Golden Pond Visitor Center.

Golden Pond Visitor Center and Planetarium

For the best overview of the history, nature, and significance of the Land Between the Lakes, stop at the **Golden Pond Visitor Center and Planetarium** (239 Visitor Center Dr., 270/924-2000, 9am-5pm daily, visitors center free, planetarium adults $5, children 5-12 $3, children under 4 free; evening shows $7 for all ages). The visitors center is home to a small museum about the park, where you can also watch a video about the elk that have been restored on the Elk and Bison Prairie. You'll also find a gift shop, restrooms, and picnic area.

The **planetarium** (10am-5pm daily) screens at least four programs daily about astronomy and nature, with more during the holidays. On Saturdays and Sundays at 1pm, you can get a sneak peek at the night sky above.

Golden Pond was the name of Land Between the Lakes' largest town before the park was created. Golden Pond, also called Fungo, was a vibrant town that, at its peak, had a hotel, bank, restaurants, and other retail outlets. During Prohibition, farmers made moonshine in the woods and sold it in Golden Pond. Golden Pond whiskey was sought after in back-alley saloons as far away as Chicago. When Land Between the Lakes was created in 1963, Golden Pond had a population of about 200 people. Families moved their homes and relocated to communities outside the park. In 1970, when the historical society unveiled a marker at the site of Golden Pond, the strains of "Taps" rang out over the hills.

You can visit the site of Golden Pond by driving a few miles east of the visitors center on Highway 80. There is a picnic area.

Woodlands Nature Station

The final major attraction in Land Between the Lakes is the **Woodlands Nature Station** (north of the visitors center on the Trace, 3146 Silver Trail Rd., Cadiz, Kentucky, 270/924-2020, 10am-5pm daily Apr.-Oct., 9am-5pm Wed.-Sat., 10am-5pm Sun. Nov. and Mar., $5 ages 13 and up, $3 children 5-12, free for children 4 and under). Geared to children, the nature station introduces visitors to animals including bald eagles, coyotes, opossum, and deer. There are also opportunities for staff-led hiking trips. Special events and activities take place nearly every weekend, and during the week in summertime.

Center Furnace

You can see the ruins of **Center Furnace,** once the largest iron furnace in the Land Between the Lakes, along the **Center Furnace Trail.** On the short (0.3 mi.) walk you will see signs that describe the process of making iron and explain why it was practiced in Between the Rivers. The trailhead is just south of Silver Trail Road, near the Woodlands Nature Station. It's about 12 miles northeast of the Golden Pond Visitor Center.

Center Furnace was built around 1852. It continued to operate until 1912, much longer than any other furnace in the area.

RECREATION

Promoting outdoor recreation is one of the objectives of Land Between the Lakes. Visitors can enjoy hiking, biking, paddling, horseback riding, hunting, fishing, and camping. An area is even specially designated for all-terrain vehicles.

Trails

Land Between the Lakes has 200 miles of scenic roads and 500 miles of hiking trails. Some of these are also open for mountain biking and horseback riding.

The **Fort Henry Trails** are a network of 26 miles of trails near the southern entrance to the park, some of which follow the shoreline of Kentucky Lake. The intricate network of six trails allows hikers to choose anywhere from a three-mile loop to much longer, and they follow General Grant's troop routes from Fort Henry over to Fort Donelson during the Civil War.

Driving south to north along the scenic main road, or Trace, that runs along the middle of the park, you will find the major attractions within Land Between the Lakes.

Access the trails from the south welcome station, or from the Fort Henry Trails parking area, at the end of Fort Henry Road. These trails crisscross the grounds once occupied by the Confederate Fort Henry. They are for bikers and hikers only.

The **North-South Trail** treks the entire length of the Land Between the Lakes. From start to finish, it is 58.6 miles. Three backcountry camping shelters are available along the way for backpackers. The trail crosses the main road in several locations. Portions of the trail are open to horseback riders, and the portion from the Golden Pond Visitor Center to the northern end is also open to mountain bikers.

The 4.5-mile **Honker Lake Loop Trail** begins at the Woodlands Nature Station. This trail is open to hikers only. Sightings of fallow deer and giant Canada geese are common along this trail. The banks of nearby Hematite Lake are littered with bits of blue stone, remnants of slag from the Center Furnace.

Finally, at the northern end of the park are the **Canal Loop Trails,** a network of hike/bike trails that depart from the north welcome station. These trails meander along the shores of both Kentucky Lake and Lake Barkley. The entire loop is 11 miles, but connector trails enable you to fashion a shorter hike or ride (1.5 miles and up) if you want.

A detailed map showing all hiking, biking, and horseback trails can be picked up at any of the park visitors centers. You can rent bikes at Hillman Ferry and Piney Campgrounds.

Off-Highway Vehicles

There are more than 100 miles of trail for off-highway vehicles (OHVs). OHV permits are available for $20 for 3 days and $75 for an annual pass. Note: There are a limited number of annual passes available and they often sell out early in the year. The nontransferable passes may be purchased at any Land Between the Lakes visitors center. Call 270/924-2000 in advance to find out if any of the trails are closed because of bad weather or poor conditions.

Fishing and Boating

Land Between the Lakes offers excellent fishing. The best season for fishing is spring, April-June, when fish move to shallow waters to spawn. Crappie, largemouth bass, and a variety of sunfish may be caught at this time.

Summer and fall offer good fishing, but winter is fair. A fishing license from the state in which you will be fishing is required; these may be purchased from businesses outside the park. Specific size requirements and open dates may be found at any of the visitors centers.

There are 19 different lake access points where you can put in a boat. Canoe rentals are available at the Energy Lake Campground, which is over the border in Kentucky. Energy Lake is a no-wake lake and perfect for paddling and fishing.

Hunting

Controlled hunting is one of the tools that the Forest Service uses to manage populations of wild animals in Land Between the Lakes. Hunting also draws thousands of visitors each year. The annual spring turkey hunt and fall deer hunts are the most popular.

Specific rules govern each hunt, and in many cases hunters must apply in advance for a permit. Hunters must also have a $25 LBL Hunter Use Permit, as well as the applicable state licenses. For details on hunting regulations, call the park at 270/924-2065.

Camping

There are nine campgrounds at Land Between the Lakes. All campgrounds have facilities for tent and trailer camping.

Most campgrounds are open March 1-November 1, but some are open year-round. There's a complicated formula for figuring out the price of campsites, based on which campground it is, the day of the week, and the month of the year. In general, camping costs $10 per night; RV sites range $6-32, depending on whether there is access to electricity, water, and sewer services.

Reservations are accepted for select campsites at Piney, Energy Lake, Hillman Ferry, and Wrangler Campgrounds up to six months in advance. Call the LBL headquarters in Kentucky at 270/924-2000 or visit the website at http://lbl.org to make a reservation. Cravens Bay, Gatlin Point, Fenton, and Turkey Bay are all self-service.

PINEY CAMPGROUND

Located on the southern tip of Land Between the Lakes, **Piney Campground** (621 Fort Henry Rd., Dover, 931/232-5331) is convenient to visitors arriving from the Tennessee side of the park and, as a result, can be one of the most crowded campgrounds in LBL. Piney has more than 300 campsites; 283 have electricity; 44 have electricity, water, and sewer; and 57 are primitive tent sites.

Nine rustic one-bedroom camping shelters have a ceiling fan, table and chairs, electric outlets, and large porch. Sleeping accommodations are one double bed and a bunk bed. Outside there is a picnic table and fire ring. There are no bathrooms; shelter guests use the same bathhouses as other campers. Camp shelters cost $50 per night and sleep up to four people.

Piney's amenities include a camp store, bike rental, archery range, playground, swimming beach, boat ramp, and fishing pier.

ENERGY LAKE CAMPGROUND

Near the midpoint of Land Between the Lakes, **Energy Lake Campground** (5501 Energy Lake Dr., Golden Pond, KY, 270/924-2270) has tent and trailer campsites, electric sites, and group camp facilities. It tends to be less crowded than some of the other campgrounds and has nice lakeside sites, with a swimming area, volleyball, and other kid-friendly activities. The assembly house has a washer and dryer and offers canoe rentals.

Distillery Tours

See how bourbon is made at the Jack Daniel's Distillery.

This region of Tennessee has a history of distilling spirits (both legal and illegal). Rather than roam the hills on your own to find some moonshine, take a tour of one of these distilleries:

- **George Dickel** (1950 Cascade Hollow Rd., Tullahoma, 931/857-4110, www.georgedickel.com, 9am-4:30pm Mon.-Sat., 11:30am-5pm Sun., $10) makes Tennessee whisky (spelled without the "e") and rye. The distillery is on the National Register of Historic Places.

- **Jack Daniel's Distillery** (280 Lynchburg Hwy./Hwy. 55, 931/759-6357, http://jackdaniels.com, 9am-4:30pm daily) is the best-known still in the Volunteer State.

- **Leiper's Fork Distillery** (3381 Southhall Rd., Franklin, 615/465-6456, http://leipersforkdistillery.com, 9:30am-5pm Tues.-Sat., tours offered on the hour 10am-4pm) opened in 2016 and is focused on small-batch whiskey. Arrive 15 minutes prior to your tour start time.

- **Tenn South** (1800 Abernathy Rd., Lynnville, 931/528-0027, http://tennsouthdistillery.com, tours and tastings 9am-5pm Mon.-Sat.) is the maker of Clayton James whiskey, Big Machine Platinum vodka, and All Mighty Shine (high-proof corn spirit).

HILLMAN FERRY CAMPGROUND

Located near the northern end of Land Between the Lakes, **Hillman Ferry Campground** (820 Hillman Ferry Rd., Grand Rivers, KY, 270/924-2181) has 374 tent and RV campsites. It is nestled on the shores of Kentucky Lake, between Moss Creek and Pisgah Bay.

Electric and nonelectric sites are available. There is a dumping station, bathhouses with showers and flush toilets, drinking water, a camp store, swimming area, a disc golf practice basket, coin-operated laundry, and bike rentals.

EXCURSIONS
LAND BETWEEN THE LAKES

Boat and Horse Camping

In addition to the campgrounds already listed, Land Between the Lakes operates five lakeside camping areas that are designed for boaters who want to spend the night. Rushing Creek/Jones Creek is the most developed of these camping areas; it has 40 tent or RV sites and a bathhouse with showers and flush toilets. Other campsites, including Birmingham Ferry/Smith Bay, Cravens Bay, Fenton, and Gatlin Point, have chemical toilets, tent camping sites, and grills.

LBL also oversees **Wrangler's Campground** (5100 Laura Furnace Rd., Golden Pond, KY, 270/924-2201), designed for horseback riders. In addition to tent and RV sites, it has camping shelters and horse stalls. Amenities include a camp store, bathhouses, coin laundry, and playground. Horse day riding permits are required for all horse trailers entering the area ($7 for 1-day, $75 annual)

Backcountry Camping

Backcountry camping is allowed year-round in Land Between the Lakes. All you need is a basic camping permit (formerly called a backcountry permit, $7 for 3 days, $30 annual) and the right gear to enjoy unlimited choices of campsites along the shoreline or in the woodlands.

INFORMATION

The park headquarters is located at the **Golden Pond Visitor Center** (239 Visitor Center Dr., 270/924-2000, 9am-5pm daily). When you arrive, stop at the nearest welcome or visitors center for up-to-date advisories and activity schedules. All of the welcome centers and the visitors center are open 9am-5pm daily.

Friends of Land Between the Lakes (800/455-5897, http://friendsoflbl.org) organizes volunteer opportunities and publishes a detailed tour guide to the park, which includes historical and natural anecdotes.

Background

The Landscape

The Cumberland River winds its way through Nashville, bending and turning through its neighborhoods and skyline. The river and its banks provide Music City with the water for its lush, green open spaces. It's also responsible for some of the traffic congestion, as streets curve along its meanders. Sometimes heading to the next neighborhood requires finding a bridge.

That said, Nashville's location in the Cumberland River basin is part of its appeal. The river gives even Music City's most urban areas a bucolic quality. The neighborhoods are full of hustle and bustle, but it doesn't take much effort to escape when you need some R&R.

GEOGRAPHY

Middle Tennessee is home to Tennessee's capital city, Nashville, and some of its most fertile farmland. Before the Civil War, great plantation mansions dotted the countryside south of Nashville. Today, Tennessee Walking Horse farms, new industries, and the economic success of Nashville continue to make Middle Tennessee prosperous.

Geographically, Middle Tennessee begins with the Cumberland Plateau, which rises to about 2,000 feet above sea level and lies west of East Tennessee's Great Valley. Despite its name, the plateau is not flat; there are a number of steep valleys in the plateau, the largest being the Sequatchie Valley.

The Highland Rim is a region of hills, valleys, and fertile farmland that lies west of the plateau. The largest physical region of Tennessee, the Highland Rim contains 10,650 square miles of land, or almost 25 percent of the state. Almost entirely surrounded by the Highland Rim is the Central Basin, a low, flat, and fertile region in north-central Tennessee. Nashville is located in the Central Basin.

Nashville itself sits at 550 feet above sea level. It is the U.S. city with the second-largest landmass: more than 500 square miles.

CLIMATE

Nashville enjoys a relatively mild climate, with average temperatures ranging from 38°F to 89°F. Summer days can feel very hot, however, and a run of humid 100°F days in August is not unusual. A few flakes of snow may fall in the winter, and the city essentially shuts down when there is any accumulation (average snowfall for the year is 7 inches, but the school closures will suggest much more). Generally, an evening's snowfall has evaporated by midmorning.

The city receives an average of 47 inches of rain per year. Long springs

Previous: attendees camped out at arts and music festival Bonnaroo; the CMA Music Fest, one of Nashville's major annual events.

and falls mean a long season for beautiful flowers, but also a long season for allergy sufferers.

Floods

A devastating flood in Nashville and Middle Tennessee in May 2010 brought the issue of global climate changes, combined with human development and water management, to the forefront of the minds of city planners and residents. The flood caused more than $1.5 billion of damage to the Music City, followed by considerable rebuilding and redevelopment.

History

THE FIRST TENNESSEANS

The first humans settled in what is now Tennessee 12,000-15,000 years ago. Descended from people who crossed into North America during the last ice age, these Paleo-Indians were nomads who hunted large game animals, including mammoth, mastodon, and caribou. Remains of these extinct mammals have been found in West Tennessee, and Native American arrowheads and spear points have been found all over the state. The ice age hunters camped in caves and under rock shelters but remained predominantly nomadic.

About 10,000 years ago, the climate and vegetation of the region changed. The deciduous forest that still covers large parts of the state replaced the evergreen forest of the fading ice age. Large game animals disappeared, and deer and elk arrived, attracted by the forests of hickory, chestnut, and beech. Descendants of the Paleo-Indians gradually abandoned the nomadic lifestyle of their ancestors and established settlements, often near rivers. They hunted deer, bear, and turkey; gathered nuts and wild fruit; and harvested freshwater fish and mussels. They also took a few tentative steps toward cultivation by growing squash and gourds.

This Archaic Period was replaced by the Woodland Period about 3,000 years ago. The Woodland Indians adopted the bow and arrow for hunting and—at the end of their predominance—began cultivating maize and beans as staple crops. Ceramic pottery appeared, and ritualism took on a greater importance in the society. Pinson Mounds, burial mounds near Jackson in West Tennessee, date from this period, as does the misnamed Old Stone Fort near Manchester, believed to have been built and used for ceremonies by the Woodland Indians of the area.

The development of a more complex culture continued, and at about AD 900 the Woodland culture gave way to the Mississippian Period, an era marked by population growth, an increase in trade and warfare, the rise of the chieftain, and cultural accomplishments. The Mississippian era is best known for the impressive large pyramid mounds that were left behind in places such as Etowah and Toqua in Tennessee and Moundville in Alabama. Mississippian Indians also created beautiful ornaments and symbolic objects including combs, pipes, and jewelry.

EUROPEANS ARRIVE

Having conquered Peru, the Spanish nobleman Hernando de Soto embarked on a search for gold in the American southeast in 1539. De Soto's band wandered through Florida, Georgia, and the Carolinas before crossing into what is now Tennessee, probably in June 1540. His exact route is a source of controversy, but historians believe he made his way through parts of East Tennessee before heading back into Georgia.

It was more than 100 years until another European was reported in the Tennessee wilderness, though life for the natives was already changing. De Soto and his men brought firearms and disease, and there was news of other Caucasians living to the east. Disease and warfare led to a decline in population for Tennessee's Native Americans during the presettlement period. As a result, Native American communities formed new tribes with each other: The Creek Confederacy and Choctaws were two such groups. In Tennessee, the Shawnee moved south into the Cumberland River country—land previously claimed as hunting ground by the Chickasaw Nation. Also at this time, a new tribe came over the Smoky Mountains from North Carolina, possibly to escape the encroachment of European settlers, to form what would become the most important Native American group in modern Tennessee: the Overhill Cherokees.

In 1673 European scouts entered Tennessee at its eastern and western ends. Englishmen James Needham and Gabriel Arthur and eight hired Native American guides were the first party to enter East Tennessee. Needham did not last long; he was killed by his Native American guides early in the outing. Arthur won over his traveling companions and joined them on war trips and hunts before returning to Virginia in 1674. Meanwhile, on the western end of the state, French explorers Father Jacques Marquette and Louis Joliet came down the Mississippi River and claimed the surrounding valley for the French.

THE LONG HUNTERS

The first Europeans to carve out a foothold in the unknown frontier of Tennessee were traders who made journeys into Native American territory to hunt and trade. These men disappeared for months at a time into the wilderness and were therefore known as long hunters. They left with European-made goods and returned with animal skins. They led pack trains of horses and donkeys over narrow, steep, and crooked mountain trails and through sometimes hostile territory. It was a lonely, hard life, full of uncertainty. Some of the long hunters were no better than crooks; others were respected by both the Native Americans and Europeans.

The long hunters included men like Elisha Walden, Kasper Mansker, and Abraham Bledsoe. Daniel Boone, born in North Carolina, was in present-day Washington County in northeastern Tennessee when, in 1760, he carved on a beech tree that he had "cilled" a "bar" nearby. Thomas Sharp Spencer became known as Big Foot and is said to have spent the winter in a hollowed-out sycamore tree. Another trader, a Scotch-Irish man named James Adair, traded with the Native Americans for years and eventually wrote *A History of the American Indian* (published in London in 1775), one of the first such accounts.

The animal skins and furs that were the aim of these men's exploits were eventually sold in Charleston and exported to Europe. In 1748 alone, South Carolina merchants exported more than 160,000 skins worth $250,000. The trade was profitable for merchants and, to a lesser extent, the traders themselves. But it was rarely profitable for the Native Americans, and it helped to wipe out much of Tennessee's native animal life.

THE FRENCH AND INDIAN WAR

In 1754 the contest between the French and the British for control of the New World boiled over into war. Native American alliances were seen as critical to success, and so the British set out to win the support of the Cherokee. They did this by agreeing to build a fort in the land over the mountain from North Carolina—territory that came to be known as the Overhill country. The Cherokee wanted the fort to protect their women and children from French or hostile Native American attack while the men were away. The fort was begun in 1756 near the fork of the Little Tennessee and Tellico Rivers, and it was named Fort Loudoun after the commander of British forces in North America. Twelve cannons were transported over the rough mountain terrain by horse to defend the fort from enemy attack.

The construction of Fort Loudoun did not prove to be the glue to hold the Cherokee and British together. In fact, it was not long before relations deteriorated to the point where the Cherokee chief Standing Turkey directed an attack on the fort. A siege ensued. Reinforcements were called for and dispatched, but the British colonel and 1,300 men turned back before reaching the fort. The English inside the fort were weakened by lack of food and surrendered. On August 9, 1760, 180 men, 60 women, and a few children marched out of Fort Loudoun, the first steps of a 140-mile journey to the nearest British fort. The group had been promised to be allowed to retreat peacefully. But on the first night of the journey it was ambushed, and 3 officers, 23 privates, and 3 women were killed. The rest were taken prisoner. The Native Americans said they were inspired to violence upon finding that the British had failed to surrender all of their firepower as promised.

The Cherokees' action was soon avenged. A year later, Col. James Grant led a party into the Lower Cherokee territory, where they destroyed villages, burned homes, and cut down fields of corn.

The French and Indian War ended in 1763, and in the Treaty of Paris the French withdrew any claims to lands east of the Mississippi. This result emboldened European settlers and land speculators who were drawn to the land of the Overhill country. The fact that the land still belonged to the Native Americans did not stop the movement west.

EARLY SETTLERS

With the issue of French possession resolved, settlers began to filter into the Overhill country. Early settlers included William Bean, on the Holston River; Evan Shelby, at Sapling Grove (later Bristol); John Carter, in the Carter Valley; and Jacob Brown, on the Nolichucky River. By 1771 the settlers at Watauga and Nolichucky won a lease from the Cherokee, and the next year they formed the Watauga Association, a quasi government and the first such in Tennessee territory.

The settlers' success in obtaining land concessions from the Native Americans was eclipsed in 1775 when the Transylvania Company, led by Richard Henderson of North Carolina, traded £10,000 of goods for 20 million acres of land in Kentucky and Tennessee. The agreement, negotiated at a treaty conference at Sycamore Shoals, was opposed by the Cherokee chief Dragging Canoe, who warned that the Cherokee were paving the way for their own extinction. Despite his warning, the treaty was signed.

Dragging Canoe remained the leader of the Cherokee's resistance to European settlement. In 1776 he orchestrated assaults on the settlements of Watauga, Nolichucky, Long Island, and Carter's Valley. The offensive, called by some the Cherokee War, had limited success at first, but it ended in defeat for the natives. In 1777 the Cherokee signed a peace treaty with the settlers that ceded more land to the Europeans.

Dragging Canoe and others did not accept the treaty and left the Cherokee as a result. He and his followers moved south, near Chickamauga Creek, where they became known as the Chickamauga tribe. Over time, this tribe attracted other Native Americans whose common purpose was opposition to new settlements.

The Native Americans could not, however, overpower the increasing tide of settlers, who brought superior firepower and greater numbers. Pressure on political leaders to free up more and more land for settlement made relations with the Native Americans and land agreements with them one of the most important features of political life on the frontier.

In the end, these leaders delivered. Europeans obtained Native American land in Tennessee through a series of treaties and purchases, beginning with the Sycamore Shoals purchase in 1775 and continuing until 1818 when the Chickasaw ceded all control to their land west of the Mississippi. Negotiating on behalf of the settlers were leaders including William Blount, the territorial governor, and Andrew Jackson, the first U.S. president from Tennessee.

Nashville itself was settled on Christmas Day in 1796.

NATIVE AMERICAN REMOVAL

Contact with Europeans had a significant impact on the Cherokee way of life. Christian missionaries introduced education, and in the 1820s Sequoyah developed a Cherokee alphabet, allowing the Native Americans to read and write in their own language. The Cherokee adopted some of the Europeans' farming practices, as well as some of their social practices, including slavery. Adoption of the European lifestyle was most common among the significant number of mixed-race Cherokee. In 1827 the Cherokee Nation was established, complete with a constitutional system of government and a capital in New Echota, Georgia. From 1828 until 1832, its newspaper, the *Cherokee Phoenix,* was published in both English and Cherokee.

The census of 1828 counted 15,000 Cherokee remaining in Tennessee. They owned 1,000 slaves, 22,400 head of cattle, 7,600 horses, 1,800 spinning wheels, 700 looms, 12 sawmills, 55 blacksmith shops, and 6 cotton gins.

Despite these beginnings of assimilation, or perhaps because of them, the Cherokee were not welcome to remain in the new territory. Settlers pushed for a strong policy that would lead to the Cherokees' removal, and they looked over the border to Georgia to see that it could be done. There, in 1832, authorities surveyed lands owned by Cherokee and disposed of them by lottery. Laws were passed to prohibit Native American assemblies and bar Native Americans from bringing suit in the state. The majority of Tennessee settlers, as well as Georgia officials, pushed for similar measures to be adopted in Tennessee.

The Cherokee were divided in their response: Some felt that moving west represented the best future for their tribe, while others wanted to stay and fight for their land and the Cherokee Nation. In the end, the Cherokee leaders lost hope of remaining, and on December 29, 1835, they signed the removal treaty. Under the agreement, the Cherokee were paid $5 million for all their lands east of the Mississippi, and they were required to move west within two years. When that time expired in 1838 and only a small number of the Cherokee had moved, the U.S. Army evicted the rest by force.

STATEHOOD

Almost as soon as settlers began living on the Tennessee frontier there were movements to form government. Dissatisfied with the protection offered by North Carolina's distant government, settlers drew up their own governments as early as the 1780s. The Watauga Association and Cumberland Compact were early forms of government. In 1785, settlers in northeastern Tennessee seceded from North Carolina and established the State of Franklin. The experiment was short-lived, but foretold that in the future the lands west of the Smoky Mountains would be their own state.

Before Tennessee could become a state, however, it was a territory of the United States. In 1789 North Carolina ratified its own constitution and in doing so ceded its western lands, the Tennessee country, to the U.S. government. These lands eventually became known as the Southwest Territory, and in 1790 President George Washington appointed William Blount its territorial governor.

Blount was a 41-year-old land speculator and businessman who had campaigned actively for the position. A veteran of the War for Independence, Blount knew Washington and was one of the signers of the U.S. Constitution in 1787.

BACKGROUND HISTORY

At the time of its establishment, the Southwest Territory was 43,000 square miles in area. The population of 35,000 was centered in two main areas: the northeastern corner and the Cumberland settlements near present-day Nashville.

Tennessee's request to become a state was debated in Washington DC, where finally, on June 1, 1796, President Washington signed the statehood bill and Tennessee became the 16th state in the Union.

FRONTIER LIFE

The new state of Tennessee attracted settlers who were drawn by cheap land and the opportunity it represented. Between 1790 and 1800 the state's population tripled, and by 1810 Tennessee's population had grown to 250,000. The expansion caused a shift in power as the middle and western parts of the state became more populated. The capital moved from Knoxville to Nashville in 1812. It was made the permanent capital of the state in 1843.

Life during the early 19th century in Tennessee was largely rural. For the subsistence farmers who made up the majority of the state's population, life was a relentless cycle of hard work. Many families lived in one- or two-room cabins and spent their days growing food and the fibers needed to make their own clothes; raising animals that supplied farm power, meat, and hides; building or repairing buildings and tools; and cutting firewood in prodigious quantities.

Small-hold farmers often owned no slaves. Those who did only owned one or two and worked alongside them.

Children provided valuable labor on the Tennessee farm. Boys often plowed their first furrow at age nine, and girls of that age were expected to mind younger children, help cook, and learn the skills of midwifery, sewing, and gardening. While women's time was often consumed with child rearing, cooking, and sewing, the housewife also worked in the field alongside her husband when she was needed.

EDUCATION AND RELIGION

There were no public schools on the frontier, and the few private schools that existed were not accessible to the farming class. Religious missionaries were often the only people who could read and write in a community, and the first schools were established by churches. Presbyterian, Methodist, and Baptist ministers were the first to reach many settlements in Tennessee.

Settlements were spread out, and few had established churches. As a result, the camp meeting became entrenched in Tennessee culture. The homegrown spirituality of the camp meeting appealed to Tennesseans' independent spirit, which looked suspiciously at official religion and embraced the informal and deeply personal religion of the camp meeting.

The meetings were major events drawing between a few hundred and thousands of people. Camp services were passionate and emotional, reaching a feverish pitch as men and women were overtaken by the spirit.

Many camp meetings attracted both African American and Caucasian
participants.

THE WAR OF 1812

Tennesseans were among the "War Hawks" in Congress who advocated for war with Great Britain in 1812. The conflict was seen by many as an opportunity to rid their borders once and for all of Native Americans. The government asked for 2,800 volunteers, and 30,000 Tennesseans offered to enlist. This is when Tennessee's nickname as the Volunteer State was born.

Nashville lawyer, politician, and businessman Andrew Jackson was chosen as the leader of the Tennessee volunteers. Despite their shortage of supplies and lack of support from the War Department, Jackson's militia prevailed in a series of lopsided victories. Given command of the southern military district, Jackson led U.S. forces at the Battle of New Orleans on January 8, 1815. The ragtag group inflicted a crushing defeat on the British, and despite its having occurred after the signing of the peace treaty with Great Britain, the battle was the victory that launched Jackson onto the road to the presidency.

GROWTH OF SLAVERY

The state's first settlers planted the seed of slavery in Tennessee, and the state's westward expansion cemented the institution. In 1791 there were 3,400 black people in Tennessee—about 10 percent of the general population. By 1810, African Americans constituted more than 20 percent of Tennessee's people. The invention of the cotton gin and subsequent rise of King Cotton after the turn of the 19th century also caused a rapid expansion of slavery.

Slavery was most important in West Tennessee; eastern Tennessee, with its mountainous landscape and small farms, had the fewest slaves. In Middle Tennessee the slave population was concentrated in the Central Basin, in the counties of Davidson, Maury, Rutherford, and Williamson. By 1860, 40 percent of the state's slave population was in West Tennessee, with the greatest concentration in Shelby, Fayette, and Haywood Counties, where cotton was grown on plantations somewhat similar to those of the Deep South.

As slavery grew, slave markets were established in Nashville and Memphis. The ban on the interstate sale of slaves was virtually ignored.

From 1790, when the territory was established, until 1831, Tennessee's slave code was relatively lenient. The law recognized a slave as both a chattel and a person, and slaves were entitled to expect protection against the elements and other people. Owners could free their slaves for any reason, and many did, causing growth in Tennessee's free African American population in the first half of the 1800s. These free African Americans concentrated in eastern and Middle Tennessee, and particularly the cities of Nashville, Memphis, and Knoxville, where they worked as laborers and artisans.

There were vocal opponents to slavery in Tennessee, particularly in the eastern part of the state. The first newspaper in the United States devoted to emancipation was established in 1819 in Jonesborough by Elihu Embree. Charles Osborne, a Quaker minister, preached against slavery shortly after the turn of the 19th century in Tennessee. Emancipationists formed societies in counties including Washington, Sullivan, Blount, Grainger, and Cocke. Many of these early abolitionists opposed slavery on religious grounds, arguing that it was incompatible with the spirit of Christianity.

These abolitionists often argued for the gradual end of slavery and sometimes advocated for the removal of freed slaves to Africa.

SLAVE EXPERIENCES

There was no single slave experience for Tennessee's slaves. On the farm, a slave's experience depended on the size of the farm, the type of crops that were grown, and the number of slaves on the farm.

Most Tennessee slaves lived on small- or medium-sized farms. The 1860 census showed that only one person in the state owned more than 300 slaves, and 47 owned more than 100. More than 75 percent of all slave owners had fewer than 10 slaves. Work assignments varied, but almost all slaves were expected to contribute to their own subsistence by keeping a vegetable garden. Slaves with special skills in areas like carpentry, masonry, blacksmithing, or weaving were hired out.

Urban slaves were domestics, coachmen, house painters, launderers, and midwives. In cities, many families owned just one or two slaves, and it was common for slaves to be hired out to others in order to provide a source of income for the slave owner. It became customary in some cities for a market day to be held on New Year's Day, when employers bargained for slave labor over the coming year.

Slaves sought to overcome their circumstances by building close-knit communities. These communities acted as surrogate families for slaves whose own spouse, parents, siblings, and children were often sold, causing lifelong separation.

Religion also served as a survival mechanism for Tennessee's slaves. Methodist and Baptist churches opened their doors to slaves, providing a space where slaves could be together. The musical tradition that resulted is today's gospel music. Religion also provided a vehicle for some slaves to learn how to read and write.

THE CIVIL WAR

In the 1830s, Tennessee's position on slavery hardened. The Virginia slave uprising led by Nat Turner frightened owners, who instituted patrols to search for runaway slaves and tightened codes on slave conduct. In 1834, the state constitution was amended to bar free African Americans from voting, a sign of Caucasians' increasing fear of the African American people living in their midst.

The division between East and West Tennessee widened as many in the east were sympathetic with the antislavery forces that were growing in Northern states. In the west, the support for slavery was unrelenting.

Despite several strident secessionists, including Tennessee governor Isham Harris, Tennessee remained uncertain about separating from the United States. In February 1861, the state voted against a convention on secession. But with the attack on Fort Sumter two months later, followed by President Abraham Lincoln's call for volunteers to apply force to bring the seceded states back to the Union, public opinion shifted. On June 8, 1861, Tennesseans voted 105,000 to 47,000 to secede.

A Border State

Tennessee was of great strategic importance during the Civil War. It sent an estimated 186,000 men to fight for the Confederacy, more than any other state. Another 31,000 are credited with having joined the Union army.

Tennessee had resources that both the Union and Confederacy deemed important for victory, including agricultural and manufacturing industries, railroads, and rivers. And its geographic position as a long-border state made it nearly unavoidable.

Tennessee Battles

Some 454 battles and skirmishes were fought in Tennessee during the war. Most were small, but several key battles took place on Tennessee soil.

The first of these was the Union victory at Forts Henry and Donelson in January 1862. Gen. Ulysses S. Grant and 15,000 Union troops steamed up the Tennessee River and quickly captured Fort Henry. They then marched overland to Fort Donelson, and 10 days later, this Confederate fort fell as well. The battle of Fort Donelson is where "U. S. Grant" (or "Unconditional Surrender" Grant) earned this sobriquet: He was asked by the Confederate general the terms of capitulation, and he replied, "unconditional surrender."

The Battle of Shiloh was the bloodiest and largest to take place in Tennessee. The battle happened near Pittsburgh Landing (the Federal name for the struggle), on the Mississippi River about 20 miles north of the Mississippi state line. More than 100,000 men took part in this battle, and there were more than 24,000 casualties.

The battle began with a surprise Confederate attack at dawn on April 6, 1862, a Sunday. For several hours, victory seemed within reach for the Southern troops, but the Union rallied and held. They built a strong defensive line covering Pittsburgh Landing, and on April 7 they took the offensive and swept the Confederates from the field. The Confederates' loss was devastating, and Shiloh represented a harbinger of the future bloodletting between Blue and Gray.

Another important Tennessee battle was at Stones River, near Murfreesboro, on December 31, 1862. Like at Shiloh, the early momentum here was with the Confederates, but victory belonged to the Union. The Battle of Chickamauga Creek, fought a few miles over the state line in

Georgia, was a rare Confederate victory. It did not come cheaply, however, with 21,000 members of the Army of Tennessee killed.

Federal forces retreated and dug in near Chattanooga, while Confederates occupied the heights above the town. Union reinforcements led by General Grant drove the Confederates back into Georgia at the Battle of Lookout Mountain, also known as the "Battle Above the Clouds," on November 25, 1863.

Wartime Occupation

Battles were only part of the wartime experience in Tennessee. The Civil War caused hardship for ordinary residents on a scale that many had never before seen. There was famine and poverty. Schools and churches were closed. Harassment and recrimination plagued the state, and fear was widespread.

In February 1863, one observer described the population of Memphis as "11,000 original whites, 5,000 slaves, and 19,000 newcomers of all kinds, including traders, fugitives, hangers-on, and negroes."

Memphis fell to the Union on June 6, 1862, and it was occupied for the remainder of the war. The city's experience during this wartime occupation reversed decades of growth and left it struggling for years.

Those who could fled the city. Many of those who remained stopped doing business (some of these because they refused to pledge allegiance to the Union and were not permitted). Northern traders entered the city and took over many industries, while African Americans who abandoned nearby plantations flooded into it.

As the military focused on punishing Confederate sympathizers, conditions in Memphis deteriorated. Crime and disorder abounded, and guerrilla bands developed to fight the Union occupation. The Federal commander responsible for the city was Maj. Gen. William T. Sherman, and he adopted a policy of collective responsibility, which held civilians responsible for guerrilla attacks in their neighborhoods. Sherman destroyed hundreds of homes, farms, and towns in the exercise of this policy.

The war was equally damaging in other parts of Tennessee. In Middle Tennessee, retreating Confederate soldiers after the fall of Fort Donelson demolished railroads and burned bridges so as not to leave them for the Union. Union troops also destroyed and appropriated the region's resources. Federals took horses, pigs, cows, corn, hay, cotton, fence rails, firearms, and tools. Sometimes this was carried out through official requisitions, but at other times it amounted to little more than pillaging.

Criminals took advantage of the loss of public order, and bands of thieves and bandits began roaming the countryside.

The experience in East Tennessee was different. Because of the region's widespread Union sympathies, it was the Confederacy that first occupied the eastern territory. During this time hundreds of alleged Unionists were charged with treason and jailed. When the Confederates began conscripting men into military service in 1862, tensions in East Tennessee grew.

Many East Tennesseans fled to Kentucky, and distrust, bitterness, and violence escalated. In September 1863 the tables turned, however, and the Confederates were replaced by the Federals, whose victories elsewhere enabled them to focus then on occupying friendly East Tennessee.

The Effects of the War

Tennessee lost most of a generation of young men to the Civil War. Infrastructure was destroyed, and thousands of farms, homes, and other properties were razed. The state's reputation on the national stage had been tarnished, and it would be decades until Tennessee had the political power that it had enjoyed during the Age of Jackson. But while the war caused tremendous hardships for the state, it also led to the freeing of 275,000 African American Tennesseans from slavery.

RECONSTRUCTION

Tennessee was no less divided during the years following the Civil War than it was during the conflict. The end to the war ushered in a period where former Unionists—now allied with the Radical Republicans in Congress—disenfranchised and otherwise marginalized former Confederates and others who had been sympathetic with the Southern cause.

They also pushed through laws that extended voting and other rights to the newly freed African Americans, changes that led to a powerful backlash and the establishment of such shadowy groups as the Ku Klux Klan.

The greatest legacy of the Civil War was the emancipation of Tennessee's slaves. Following the war, many freed African Americans left the countryside and moved to cities, including Memphis, Nashville, Chattanooga, and Knoxville, where they worked as skilled laborers, domestics, and more. Other African Americans remained in the countryside, working as wage laborers on farms or sharecropping in exchange for occupancy on part of a former large-scale plantation.

The Freedmen's Bureau worked in Tennessee for a short period after the end of the war, and it succeeded in establishing schools for African Americans. During this period the state's first African American colleges were established: Fisk, Tennessee Central, LeMoyne, Roger Williams, Lane, and Knoxville.

As in other states, African Americans in Tennessee enjoyed short-lived political power during Reconstruction. The right to vote and the concentration of African Americans in certain urban areas paved the way for African Americans to be elected to the Tennessee House of Representatives, beginning with Sampson Keeble of Nashville in 1872. In all, 13 African Americans were elected as representatives between 1872 and 1887, including James C. Napier, Edward Shaw, and William Yardley, who also ran for governor.

Initially, these pioneers met mild acceptance from Caucasians, but as time progressed Caucasians became uncomfortable sharing political power with African Americans. By the 1890s, racist Jim Crow policies of segregation, poll taxes, secret ballots, literacy tests, and intimidation prevented African Americans from holding elected office—and in many cases, voting—in Tennessee again until after the civil rights movement of the 1960s.

The Republican Party saw the end of its influence with the end of the Brownlow governorship. Democrats rejected the divisive policies of the Radical Republicans, who sought to protect the racial order that set African Americans at a disadvantage to Caucasians, and were less concerned about the state's mounting debt than the Republicans.

ECONOMIC RECOVERY

The social and political upheaval caused by the Civil War was matched or exceeded by the economic catastrophe that it represented for the state. Farms and industry were damaged or destroyed, public infrastructure was razed, schools were closed, and the system of slavery that underpinned most of the state's economy was gone. During this period Nashville flourished, as the city grew to become an essential business hub. The Nashville population skyrocketed from less than 17,000 in 1860 to more than 80,000 just 40 years later. In Nashville, new distilleries, sawmills, paper mills, stove factories, and an oil refinery led the way to industrialization.

The economic setback was seen as an opportunity by proponents of the "New South," who advocated for an industrial and economic revival that would catapult the South to prosperity impossible under the agrarian and slavery-based antebellum economy. The New South movement was personified by carpetbagging Northern capitalists who moved to Tennessee and set up industries that would benefit from cheap labor and abundant natural resources. Many Tennesseans welcomed these newcomers and advocated for their fellow Tennesseans to put aside regional differences and also welcome the Northern investors. Mines were opened in Cleveland, flour mills in Jackson, and textile factories in Tullahoma and other parts of the state.

WORLD WAR I

True to its nickname, Tennessee sent a large number of volunteer troops to fight in World War I. Most became part of the 30th "Old Hickory" Division, which entered the war on August 17, 1918. The most famous Tennessee veteran of World War I was Alvin C. York, a farm boy from the Cumberland Mountains who staged a one-man offensive against the German army after becoming separated from his own detachment. Reports say that York killed 20 German soldiers and persuaded 131 more to surrender.

WOMEN'S SUFFRAGE

The movement for women's suffrage had been established in Tennessee prior to the turn of the 20th century, and it gained influence as the century progressed. The Southern Woman Suffrage Conference was held in Memphis in 1906, and a statewide suffrage organization was established. State bills to give women the right to vote failed in 1913 and 1917, but support was gradually growing. In the summer of 1920, the 19th Amendment had been ratified by 35 states, and one more ratification was needed to make it law. Tennessee was one of five states yet to vote on the measure, and on August 9, Governor Roberts called a special sitting of the legislature to consider the amendment.

Furious campaigning and public debate led up to the special sitting. The Senate easily ratified the amendment 25 to 4, but in the House of Representatives the vote was much closer: 49 to 47. Governor Roberts certified the result and notified the secretary of state: Tennessee had cast the deciding vote for women's suffrage. A sculpture of four of the women who worked hardest to make this power a reality stands in the center of Centennial Park, erected in 2016 and designed by local artist Alan LeQuire.

THE DEPRESSION

The progress and hope of the 1920s were soon forgotten with the Great Depression. Tennessee's economic hard times started before the 1929 stock market crash. Farming in the state was hobbled by low prices and low returns during the 1920s. Farmers and laborers displaced by this trend sought work in new industries like the DuPont plant in Old Hickory, Eastman-Kodak in Kingsport, or the Aluminum Company of America in Blount County. But others, including many African Americans, left Tennessee for northern cities such as Chicago.

The Depression made bad things worse. Farmers tried to survive, turning to subsistence farming. In cities, unemployed workers lined up for relief. Major bank failures in 1930 brought most financial business in the state to a halt.

President Roosevelt's New Deal provided some relief for Tennesseans. The Civilian Conservation Corps (CCC), Public Works Administration (PWA), and Civil Works Administration (CWA) were established in Tennessee. Through the CCC, more than 7,000 Tennesseans planted millions of pine seedlings, developed parks, and built fire towers. Through the PWA, more than 500 projects were undertaken, including bridges, housing, water systems, and roads. Hundreds of Tennesseans were employed by the CWA to clean public buildings, landscape roads, and do other work.

But no New Deal institution had more impact on Tennessee than the Tennessee Valley Authority (TVA). Architects of TVA saw it as a way to improve agriculture along the Tennessee River, alleviate poverty, and produce electrical power. The dam system would also improve navigation along what was then an often dangerous river. The law establishing TVA was introduced by Sen. George W. Norris of Nebraska and passed in 1933. Soon after, dams were under construction, and trade on the river increased because of improved navigability. Even more importantly, electric power was now so cheap that even Tennesseans in remote parts of the state could afford it. By 1945, TVA was the largest electrical utility in the nation, and new industries were attracted by cheap energy and improved transportation. Tourists also came to enjoy the so-called Great Lakes of the South.

BACKGROUND HISTORY

WORLD WAR II

Tennessee, like the rest of the country, was changed by World War II. The war effort transformed the state's economy and led to a migration to the cities unprecedented in Tennessee's history. The tiny mountain town of Oak Ridge became the state's fifth-largest city almost overnight when it became a production site for the Manhattan Project. The city, nicknamed "Atomic City," became nearly synonymous with the atomic bomb that was dropped on Hiroshima at the final stage of the war.

More than 300,000 Tennesseans served in World War II, and just under 6,000 died. During the war, Camps Forrest, Campbell, and Tyson served as prisoner of war camps. Several hundred war refugees settled in Tennessee, many in the Nashville area.

POSTWAR TENNESSEE

Tennessee's industrialization continued after the war. By 1960 there were more city dwellers than rural dwellers in the state, and Tennessee was ranked the 16th most industrialized state in the United States. Industry that had developed during the war transformed to peacetime operation.

Ex-servicemen were not content with the political machines that had controlled Tennessee politics for decades. In 1948 Congressman Estes Kefauver won a U.S. Senate seat, defeating the candidate chosen by Memphis mayor Ed Crump. The defeat signaled an end to Crump's substantial influence in statewide elections. In 1953 Tennessee repealed the state poll tax, again limiting politicians' ability to manipulate the vote. The tide of change also swept in Sen. Albert Gore Sr. and Gov. Frank Clement in 1952. Kefauver, Gore, and Clement were moderate Democrats of the New South.

CIVIL RIGHTS IN TENNESSEE

The Nashville lunch counter sit-ins of 1960 were an important milestone in both the local and national civil rights movements. Led by students from the city's African American universities, the sit-ins eventually forced an end to racial segregation of the city's public services. Over two months, hundreds of African American students were arrested for sitting at Caucasian-only downtown lunch counters. African American consumers' boycott of downtown stores put additional pressure on the business community. On April 19, thousands of protesters marched in silence to the courthouse to confront city officials, and the next day Rev. Martin Luther King Jr. addressed Fisk University. On May 10, 1960, several downtown stores integrated their lunch counters, and Nashville became the first major city in the South to begin desegregating its public facilities.

MODERN TENNESSEE

The industrialization that began during World War II has continued in modern-day Tennessee. In 1980 Nissan built what was then the largest truck assembly plant in the world at Smyrna, Tennessee. In 1987 Saturn Corporation chose Spring Hill as the site for its $2.1 billion automobile plant.

Nashville Sit-ins

Greensboro, North Carolina, is often considered the site of the first sit-ins of the American civil rights movement. But in truth, activists in Nashville carried out the first "test" sit-ins in late 1959. In these test cases, protesters left the facilities after being refused service and talking to management about the injustice of segregation. In between these test sit-ins and the moment when Nashville activists would launch a full-scale sit-in campaign, students in Greensboro took that famous first step.

The Nashville sit-ins began on February 13, 1960, when a group of African American students from local colleges and universities sat at a downtown lunch counter and refused to move until they were served. The protesting students endured verbal and physical abuse and were arrested.

Community members raised money for the students' bail, and African American residents of the city began an economic boycott of downtown stores that practiced segregation. On April 19, the home of Z. Alexander Looby, an African American lawyer who was representing the students, was bombed. Later the same day, students led a spontaneous, peaceful, and silent march through the streets of downtown Nashville to the courthouse. Diane Nash, a student leader, asked Nashville mayor Ben West if he thought it was morally right for a restaurant to refuse to serve someone based on the color of his or her skin, Mayor West said, "No."

The march was an important turning point for the city. The combined effect of the sit-ins, the boycott, and the march caused, in 1960, Nashville to be the first major Southern city to experience widespread desegregation of its public facilities. The events also demonstrated to activists in other parts of the South that nonviolence was an effective tool of protest.

The story of the young people who led the Nashville sit-ins is told in the book *The Children* by David Halberstam. In 2001, Nashville resident Bill King was so moved by the story of the protests that he established an endowment to raise funds for a permanent civil rights collection at the Nashville Public Library. In 2003, the Civil Rights Room at the Nashville Public Library was opened. It houses books, oral histories, audiovisual records, microfilm, dissertations, and stunning photographs of the events of 1960 and is one of the must-visit city sights. The words of one student organizer, John Lewis, who went on to become a congressman from Georgia, are displayed over the entryway: "If not us, then who; if not now, then when?"

At the same time, however, the state's older industries—including textiles and manufacturing—have suffered losses over the past three decades, in part because of the movement of industry outside of the United States.

During the 1950s and beyond, Tennessee developed a reputation as a hotbed of musical talent. The Grand Ole Opry in Nashville was representative of a second musical genre that came to call Tennessee home—country music. Country legend Roy Acuff helped put the city and its music scene on the map. He founded one of the city's first music publishing companies and later ran for governor of the state.

Nashville is still home to North America's largest-volume vinyl pressing plant. This, literally, is where the music is made.

GOVERNMENT

Tennessee is governed by its constitution, unchanged since 1870 when it was revised in light of emancipation, the Civil War, and Reconstruction.

Tennessee has a governor who is elected to four-year terms, a legislature, and a court system. The lieutenant governor is not elected statewide; he or she is chosen by the Senate and also serves as its speaker.

The legislature, or General Assembly, is made up of the 99-member House of Representatives and the 33-member Senate. The Tennessee State Supreme Court is made up of five justices, with no two from the same Grand Division. The Supreme Court chooses the state's attorney general.

The executive branch consists of 22 cabinet-level departments, which employ 43,500 state workers. Departments are led by a commissioner who is appointed by the governor and serves as a member of his or her cabinet.

Tennessee has 95 counties; the largest is Shelby County, which includes Memphis. The smallest county by size is Trousdale, with 114 square miles; the smallest population is in Pickett County.

The state has 11 electoral college votes in U.S. presidential elections.

Modern Politics

Like other Southern states, Tennessee has seen a gradual shift to the political right since the 1960s. The shift began in 1966 with Howard Baker's election to the U.S. Senate, and it continued with Tennessee's support for Republican presidential candidate Richard Nixon in 1968 and 1972. Despite a few exceptions, the shift has continued into the 21st century, although Nashville, Memphis, and other parts of Middle and West Tennessee remain Democratic territory.

East Tennessee holds the distinction as one of a handful of Southern territories that has consistently supported the Republican Party since the Civil War. Today, Republicans outpoll Democrats in this region by as much as three to one.

The statewide trend toward the Republican Party continued in 2008, with Tennessee being one of only a handful of states where Democrat Barack Obama received a lesser proportion of votes than did Senator John Kerry four years earlier. State Republicans also succeeded in gaining control of both houses of the state legislature. The general shift to the right has continued in the governor's office. Previous governor Phil Bredesen is a Democrat, but he was succeeded by Republican Bill Haslam. Since 1967, no party has been able to keep the governor's seat for more than two terms, but term limits prevent incumbents from staying in office for more than two terms.

Andrew Jackson may still be the most prominent Tennessean in American political history, but Tennessee politicians continue to play a role on the national stage. Albert Gore Jr., elected to the U.S. House of Representatives in 1976, served as vice president under President Bill Clinton from 1992 until 2000, and he lost the highly contested 2000 presidential contest to George W. Bush. Gore famously lost his home state to Bush, further evidence of Tennessee's move to the right. Gore went on to champion global climate change and win the Nobel Peace Prize, and he is often seen around Nashville.

Lamar Alexander, a former governor of Tennessee, was appointed secretary of education by the first President Bush in 1990. Alexander—famous for his flannel shirts—ran unsuccessfully for president and was later elected senator from Tennessee. Bill Frist, a doctor, was also elected senator and rose to be the Republican majority leader during the presidency of George W. Bush, before quitting politics for medical philanthropy.

The most recent Tennessean to seek the Oval Office was former senator and *Law and Order* star Fred Thompson, from Lewisburg in Middle Tennessee. Thompson passed away in 2015.

One of the most persistent political issues for Tennesseans in modern times has been the state's tax structure. The state first established a 2 percent sales tax in 1947, and it was increased incrementally over the years, eventually reaching 7 percent in 2013. With local/city takes on top of that, it is one of the highest sales tax rates in the country, ringing in at 9.25 percent in Nashville. (The state sales tax on food is 5.5 percent.) At the same time, the state has failed on more than one occasion—most recently with a state constitutional amendment in 2014—to establish an income tax that would provide greater stability to the state's revenues.

Like much of the country, in 2008 Tennessee faced a serious budget crunch that led to the elimination of thousands of state jobs, cutbacks at state-funded universities, and the scaling back of the state health insurance program.

Nashville and Davidson County have a consolidated government, and half a century ago were the first municipalities to choose this government structure. The system, which celebrated its 50th anniversary in 2013, is often thought of as being more efficient and reducing redundancy. In September 2015 the consolidated government elected its first female mayor, Megan Barry.

ECONOMY

Tennessee has the 18th-largest economy in the United States. Important industries include health care, education, farming, electrical power, and tourism. In the past few years, most job growth has been recorded in the areas of leisure, hospitality, education, and health care. Manufacturing, mining, and construction jobs have declined, but auto- and auto-park manufacturing have increased in recent years.

Tennessee's unemployment rate fluctuates, but in recent years has been below the national average. In 2017, the jobless rate was about 3.4 percent.

Per 2015 statistics, about 18.3 percent of Tennessee families live in poverty, the state ranking 45th out of 50. The median household income in 2015 was $47,275.

All of Tennessee's cities have poverty rates higher than the state or national average. The percentage of Memphis families living below the poverty level is the state's highest: 27.6 percent of Memphis families are poor. The U.S. Census calls Memphis one of the poorest cities in the nation. Knoxville's family poverty rate is 25.7 percent.

Agriculture

Farming accounts for 10.4 percent, or $50.4 billion, of the Tennessee economy. More than 42 percent of the state's land is used in farming; 63.6 percent of this is cropland.

Soybeans, tobacco, corn, and hay are among Tennessee's most important agricultural crops. Cattle and calf production, chicken farming, and cotton cultivation are also important parts of the farm economy.

Greene County, in northeastern Tennessee, is the leading county for all types of cow farming; Giles and Lincoln Counties, in the south-central part of the state, rank second and third. The leading cotton producer is Haywood County, followed by Crockett and Gibson, all three of which are located in West Tennessee. Other counties where agriculture figures largely into the economy are Obion, Dyer, Rutherford, and Robertson.

Tennessee ranks sixth among U.S. states for equine production, and walking or quarter horses account for more than half of the state's estimated 210,000 head of equine. The state ranks sixth for tomatoes, fourth for tobacco, and sixth for cotton.

Some farmers have begun converting to corn production in anticipation of a biofuel boom.

Tourism

According to the state tourism department, the industry generated $19 billion in economic activity in 2016. More than 175,000 Tennessee jobs are linked to tourism. The state credits the industry with generating more than $1.6 billion in state and local tax revenue.

In addition to tourism, people typically assume that music is job number one in Nashville. It is true that the music industry is important to the city, but health care, real estate, and education are bigger industries in Music City.

DEMOGRAPHICS

Nashville's population as of 2016 was 684,410 people, according to the U.S. Census. When you look at the entire 13-county metropolitan area, the population is more than 1.8 million. An oft-cited statistic is that the population of the greater Nashville area will increase by an additional 1 million people by the year 2020. Approximately 78 percent of Tennesseans are Caucasian, 17 percent are African American, and 5 percent are Latino or Hispanic. Nashville's foreign-born population tripled during the decade between 1990 and 2000, and 11 percent of the city's population was born outside of the United States. This includes large populations from Mexico, Vietnam, Laos, and Somalia. Nashville is also home to more than 11,000

Famous Nashvillians

Since its earliest days, Nashville's siren song has attracted those who wanted to see (or more likely, hear) their name in lights. The wannabe famous come here to get their break, and they stay here because, for the most part, it is an easy place to be famous. Über-stars like Keith Urban and Nicole Kidman can shop at Whole Foods and take their kids to the library without being harassed by paparazzi.

- Tons of the music industry's elite call Nashville (or more often than not, suburban Leiper's Fork and Franklin) home. In addition to Keith Urban, Taylor Swift, Brad Paisley, Robert Plant, Ben Folds, members of The Black Keys and the Kings of Leon, Jack White and Peter Frampton live here at least part of the year.

- But it isn't just the musicians who can be seen around town. Since the TV drama *Nashville* started airing in 2012, its actors could be seen here, too, including Connie Britton. Finance guru Dave Ramsey's office is located in suburban Brentwood. Travis Stork, of *The Bachelor* and *The Doctors* fame, is often sighted in the 12 South neighborhood. Another famous-for-being-on-*The Bachelor* couple, Carly Waddell and Evan Bass, live in Brentwood.

- Al Gore Jr., though born in Washington DC and raised in Carthage, Tennessee, is closely associated with Nashville. After the Vietnam War he attended Vanderbilt University for one year and then spent five years as a reporter for *The Tennessean*. The former U.S. vice president has had a home in Nashville for many decades and is frequently seen around town.

- Remember that celebrities like to live in Nashville because they get a chance to be "normal." Use discretion when asking for autographs or taking photos. Most importantly, don't overlook seeing the next soon-to-be-star by searching only for the big-name celebs.

Iraqi Kurds. Nashville surpassed Memphis in population to become the state's largest city in 2016.

RELIGION

Nashville is part of the U.S. Bible Belt; conservative Christian faith is both prevalent and prominent all over the state. Of Nashvillians 58 percent call themselves Christians, and 27 percent identify as Baptist. Nashville is the headquarters of the Southern Baptist Convention, the National Baptist Convention, and the United Methodist Church. The city has growing populations that practice Judaism and Islam.

One practical effect of Tennessee's Christian bent is that wine and spirits are not sold on Sunday in stores, but can be served in restaurants and bars. Beer can be purchased on Sundays in grocery stores, convenience stores, and gas stations from noon to midnight.

LANGUAGE

Nashvillians speak English, of a kind. Many have a Tennessee drawl, though with so many transplants from across the world, there's not really a Music City accent.

Speech patterns have been documented throughout the state, outlined by Michael Montgomery of the University of South Carolina in the *Tennessee Encyclopedia of History and Culture.* Montgomery writes that Tennesseans tend to pronounce vowels in the words *pen* and *hem* as *pin* and *him;* they shift the accent to the beginning of words, so *Tennessee* becomes *TIN-isee;* they clip or reduce the vowel in words like *ride* so it sounds more like *rad;* and vowels in other words are stretched, so that a single-syllable word like *bed* becomes *bay-ud.*

Local speech patterns are not limited to word pronunciation. Tennesseans also tend to speak with folksy and down-home language. Speakers often use colorful metaphors, and greater value is placed on the quality of expression rather than the perfection of grammar.

Essentials

Getting There

Thanks to a friendly, accessible airport, easy access to several interstates, reliable bus services, and a plethora of rental cars, getting to Music City shouldn't be a hassle (although no guarantees about the traffic once you arrive).

Many visitors to Nashville drive their own cars. The highways are good, distances are manageable, and many, if not most, destinations in the city and surrounding area are not accessible by public transportation.

If you're coming to Nashville for a weekend getaway or a conference and staying downtown or in Music Valley, you may be able to manage without a car. Many of the major attractions are within walking distance of downtown, and a majority of Music Valley hotels have shuttles. But the lack of wheels will limit your ability to visit attractions outside the main tourist areas. If you will have significant time outside your conference room, consider bringing or renting a car or budget for your taxi tab or use a ride-hailing app like Uber or Lyft.

AIR

The **Nashville International Airport** (BNA, http://flynashville.com) brings back some of the pleasure to air travel. Despite shuttling 12 million passengers annually, it is easy to navigate, affordable to park at, and only overwhelmingly crowded during big events like CMA Music Festival. BNA offers email updates that tell travelers when to expect congestion, so they can plan accordingly. BNA is about nine miles east of downtown, a 20-minute drive in average traffic.

The four-runway airport is filled with local art and live music and comfortable waiting areas for those picking up inbound passengers. There's even a health clinic for routine medical care.

At the Nashville International Airport, you can exchange currency at **SunTrust Bank** (615/275-0236) near A/B concourse or at the **Business Service Center** (Wright Travel, 615/275-2658) near C/D concourse.

Many of the major hotels offer shuttles from the airport; a kiosk on the lower level of the terminal can help you find the right one.

BNA was the first airport in the United States to include "transportation network companies" such as Lyft and Uber in their plans. A designated ride-hailing area is on the ground floor where hotel shuttles wait.

Taxis are also a feasible option for ground transport from BNA. Rates start at $7 plus $2.10 per mile. To downtown or Opryland, the flat rate is $25.

Previous: the *General Jackson* showboat; Leiper's Fork Distillery, producer of small-batch spirits.

BUS

Greyhound (709 5th Ave. S., 615/255-3556, www.greyhound.com) fully serves Music City, with daily routes that crisscross the state in nearly every direction. The environmentally friendly depot has parking for those awaiting passengers, a restaurant, a vending machine area, and ample space for buses coming and going. Service goes to major cities in most directions, including Atlanta, Chattanooga, Memphis, and Louisville.

Budget-friendly **Megabus** (http://us.megabus.com) also leaves from the same station. Megabus boasts free Wi-Fi on board and, perhaps because of that, attracts a younger clientele.

CAR

If you don't bring your own car, a dozen different major rental agencies have a fleet of cars, trucks, and SUVs at the airport. Agencies include **Alamo** (844/370-2402, www.alamo.com), **Avis** (615/361-1212, www.avis.com), and **Hertz** (615/275-2600, www.hertz.com). For the best rates, use an online travel search tool, such as **Expedia** (www.expedia.com), **Kayak** (www.kayak.com), or **Travelocity** (www.travelocity.com), and book the car early, along with your airline tickets.

Getting Around

DRIVING

A reliable road map or GPS is essential for exploring Nashville by car. The city is only vaguely laid out on a grid, and even then, the numeric grid is a suggestion, rather than the rule. Roads frequently change names and merge into other roads (even numbered streets that seem like they ought to be parallel do this). Locals know this and are more than willing to give directions, but they often do so using landmarks ("Turn left where the Shoney's used to be") rather than street names.

The interstates are a little easier to navigate than side streets. I-65 and I-24 create a tight inner beltway that encircles the heart of the city. I-440 is an outer beltway that circles the southern half of the city, while I-40 runs horizontally, from east to west. Briley Parkway, shown on some maps as TN 155, is a highway that circles the north and east perimeters of the city.

City residents use the interstates not just for long journeys but for short crosstown jaunts as well. Most businesses give directions according to the closest interstate exit.

Non-interstate thoroughfares emanate out from Nashville like spokes in a wheel. Many are named for the communities that they eventually run into. Murfreesboro Pike runs southeast from the city; Hillsboro Pike (Rte. 431) starts out as 21st Avenue South and takes you to Hillsboro Village and Green Hills and eventually to Leiper's Fork. Broadway becomes West End Avenue and takes you directly to Belle Meade and, eventually, The Loveless

Cafe. It does not take long to realize that roads in Nashville have a bad habit of changing names all of a sudden, so be prepared and check the map to avoid getting too confused.

For real-time traffic advisories and road construction closures, dial 511 or go to www.tn511.com.

PARKING

Metered parking is available on most downtown streets, but some have prohibited-parking signs effective during morning and afternoon rush hours. Always read the fine print carefully.

There is plenty of off-street parking in lots and garages. Expect to pay about $22 a day for garage parking. **Park It! Downtown** (www.parkitdown-town.com) is a great resource for finding downtown parking deals, plus information about the **Music City Circuit,** a free downtown shuttle operated by the MTA. The Metro Courthouse Garage and the Public Library Garage typically have discounted rates at night and on weekends.

TRAFFIC REPORTS

Nashville traffic is among the worst in the nation, and the city's growing population has only made it worse. For current traffic and road reports, including weather-related closures, construction closures, and traffic jams, dial 511 from any mobile or landline. You can also check online at www.tn511.com.

TAXIS

Licensed taxicabs will have an orange driver permit, usually displayed on the visor or dashboard.

Several reliable cab companies are **Allied Cab/Nashville Cab** (615/333-3333, www.nashvillecab.com), **Checker Cab** (615/256-7000, http://nashvillecheckercab.com), **American Music City Taxi Inc.** (615/865-4100, www.musiccitycab.com), and **United Cab** (615/228-6969, www.unitedcabnashville.com). Taxi rates are $2.10 per mile.

If cruising around in a stretch limo is more your style, call **Basic Black Limo** (615/430-8157, www.basicblacklimo.com). The rate is $125 per hour on Saturday nights; the limo seats up to 14 passengers.

Ride-hailing companies, including **Lyft** and **Uber,** are popular in Nashville. Download their apps to find a local to drive you to your destination. **Joyride Nashville** (615/285-9835, http://joyrideus.com/nashville) offers licensed rides around downtown in a golf cart for a pay-what-you-wish model. Many of the drivers are happy to provide recommendations and tours as well as transportation.

PUBLIC TRANSPORTATION

Nashville's **Metropolitan Transit Authority** (www.nashvillemta.org) operates city buses. Pick up a map and schedule from either of the two downtown visitors centers or online.

Improvements to the city's public transport system have made it easier to use, but few tourists ride the buses because they can be difficult to understand if you're new to the city. One favorite is the **Music City Circuit,** a free bus that runs between downtown and The Gulch. These Blue and Green Circuit buses stop at 75 different spots on two different routes. One other bus route that is helpful, however, is the **Opry Mills Express** that travels from downtown Nashville to Music Valley, home of the Grand Ole Opry, Gaylord Opryland Resort, and Opry Mills, the shopping mall. The Opry Mills Express departs the Bridgestone Arena 13 times a day on weekdays. Fare is $1.70 one way; $0.85 for senior citizens. You can pick up a detailed route timetable from either of the two downtown visitors centers or online.

COMMUTER RAIL

In 2006 Nashville debuted the **Music City Star Rail** (108 1st Ave., 615/862-8833, www.musiccitystar.org), a commuter rail system designed to ease congestion around the city. With service Monday-Friday, several times a day, trains connect Donelson, Hermitage, Mount Juliet, and Lebanon to downtown Nashville. Service is often bumped up during special events, such as the 4th of July celebration downtown. More routes are planned for the future.

One-way tickets can be purchased for $2-5.45 each from vending machines at any of the stations. You can prepurchase single-trip tickets, 10-trip packs, and monthly passes at a discount online. For a complete list of ticket outlets, contact the railway.

BICYCLING

Riding a bike as transportation, rather than exercise, is still a growing pursuit in Nashville, with more activity in some neighborhoods than others.

Many roadways lack dedicated bike lanes, and while some businesses have bike racks out front, many do not. That said, both those who want to ride their own bikes and those who want to rent will discover that two wheels are a good way to see Music City. Check out **Nashville GreenBikes** (www.nashville.gov) or **B-Cycle** (http://nashville.bcycle.com) for options if you aren't bringing your own set of wheels.

The **Music City Bikeway** (www.nashville.gov/bikeways) website offers a downloadable route map of the 26-mile bike-friendly route in Nashville. Another good set of downloadable maps is available from **Walk/Bike Nashville** (www.walkbikenashville.org).

The **Harpeth Bike Club** (www.harpethbikeclub.com) is Nashville's largest bike club. It organizes weekend and weekday group rides April-October, plus races and social events where you can meet other bike enthusiasts. Its website is also a good resource for traffic laws for bicyclists and other helpful info.

TRAVELING WITH CHILDREN

It is hard to imagine a place better for family vacations than Music City. There are museums and kid-friendly exhibits at most of the major attractions. And don't forget the zoo and railroad excursions. Nearby state parks provide numerous places to camp, hike, swim, fish, and explore.

Many hotels and inns offer special discounts for families, and casual restaurants almost always have a children's menu with lower-priced, kid-friendly choices.

SENIOR TRAVELERS

Road Scholar (800/454-5768, www.roadscholar.org), formerly called Elderhostel, organizes educational tours for people over 55 in Memphis and Nashville.

For discounts and help with trip planning, try **AARP** (866/654-5572, www.aarp.org), which offers a full-service travel agency, trip insurance, a motor club, and the AARP Passport program, which provides you with senior discounts for hotels, car rentals, and other things.

Persons over 55 should always check for a senior citizen discount. Most attractions and some hotels and restaurants have special pricing for senior citizens.

LGBT TRAVELERS

Gay, lesbian, bisexual, and transgender people are presented with a mixed bag when visiting Tennessee. In 2013, Tennessee lawmakers introduced a bill, often referred to as the "Don't Say Gay" bill, that would have banned teachers from even saying the word *gay* in the classroom. (It failed to make it through the legislative process.)

On the other hand, there has been no better time to be gay in Tennessee. More and more social, civic, and political organizations are engaging the gay community, and many Nashville neighborhoods have vibrant gay scenes.

A number of different publications and websites cover the LGBT community in Nashville. Two of the best known are *Out and About* (www.outandaboutnewspaper.com), a free monthly newsmagazine, and *Unite* magazine (http://unitemag.com).

Several specific guidebooks and websites give helpful listings of gay-friendly hotels, restaurants, and bars. The **Damron guides** (www.damron.com) offer Tennessee listings; the **International Gay and Lesbian Travel Association** (IGLTA, www.iglta.org) is a trade organization with listings of gay-friendly hotels, tour operators, and much more. California-based **Now, Voyager** (www.nowvoyager.com) is a gay-owned and gay-operated travel agency that specializes in gay tours, vacation packages, and cruises.

More people with disabilities are traveling than ever before. The Americans with Disabilities Act requires most public buildings to make provisions for disabled people, although in practice accessibility may be spotty.

When you make your hotel reservations, always check that the hotel is prepared to accommodate you. Airlines will also make special arrangements for you if you request help in advance.

Several national organizations have information and advice about traveling with disabilities. **The Society for Accessible Travel and Hospitality** (www.sath.org) publishes links to major airlines' accessibility policies and publishes travel tips for people with all types of disabilities, including blindness, deafness, mobility disorders, diabetes, kidney disease, and arthritis. The society publishes *Open World,* a magazine about accessible travel.

Wheelchair Getaways (800/642-2042, www.wheelchairgetaways.com) is a national chain specializing in renting vans that are wheelchair accessible or otherwise designed for disabled drivers and travelers. Wheelchair Getaways has locations in **Memphis** (901/795-6533 or 866/762-1656) and **Knoxville** (865/622-6550 or 888/340-8267), and they will deliver to other locations in the state.

Avis offers **Avis Access,** a program for travelers with disabilities. Call the dedicated 24-hour toll-free number (888/879-4273) for help renting a car with features such as transfer boards, hand controls, spinner knobs, and swivel seats.

INTERNATIONAL TRAVELERS

Foreign travelers will find a warm welcome. Those in the music and tourist trades are used to working with people from all over the world and will be pleased that you have come from so far away to visit their home. If you are not a native English speaker, it may be difficult to understand the local accent at first. Just smile and ask the person to say it again, a bit slower. Good humor and a positive attitude will help at all times.

Most citizens of a foreign country require a visa to enter the United States. There are many types of visas, issued according to the purpose of your visit. Business and pleasure travelers apply for B-1 and B-2 visas, respectively. When you apply for your visa, you will be required to prove that the purpose of you trip is business, pleasure, or for medical treatment; that you plan to remain in the United States for a limited period; and that you have a place of residence outside the United States. Apply for your visa at the nearest U.S. embassy. For more information, contact the **U.S. Citizenship and Immigration Service** (www.uscis.gov).

Nationals of 38 countries may be able to use the Visa Waiver Program, operated by Customs and Border Protection. Presently, these countries are Andorra, Australia, Austria, Belgium, Brunei, Chile, Czech Republic, Denmark (including Greenland and Faroe Islands), Estonia, Finland, France, Germany, Greece, Hungary, Iceland, Ireland, Italy, Japan, Latvia, Liechtenstein, Lithuania, Luxembourg, Malta, Monaco, the Netherlands

ESSENTIALS
TRAVEL TIPS

(including Aruba, Bonaire, Curacao, Saba, and Sint Maarten), New Zealand, Norway, Portugal (including Azores and Madeira), San Marino, South Korea, Singapore, Slovakia, Slovenia, Spain, Sweden, Switzerland, Taiwan, and the United Kingdom, unless citizens are also nationals of Sudan, Syria, Iraq, or Iran.

Take note that in recent years the United States has begun to require visa-waiver participants to have upgraded passports with digital photographs and machine-readable information. They have also introduced requirements that even visa-waiver citizens register in advance before arriving in the United States. For more information about the Visa Waiver Program, contact the **Customs and Border Protection Agency** (www. travel.state.gov).

All foreign travelers are required to participate in U.S. Visit, a program operated by the Department of Homeland Security. Under the program, your fingerprints and photograph are taken—digitally and without ink—as you are being screened by the immigration officer.

Health and Safety

Nashville is a safe city, with the regular concerns of any urban area. Locals, both native and otherwise, are at-the-ready with Southern hospitality and willing to help a visitor who has lost his or her way.

In general, if you stay alert, you should feel free to explore the city's neighborhoods. For the most part, the neighborhoods highlighted in this guide, those that are chock-full of attractions, are safe to venture out in, although crimes that take place in high-tourist areas, like pickpocketing, do happen. Lock your valuables out of sight in your car, don't carry large amounts of cash, pay attention to your surroundings, and you'll be fine.

HOSPITALS AND PHARMACIES

Because health care is such a big industry in Nashville, there are a lot of hospitals. Should you need emergency medical care, the majority of the hospitals are clustered in the Midtown neighborhood, near Vanderbilt. **The Monroe Carell Jr. Children's Hospital** at Vanderbilt (2200 Children's Way, 615/936-1000, www.childrenshospital.vanderbilt.org) is among the best in the country. **TriStar Skyline Medical Center** (3441 Dickerson Pike, 615/769-2000, https://tristarskyline.com) is the closest hospital to Music Valley and parts of East Nashville. Others include **Saint Thomas West Hospital** (4220 Harding Pike, 615/222-2111, www.sthealth.com) and **Centennial Medical Center** (2300 Patterson St., 615/342-1000, https:// tristarcentennial.com).

Rite Aid, CVS, Walgreens, and the major grocery store chains have drugstores all over Nashville. There's a **CVS** (426 21st Ave. S., 615/321-2590, www.cvs.com) close to Midtown, the Vanderbilt and Belmont campuses, and Music Row. If you need a 24-hour option, try **Walgreens** (5555 Edmondson Pike, 615/333-2722, www.walgreens.com).

EMERGENCY SERVICES

Dial **911** for police, fire, or ambulance in an emergency. The local number for "urgency without emergency" is 615/862-8600. For help with a traffic accident, call the **Tennessee Highway Patrol** at 615/741-3181. The concierge at major hotels can also help direct you in the event of an emergency.

Nashville Veterinary Specialists (2971 Sidco Dr., 615/386-0107, www.nashvillevetspecialists.com) has an emergency staff ready and waiting for anything that happens to your pet while you are traveling. The Wi-Fi and snacks help keep worried humans occupied while waiting.

Communications and Media

INTERNET SERVICES

You can go online free at the **Nashville Public Library** (615 Church St., 615/862-5800, https://library.nashville.org). There is free wireless access at the **5th and Broadway visitors center** (501 Broadway, 615/259-4747, www.visitmusiccity.com). Many local restaurants, coffee shops, and hotels also offer free wireless internet.

MAIL SERVICES

The **United States Postal Service** maintains a branch in almost every Nashville neighborhood. Search for specific locations at www.usps.gov. If you need to mail a letter or buy stamps while downtown, you have a few options. The post office at 901 Broadway (615/255-3613) is found on the basement level of the **Frist Center for the Visual Arts,** which itself used to be a post office before it was renovated for the museum space. There is also a post office in the downtown Arcade and at 1718 Church Street.

Both **FedEx** (800/463-3339, www.fedex.com) and **UPS** (800/742-5877, www.ups.com) have several locations downtown and drop boxes in local hotels and businesses.

BANKS

Dozens of local and regional banks operate in Nashville. Most banks will cash travelers checks, exchange currency, and send wire transfers. Banks are generally open weekdays 9am-4pm, although some are open later and on Saturday. Automatic teller machines (ATMs) are ubiquitous at grocery stores, live music venues, and elsewhere, and many are compatible with bank cards bearing the Plus or Cirrus icons. Between fees charged by your own bank and the bank that owns the ATM you are using, expect to pay $2-5 extra to get cash from an ATM that does not belong to your own bank.

SALES TAX

Sales tax is charged on all goods, including food and groceries.

The sales tax you pay is split between the state and local governments. Tennessee's sales tax is 5.5 percent on food and groceries and 7 percent on all other goods. Cities and towns add an additional "local use tax" of 1.5-2.75 percent. In Nashville it adds up to 9.25 percent on the goods you buy.

TIPPING

You should tip waitstaff 15-20 percent in a sit-down restaurant. You can tip 5-10 percent in a cafeteria or restaurant where you collect your own food from the counter.

Tip a bellhop or bag handler $1 per bag, or more if they went out of their way to help you.

TIME ZONES

All of Middle Tennessee, including Nashville and its environs, is in the Central Time Zone. The time zone line runs a slanted course from Signal Mountain (near Chattanooga) in the south to the Big South Fork National River and Recreation Area in the north. The time zone line falls at mile marker 340 along I-40, just west of Rockwood and a few miles east of Crossville. Chattanooga, Dayton, Rockwood, Crossville, Rugby, Fall Creek Falls State Park, the Catoosa Wildlife Management Area, and Big South Fork lie close to or on the time zone line, and visitors to these areas to the east of Nashville should take special care to ensure they are on the right clock.

Resources

Suggested Reading

PHOTOGRAPHY AND ART

Escott, Colin. *The Grand Ole Opry: The Making of an American Icon.* Nashville, TN: Center Street, 2006. An authorized (and somewhat sanitized) look at the Grand Ole Opry, this makes for an attractive coffee-table book with lots of pictures, reminiscences, and short sidebars.

McDaniel, Karina. *Nashville Then and Now.* Pavilion, 2014. This is an illustrated guide of what makes Music City tick, written by an archivist for the Tennessee State Library and Archives.

McGuire, Jim. *Nashville Portraits: Legends of Country Music.* Guilford, CT: The Lyons Press, 2007. Sixty stunning photographs of country music legends, including Johnny Cash, Waylon Jennings, Doc Watson, and Dolly Parton, are found in this companion book to an eponymous exhibit that debuted in 2007.

Sherraden, Jim, Paul Kingsbury, and Elek Horvath. *Hatch Show Print: The History of a Great American Poster Shop.* San Francisco: Chronicle Books, 2001. This fully illustrated, beautiful book explores Hatch Show Print, the Nashville advertising and letter press founded in 1897.

GUIDES

Brandt, Robert. *Touring the Middle Tennessee Backroads.* Winston-Salem, NC: John F. Blair Publisher, 1995. Robert Brandt is a Nashville judge and self-professed "zealot" for Middle Tennessee. His guidebook details 15 driving tours through backroads in the heartland of Tennessee. Brandt's knowledge of local history and architecture cannot be surpassed, and his enthusiasm for his subject shines through the prose. While some of the entries are now dated, the guide remains an invaluable source of information about small towns in the region.

Van West, Carroll. *Tennessee's Historical Landscapes: A Traveler's Guide.* Knoxville: University of Tennessee Press, 1995. The editor of the *Tennessee Historical Quarterly* and a professor of history at Middle Tennessee State University, Carroll Van West guides readers along highways and byways, pointing out historical structures and other signs of history along the way. A good traveling companion, especially for students of architecture and landscape.

The WPA Guide to Tennessee. Knoxville: University of Tennessee Press, 1986. The Works Progress Administration guide to Tennessee, written in 1939 and originally published by Viking Press, is a fascinating portrait of Depression-era Tennessee. Published as part of a New Deal project to employ writers and document the culture and character of the nation, the guide contains visitor information, historical sketches, and profiles of the state's literature, culture, agriculture, industry, and more. The guide, republished as part of Tennessee's "Homecoming '86," is a delightful traveling companion.

GENERAL HISTORY

Bergeron, Paul H. *Paths of the Past: Tennessee, 1770-1970*. Knoxville: University of Tennessee Press, 1979. This is a concise, straight-up history of Tennessee, with a few illustrations and maps.

Corlew, Robert E. *Tennessee: A Short History*. Knoxville: University of Tennessee Press, 1990. The definitive survey of Tennessee history, this text was first written in 1969 and has been updated several times by writers including Stanley J. Folmsbee and Enoch Mitchell. This is a useful reference guide for a serious reader.

Dykeman, Wilma. *Tennessee*. New York: W. W. Norton & Company and the American Association for State and Local History, 1984. Novelist and essayist Wilma Dykeman says more about the people of Tennessee and the events that shaped the modern state in this slim and highly readable volume than you would find in the most detailed and plodding historical account. It becomes a companion, and a means through which to understand the Tennessee spirit and character.

SPECIALIZED HISTORY

Egerton, John. *Speak Now Against the Day: The Generation Before the Civil Rights Movement in the South*. Chapel Hill: University of North Carolina Press, 1995. Nashville native John Egerton tells the relatively unacknowledged story of Southerners, African American and Caucasian, who stood up against segregation and racial hatred during the years before the civil rights movement.

Egerton, John. *Visions of Utopia*. Knoxville: University of Tennessee Press, 1977. An accessible and fascinating portrait of three intentional Tennessee communities—Ruskin in Middle Tennessee, Nashoba in West Tennessee, and Rugby in East Tennessee—Egerton's usual sterling prose and sensitive observations make this volume well worth reading.

Sword, Wiley. *The Confederacy's Last Hurrah: Spring Hill, Franklin and Nashville.* Lawrence: University Press of Kansas, 2004. This is a well-written and devastating account of John Bell Hood's disastrous campaign through Middle Tennessee during the waning months of the Confederacy. It was a campaign that cost the South more than 23,000 men. With unflinching honesty, Sword describes the opportunities lost and poor decisions made by General Hood.

MUSIC

Carlin, Richard. *Country Music.* New York: Black Dog and Leventhal Publishers, 2006. This is a highly illustrated, well-written, and useful reference for fans of country music. It profiles the people, places, and events that contributed to country's evolution. With lots of graphic elements and photographs, it is a good book to dip into.

Chapman, Marshall. *They Came to Nashville.* Nashville, TN: Vanderbilt University Press, 2010. Singer-songwriter Chapman tells her tales, as well as those of many others, as they came to Music City and set about hitting the big time.

Escott, Colin. *Hank Williams The Biography.* Back Bay Books, 2004. No country star had a bigger impact on Nashville's evolution to Music City than Hank Williams. This detailed history shares his failings, downfall, and remarkable legacy.

Havighurst, Craig. *Air Castle of the South: WSM and the Making of Music City (Music in American Life).* Urbana and Chicago: University of Illinois Press, 2007. Havighurst is known as the preeminent Nashville music historian and this tome delves deep into an important piece in Nashville's musical hierarchy.

Kingsbury, Paul, ed. *Will the Circle Be Unbroken: Country Music in America.* London: DK Adult, 2006. An illustrated collection of articles by 43 writers, including several performing artists, this book is a useful reference on the genre's development from 1920 until the present.

Kossner, Michael. *How Nashville Became Music City: 50 Years of Music Row.* Milwaukee, WI: Hal Leonard, 2006. Forget about the stars and the singers, this profile of country music focuses on the people you've never heard of: the executives, songwriters, and behind-the-scenes technicians who really make the music happen. An interesting read for fans who don't mind seeing how the sausage is made; a good introduction for people aspiring to be a part of it.

REFERENCE

Van West, Carroll, ed. *The Tennessee Encyclopedia of History and Culture.* Nashville: Tennessee Historical Society and Rutledge Hill Press, 1998. Perhaps the most valuable tome on Tennessee, this 1,200-page encyclopedia covers the people, places, events, and movements that defined Tennessee history and the culture of its people. Dip in frequently and you will be all the wiser.

FICTION

Burton, Linda, ed. *Stories from Tennessee.* Knoxville: University of Tennessee Press, 1983. An anthology of Tennessee literature, the volume begins with a story by David Crockett on hunting in Tennessee and concludes with works by 20th-century authors such as Shelby Foote, Cormac McCarthy, and Robert Drake.

Hicks, Rover. *The Widow of the South.* New York: Warner Books, 2005. Tour guides at Carton Plantation gripe about the poetic license taken with some facts in this fictional tale. But it offers a moving story of the Battle of Franklin and the high emotional costs of the Civil War.

Taylor, Peter. *Summons to Memphis.* New York: Knopf Publishing Group, 1986. Celebrated and award-winning Tennessee writer Peter Taylor won the Pulitzer Prize for fiction for this novel in 1986. Phillip Carver returns home to Tennessee at the request of his three older sisters to talk his father out of remarrying. In so doing, he is forced to confront a troubling family history. This is a classic of American literature, set in a South that is fading away.

FOOD

Justus, Jennifer. *Nashville Eats: Hot Chicken, Buttermilk Biscuits, and 100 More Southern Recipes from Music City.* New York: Stewart, Tabori & Chang, 2015. Compiled by a former newspaper reporter, this is the guide to making all the local foods you fall in love with on your trip.

Lewis, Edna, and Scott Peacock. *The Gift of Southern Cooking: Recipes and Revelations from Two Great American Cooks.* New York: Knopf Publishing Group, 2003. Grande dame of Southern food Edna Lewis and son-of-the-soil chef Scott Peacock joined forces on this seminal text of Southern cuisine. It demystifies, documents, and inspires. Ideal for those who really care about Southern food ways.

Lundy, Ronnie, ed. *Cornbread Nation 3.* Chapel Hill: University of North Carolina Press, 2006. The third in a series of collections on Southern food and cooking. Published in collaboration with the Southern Foodways Alliance, which is dedicated to preserving and celebrating Southern food traditions, the Cornbread Nation collection is an ode to food traditions large and small. Topics include pawpaws, corn, and pork. *Cornbread Nation 2* focused on barbecue. *Cornbread Nation 1* was edited by restaurateur and Southern food celebrant John Egerton.

Stern, Jane, and Michael Stern. *Southern Country Cooking from The Loveless Cafe: Biscuits, Hams, and Jams from Nashville's Favorite Café.* Nashville, TN: Rutledge Hill Press, 2005. Road-food aficionados wrote the cookbook on Nashville's most famous pit stop: The Loveless Cafe. Located at the northern terminus of the Natchez Trace Parkway, The Loveless is quintessential Southern cooking—delectable biscuits, country ham, and homemade preserves. Now you can take some of that down-home flavor back with you.

Internet and Digital Resources

FOOD AND DRINK

Eat Drink Smile
www.eat-drink-smile.com
A fun blog about what to eat and drink in Music City.

HISTORY AND REFERENCE

Tennessee Civil War 150
A free app for iPhones and iPads provides quick-hit history lessons about Civil War battle sites, plus information about visiting them.

Tennessee Encyclopedia of History and Culture
www.tennesseeencyclopedia.net
The online edition of an excellent reference book, this website is a great starting point on all topics Tennessee. Articles about people, places, and events are written by hundreds of different experts. Online entries are updated regularly.

NEWSPAPERS AND MAGAZINES

Nashville Lifestyles
www.nashvillelifestyles.com
The website of this monthly magazine has great information about what's going on in the city, whether you want to eat, shop, dance, or all of the above.

The Nashville Scene
www.nashvillescene.com
Nashville's alternative weekly has a great website. The dining guide is fabulous, the stories interesting and archived, and the entertainment calendar is the best in town. Go to "Our Critics' Picks" for a rundown on the best

shows in town. The annual manual, reader's choice awards, and other special editions are useful for newcomers and old-timers alike.

The Tennessean
www.tennessean.com
Nashville's major newspaper posts news, entertainment, sports, and business stories online. Sign up for a daily newsletter of headlines from Music City, or search the archives.

OUTDOOR RECREATION
NashVitality
Download this free app created by the mayor's office for GPS-specific information on where to get outdoors in Music City. The app includes water launches, bike trails, greenways, and more.

Tennessee State Parks
www.tnstateparks.com
An online directory of all Tennessee state parks, this site provides useful details, including campground descriptions, cabin rental information, and the lowdown on activities. A free downloadable smart phone app is also available.

TVA Lake Info
This free iPad and iPhone app lists recreational dam release schedules for across the state.

TOURIST INFORMATION
Nashville Convention and Visitors Corporation
www.visitmusiccity.com
The official tourism website for Nashville, this site offers concert listings, hotel booking services, and useful visitor information. You can also order a visitors guide and money-saving coupons. Listen to the Highway 65 Nashville-centric music stream as you browse. There's also a free app to help you on the road.

Tennessee Department of Tourism Development
www.tnvacation.com
On Tennessee's official tourism website you can request a visitors guide, search for upcoming events, or look up details about hundreds of attractions, hotels, and restaurants. This is a great resource for suggested scenic drives. A printed guide is also available.

Restaurants Index

Nightlife Index

Shops Index

Hotels Index

Photo Credits

Title page photo: © Nashville Convention & Visitors Corp.

All photos © Margaret Littman except page 2 (top left) © Peyton Hoge, (top right) © Deone Jahnke; page 18 (top left) © Patsy Cline Museum, (top right) © Margaret Littman; page 19 © Nashville Convention & Visitors Corp.; page 20 © Nashville Convention & Visitors Corp.; page 21 © Nashville Convention & Visitors Corp.; page 23 © Sean Pavone | Dreamstime.com; page 25 (top) © Nashville Convention & Visitors Corp., (bottom) © Nashville Convention & Visitors Corporation; page 28 (top) © Jake's Bakes, (bottom) © Nashville Convention & Visitors Corp.; page 37 (top) © Nashville Convention & Visitors Corp., (bottom) © Johnny Cash Museum; page 41 © Nashville Convention & Visitors Corp.; page 52 (top left) © Nashville Convention & Visitors Corp., (top right) © Nashville Convention & Visitors Corp., (bottom) © Nashville Convention & Visitors Corp.; page 61 (top) © Andrea Behrends, (bottom) © Andrew Cebulka; page 69 (top) © A la Mode Media, (bottom) © Nashville Guru; page 72 © Emily B. Hall; page 88 © Andrew Cebulka; page 94 © Hannah Schneider Creative; page 99 (top) © Real World Tours, (bottom) © Nashville Convention & Visitors Corp.; page 116 (top) © Andrea Behrends, (bottom) © Nudie's Honky Tonk; page 120 © John Scarpati; page 127 (top) © Karyn Kipley Photography, (bottom) © 21c Museum Hotel; page 134 © Rick Malkin; page 151 (top) © Nashville Convention & Visitors Corp., (bottom) © Audrey Spillman; page 161 (top left) © Nashville Sounds, (top right) © Kerry Woo; page 172 (top) © Brett Warren, (bottom) © Jo McCauchey; page 178 (top) © Two Old Hippies, (bottom) © Gregg Roth; page 190 © Joelle Herr/Her Bookshop; page 198 (top) © Nashville Convention & Visitors Corp., (bottom) © Nashville Convention & Visitors Corp.; page 205 (top) © The Westin Nashville, (bottom) © David Phelps; page 211 (top left) © Hutton Hotel, (top right) © Laure Joliet, (bottom) © Gaylord Opryland Resort; page 216 © Peyton Hoge; page 231 © Elizabeth Looney; page 246 © The Jack Daniel Distillery; page 247 (top) © Kristin Luna/CamelsAndChocolate.com, (bottom) © Nashville Convention & Visitors Corp.

Acknowledgments

Even under the pressure of looming deadlines, stacks of photo-filled jump drives on the desk, and marked-up maps covering the floor, I'm convinced I have the world's best job. I have legitimate, work-related excuses to strap the paddleboard to my car and explore a brand new river access point. Or to call a few friends and ask them to help me check out Nashville's honky-tonks. Or taste-test the newest purveyor of hot chicken.

I'm grateful to many people who helped me synthesize what I've heard, seen, and experienced into something coherent that others could use. First and foremost, thanks go to DG Strong, who encouraged me to move back to Nashville after many years away and who not just indulges but enables my statewide whims.

Perhaps the only person who loves Music City as much as I do is Heather Middleton of the Nashville Convention and Visitors Corp. She's always available for brainstorming and, of course, providing photos (with the help of Sarah Mynatt).

Lisa Arnett is more than an excellent researcher and editorial assistant. Yes, she verifies the alphabet soup of phone numbers and URLs, and tracks down photos and permissions, but she also helps me think strategically about how to bring the best of Nashville to readers.

I first worked with the crackerjack staff of Avalon Travel on *The Dog Lover's Companion to Chicago* and decades later I'm just as grateful for their great expertise and better attitudes. Particular thanks, again, this time around to the endlessly patient Leah Gordon, Darren Alessi, Kat Bennett, Holly Birchfield, Nikki Ioakimedes, and Sierra Machado. Many thanks to those who worked on previous editions of *Moon Tennessee* and *Moon Nashville,* including Susanna Henighan Potter and Jeff Bradley.

As always, I am grateful for the help and support of my family and friends, who tolerate my working long hours on "vacation" and dragging them to sightsee wherever we are, not to mention my soundtrack of bluegrass and country music, and the ever-expanding wardrobe of cowboy boots.

MOON NATIONAL PARKS

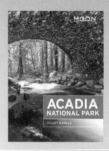

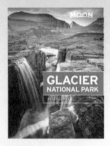

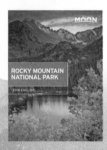

In these books:

- Full coverage of gateway cities and towns
- Itineraries from one day to multiple weeks
- Advice on where to stay (or camp) in and around the parks

PREPARE FOR ADVENTURE

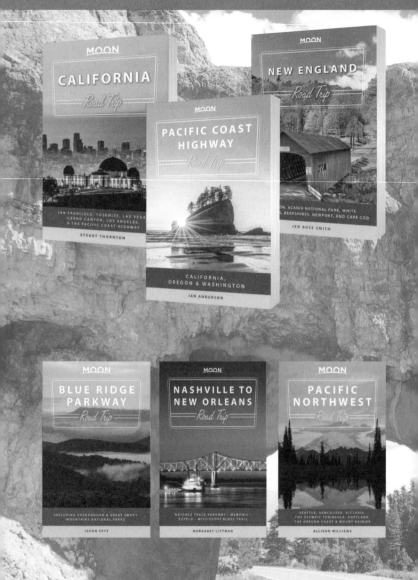

MOON ROAD TRIP GUIDES

Advice on where to sleep, eat, and explore

Detailed driving directions including mileage and drive times

Itineraries for a range of timelines

Moon Travel Guides are available from your favorite bookseller.

Join our travel community!
Share your adventures using **#travelwithmoon**

MOON.COM
@MOONGUIDES

Stunning Sights Around the World

BELIZE

COLOMBIA

ICELAND

MACHU PICCHU

MOROCCO

NORWAY

PATAGONIA

ROME, FLORENCE & VENICE

Guides for Urban Adventure

AMSTERDAM

BUENOS AIRES

HANOI

MEXICO CITY

MONTRÉAL

OSLO

VANCOUVER

WASHINGTON DC

MAP SYMBOLS

■	Sights	◉	National Capital	▲	Mountain	═══════	Major Hwy
■	Restaurants	◎	State Capital	✚	Natural Feature	─────────	Road/Hwy
■	Nightlife	○	City/Town	🦅	Waterfall	─────────	Pedestrian Friendly
■	Arts and Culture	★	Point of Interest	⚑	Park	- - - - - -	Trail
■	Sports and Activities	•	Accommodation	▲	Archaeological Site	▪▪▪▪▪▪▪	Stairs
■	Shops	▼	Restaurant/Bar	🚺	Trailhead	··············	Ferry
■	Hotels	▪	Other Location	🅿	Parking Area	━ ━ ━ ━	Railroad

CONVERSION TABLES

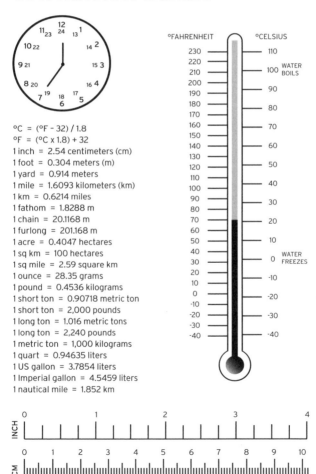

°C = (°F − 32) / 1.8
°F = (°C x 1.8) + 32
1 inch = 2.54 centimeters (cm)
1 foot = 0.304 meters (m)
1 yard = 0.914 meters
1 mile = 1.6093 kilometers (km)
1 km = 0.6214 miles
1 fathom = 1.8288 m
1 chain = 20.1168 m
1 furlong = 201.168 m
1 acre = 0.4047 hectares
1 sq km = 100 hectares
1 sq mile = 2.59 square km
1 ounce = 28.35 grams
1 pound = 0.4536 kilograms
1 short ton = 0.90718 metric ton
1 short ton = 2,000 pounds
1 long ton = 1.016 metric tons
1 long ton = 2,240 pounds
1 metric ton = 1,000 kilograms
1 quart = 0.94635 liters
1 US gallon = 3.7854 liters
1 Imperial gallon = 4.5459 liters
1 nautical mile = 1.852 km

MOON NASHVILLE
Avalon Travel
Hachette Book Group
1700 Fourth Street
Berkeley, CA 94710, USA
www.moon.com

Editor and Series Manager: Leah Gordon
Copy Editor: Ashley Benning
Production and Graphics Coordinator: Darren Alessi
Cover Design: Faceout Studios, Charles Brock
Interior Design: Domini Dragoone
Moon Logo: Tim McGrath
Map Editor: Kat Bennett
Cartographers: Albert Angulo, Brian Shotwell, Kat Bennett
Proofreader: Caroline Trefler
Indexer: Rachel Kuhn

ISBN-13: 9781640491595

Printing History
1st Edition — 2014
3rd Edition — June 2018
5 4 3 2

Front cover photo: © amesy/Getty Images
Back cover photos: Parthenon © Brenda Kean | Dreamstime.com

Printed in Canada by Friesens